Global War Game

Second Series
1984–1988

Robert H. Gile

NAVAL WAR COLLEGE
686 Cushing Road
Newport, Rhode Island

Naval War College

Newport, Rhode Island
Center for Naval Warfare Studies
Newport Paper Number Twenty
2004

Telephone: 401.841.2236
Fax: 401.841.3579
DSN exchange: 948
E-mail: press@nwc.navy.mil
Web: http://www.nwc.navy.mil/press

The Newport Papers are extended research projects that the Naval War College Press Editor, the Dean of Naval Warfare Studies, and the President of the Naval War College consider of particular interest to policy makers, scholars, and analysts.

Correspondence concerning the Newport Papers may be addressed to the Dean of Naval Warfare Studies. To request additional copies or subscription consideration, please direct inquiries to the President, Code 32A, Naval War College, 686 Cushing Road, Newport, RI 02841-1207.

I wish to express my deep appreciation to Orville "Bud" Hay, former Director of Advanced Concepts, Center for Naval Warfare Studies, Naval War College. He not only advised, read, and commented on this paper, but he provided me with access to the resources I needed to write it. Bud has been the guiding genius of the Global Games, which the London Times of 13 February 2003 referred to as "a series long seen as the apogee of military war gaming." It is my distinct pleasure to have been associated with him since 1983, to have worked with him in eighteen Globals, and to have collaborated with him in writing the first volume of Global history.

Fundamentally, this type of worldwide tabletop game has obvious potential for further development. Such a summer project could evolve into a popular and productive annual exercise.

—Hugh Nott, with reference to the 1979 Global War Game

Contents

Foreword

The Naval War College, at Newport, Rhode Island, is justifiably famous in national security and naval circles across the globe for being on the cutting edge of war gaming, and it has been for over a century. From the famous games that helped set the stage for the island-hopping campaign across the Pacific in World War II to a recent series exploring military options for U.S. homeland defense, the College's war games have kept it among the ranks of the world's premier gaming facilities. The history of the Naval War College's war-gaming efforts for the past two decades, a particularly critical period, is only now being acknowledged and analyzed.

Captain Robert H. Gile (U.S. Navy, Ret.) has in this Newport Paper provided a service for the Naval War College, the U.S. Navy, and indeed, practitioners and historians of gaming around the world. This is the second in a series of monographs synthesizing the primary sources to provide a concise, chronological summary and analysis of the prestigious Global War Games, hosted in Newport from 1984 until after the fall of the Soviet Union. The first monograph (coauthored with Bud Hay) was *Global War Game: The First Five Years,* published as Newport Paper 4 in 1993; it is available electronically in Adobe Acrobat and in limited paper copies. Planning and research is under way to complete the history of the Global series. Captain Gile's invaluable effort captures the methods, techniques, assumptions, analysis, results, and the all-important "take-aways" of this widely known game series, important today for the history of war gaming but even more so at the time, as a vital contribution to the thinking and strategy of the U.S. Navy, the other U.S. services, and its alliance counterparts in the later stages of the Cold War.

This Newport Paper, *Global War Game: Second Series, 1984-1988,* recounts a uniquely interesting and challenging period in the Naval War College's engagement with naval and national strategies through the war-gaming process. The games examined the ability of the United States to sustain conventional warfare with the Soviet Union until full mobilization of the nation's resources could be achieved. Through a sustained set of sequential and interlocking games, the Global process identified a number of important and controversial findings. For instance, as the following pages will show, these games pointed to the importance of offensive action, including maritime operations; the ability of "Blue" (the West, broadly speaking) to win without resorting to nuclear weapons; and the extensive planning necessary to conduct high-intensity combat over a lengthy period.

Fortunately for the United States and the world, the 1984–88 era was the penultimate period during which Global games would take place in the shadow of superpower conflict. As we look forward to the third and final installation of Captain Gile's narrative we can already see, in the present work, the first signs of the impact of the changing geopolitical environment on the Global series and the Naval War College's dynamic approach to war gaming.

PETER DOMBROWSKI
Editor, Naval War College Press

August 2004

Note to the Reader

This report deals with practical issues and major themes identified during the second Global War Game (GWG) Series. Its focus is on various general topics, specific force employment issues, and discrete game events. Because of the interplay of themes and issues among several theaters, some repetition is necessary to provide a more complete discussion.

The Global War Game was conceived in 1978 to build a structure to explore war-fighting issues in a larger perspective than the tactical view prevalent in the Navy at that time. These games constitute a research project that ranges from policy through strategy to operations (campaigns). It was and is an opportunity to investigate ideas and concepts that may vary from current policy or strategic "wisdom." With the understanding that game simulations were but an approximation of the behavior of governments in global war, the scenarios should be considered as a context for issues to be explored.

The first game (1979) had a distinctly naval focus, but the series quickly evolved, by obvious necessity, into a much broader military and political forum. Throughout the first series, GWG was utilized as a test bed or crucible for an emerging maritime strategy. A brief summary of these initial games and an overview of some of the major issues examined in them is included in this volume for those who do not have access to *Global War Game: The First Five Years* (Newport Paper Number 4.) While the first series involved several different geographical areas to confront current, real-world events or to test a specific concept, the second series picked up where the first terminated, with a major war between the North Atlantic Treaty Organization (NATO) and the Warsaw Pact (WP). It was a natural extension of the first series, designed for the purpose of exploring issues that would arise in waging protracted warfare in the decade of the 1990s.

Effort has been made throughout this paper to preserve the terminology that was in use when the games were conducted and to relate faithfully actual strategies pursued and campaigns implemented as well as the rationale behind them. Thus, while some of the terminology may seem archaic and some of the operations ill-advised, it is necessary to look at these efforts as a learning experience that reflects how our thinking about global war, our concepts, and our practices matured during the series.

Executive Summary

The second Global War Game Series was played at the Naval War College for three weeks each summer of the years 1984–1988. The issues that were pervasive throughout can be summarized as follows:

> What are the political, war fighting, logistical, and mobilization factors that determine the United States/NATO capability to sustain conventional against the Soviet Union/Warsaw Pact until the full military, industrial and personnel resources of the "free world" can be mobilized to secure victory? and
>
> How best can US/NATO maritime superiority be translated into strategic leverage useful in bringing the conflict to a successful conclusion?

The first game of the series, GWG '84, was a stand-alone game designed to test new gaming concepts and to ensure realistic orders of battle. The 1985, 1986, and 1987 games consisted of one continuous game, with the two latter games picking up where its predecessor had terminated. In game play, war broke out on 10 November 1990, and hostilities were played out to D+65, or 14 January 1991. As one of the purposes of the series was to ascertain the contours of protracted conventional war, use of nuclear weapons was not permitted, although "off line" excursions into the possible results and ramifications of such use did take place. The final game of the series, in 1988, was designed to study war termination. This was a planning, seminar-type game in format, without any actual moves occurring.

The games of the series involved about 600 participants (at any given time) from over 100 government departments, agencies, military commands, educational and research facilities, and business and industry. Foreign military and civilian representatives from Canada and the United Kingdom played.

Principal findings of the series can be summarized as follows:

- A NATO/Warsaw Pact war would be difficult to start but virtually impossible to conclude on a negotiated basis.

- What constitutes "victory" and "defeat" can be perceived very differently by Blue and by Red.
- Although contemplation of nuclear use tends to change for both sides with time and circumstance, early escalation by Blue is probably unnecessary and unwise.
- The huge material expenditures involved in waging modern, conventional war require pre-planning of resource management and industrial mobilization.
- Offensive use of military forces is critical in throwing Red off timeline and, at sea, creating strategic options and protecting SLOCs.
- Although maritime success is critical to Blue conduct of the war, translation of that success into negotiating leverage is elusive.
- Regardless of Blue policy preference/strategy, a NATO/Warsaw Pact war in which alliances remain firm and nuclear weapons are not used will probably become protracted.

Assuming continued domestic support and alliance cohesion, the validity of the Blue strategy of protracted, conventional war rested on two conditions that these games called into question:

- The ability of Blue to generate or to accure from other sources the equipment necessary to sustain the conflict until industrial mobilization occurred was problematic,
- There was a distinct possibility that the very success of the Blue strategy would drive Red to some form of nuclear escalation.

Review of the First Global War Game Series (1979–1983)

A Review of War Gaming

One common distinction made among war games is between *educational* (or training) and *research* games.[1] In educational games, the concern is with simulating warfare situations in which players can exercise decision-making skills. Research games, in contrast, though they frequently have instructional value, are designed to generate insights into military problems; designers and controllers attempt to inject as much realism as possible, given the inherent limitations of the medium. The Global War Game series was of the research category, and one of the premier examples of that type.

Educational war games are typically "one-sided"—that is, only one side comprises players, acting freely. In such games the control cell "plays" the opposition, usually in a scripted fashion, at least at the outset. The bounds of scenario probability commonly become elastic in such games, as control cells—gaming-center staff members who regulate game flow, devise and issue "intelligence" disclosures, and respond to the game's sponsor, the entity that requested that the game be played and set its objectives—tailor move-outcome assessments so as to confront confront with the desired challenges. Other games are "two-sided," in which both opposing sides are staffed by players, acting autonomously and mediated by the control cell, which analyzes the interaction of the opposing decisions for each "move" (below) of the two sides and chooses among the plausible outcomes those that best serve the game's objectives. A variant, of which the Global Game was a highly elaborated exemplar, is the "multisided" game, in which some of the player cells may act as "neutrals."

War games can also classified in terms of time—that is, of how "real" time (months, in the case of the Global game) is compressed into the actual, physical period available to the players (two or three weeks in the Global series). Conventional games (such as the Global games of the its first and second series) proceed in discrete stages, known as "moves." In each of these steps, players (or groups of players, in the Global case) privately assess the presented situation as they perceive it—on the basis of "intelligence" provided by the control cell, and within the scenario framework—and then report to the controllers their intentions (political initiatives, diplomatic announcements and démarches, force movements and dispositions, combat orders, etc.) for the next specified period of time. Generally, moves cover short periods of time for tactical-level games and much longer increments for operational and strategic-level ones (the Global case). There are also games that employ "moving game clocks" and confront players with continuously changing situations to which they must respond. Operational games tend to be limited to the tactical level, due to the necessarily limited spans of time they can accommodate.

All war games, of whatever kind or technological sophistication, share a basic conceptual hierarchy, of which the most fundamental dimension relates to physical location and movement.

Even complex operations, including their logistical flows, can be simulated in with physical markers or computer symbols. The value of the outcomes at higher dimensions of any war game depends on how realistically forces are played. If tactics or capabilities are used that would be impossible in the real world, any resulting assessments will be invalid. The next dimension is assessment of outcomes—what "happens" as forces (or political enties) confront or otherwise deal with each other. Some outcomes can be reduced to a roll of the dice, others to complex software algorithms, and yet others (certainly at the strategic level) the judgment of human umpires. Here again, fidelity to real-world phenomena is necessary in order to prevent distortions at the dimension of player decisions. Skewed assessments can lead to faulty analysis and to decisions that yield no useful insights.

The topmost dimension is the analysis of player decisions. Frequently it is not the decisions themselves that are of most interest to a sponsor but, for example, the courses of action that seemed possible to the players, the constraints they perceived, or the effect of the "fog of war" or uncertainty—induced by deliberate ambiguity or lacunae in the information disclosed by the control cell. Typically players are typically provided not actual, precise, and complete outcome assessments—the "ground truth," known only to the control cell—but only those elements (or indications of them) that might realistically be observable, given the capabilities being gamed. Research games do not often deal with this dimension, because of its indeterminate and unpredictable nature; the Global War Game series, for which such indeterminacy was of the essence, was a notable exception.

The annual Global War Game (GWG) in Newport, Rhode Island, was, until its final iterations early in the present century, a multisided, conventionally organized, research game. Initiated in 1978, it soon became one of the preeminent analytic resources of the U.S. national security community. Throughout its history it represented "an opportunity to investigate ideas and concepts that may vary from current strategy or policy wisdom." From its inception in 1978, the game series confronted defining issues. As seen in the previous study of which the present work is a continuation, the Global series constituted a "test bed or crucible for an emerging maritime strategy," a strategy that was to be the U.S. Navy's fundamental concept of global warfare until the dissolution of the Soviet Union.[2]

Series Development

The 1979 Global War Game was the first of a five-year series that reintroduced a concept largely neglected since the 1930s, when the Orange War Plans were gamed at the Naval War College. These first five games played out five Blue/Red scenarios with force levels postulated for the respective sides in the year 1985. Each game was a separate entity with no direct tie-in to the previous or succeeding game. Although scenarios did not necessarily relate to each other, issues identified in one game were incorporated into those that followed. This, in effect, created a "series" through the establishment of a longitudinal approach that promoted the examination of problems over time, in different circumstances, and permitted detailed study in the intervals between games.

This game-study-game cycle, which evolved during the first GWG series, was to become a most important aspect of the second series. Issues raised in one year's game could be researched during the intervening eleven months and the results incorporated into the next game. This process was greatly facilitated by the presence of Army and Air Force officers at the Naval War College. Their work, along with that of their Navy and Marine Corps contemporaries, often in inter-service combinations, contributed importantly to both game development and the attainment of game objectives.

The first game was held in the summer of 1979 at the Naval War College under the sponsorship of the Center for Advanced Research. It was structured as an experimental concept with limited personnel and material resources. Scenarios and strategies appropriate to worldwide conflict were developed, and, because of the experimental nature of the undertaking, a manual, chart-type game format was selected. Some 50 officers (mostly NWC students) and a half-dozen senior defense officials played. Initially, there was concern as to whether this level of participation was sufficient to properly execute a simulation that was global in scope. GWG '79 was in fact more successful than expected. It was also evident, however, that a more thorough examination of global conflict was required and that the effort needed to be populated by more senior players and experts.

From these modest beginnings, the Global War Game experienced substantial growth both in terms of personnel and the level of sophistication. Midway through the first series, the GWG had become a complex operation involving over two hundred participants from all the military services, several intelligence organizations, numerous government departments and agencies as well as representatives from academia and industry. Experts were employed to ensure game fidelity in such areas as logistics, advanced technology and command, control and communications (C3).

Each game of the first series stressed strategy and maneuver. Standard data values and models for weapons systems and sensors were utilized to determine the outcome of specific force interactions.

As is suggested by its name, the Global War Game is a large operation, and by 1983 required many players and controllers. These participants were organized into six primary teams and several supporting tables. Primary cells were:

Blue and Red National Command Authority (NCA)/Supreme High Command (VGK)

Blue and Red Commanders in Chief (CINCs)/Theater Commanders (TVD)

Blue and Red players on the game floor.

Supporting tables covered such subjects as logistics, weather, intelligence and political/military decisions by nations not allied with Blue or Red.

The Global War Game is a hybrid. It includes aspects of a research game, a logistics game and an operational game. Both manual and automated gaming systems have been employed. As later games grew larger and more complex, there was a shift toward increasing reliance on computer-based systems. Whereas GWG 1979 was essentially a manual game, GWG '83 incorporated the new Naval Warfare Gaming System (NWGS), the U.S. Army War College's Theater and Corps Operations and Planning Simulation (TACOPS) and number of smaller models used to perform functions such as battle damage assessment (BDA). Some inputs for the game itself, such as logistics plans, were generated by computer runs made prior to the start on the game.

Game Scenarios 1979–1983

1979

The scenario for the first Global War Game was set in 1985. Consistent with concerns over the security of oil supplies that were prevalent in 1979, the area of initial conflict between Blue and Red was Southwest Asia. An insurgency was in progress in Saudi Arabia, and international tension was high along that nation's northern border. Blue supported Saudi Arabia by sending a brigade of the 82nd Airborne Division along with a contingent of airborne warning and control system (AWACS) aircraft and an F-15 squadron. Two aircraft carrier battle groups (CVBGs) were transferred from the Indian Ocean to proceed around Africa and join the Atlantic Fleet. Worldwide defensive measures included the forward positioning of additional maritime patrol (VP) squadrons and the movement of two CVBGs from the East Coast to positions in the North Atlantic. As the crisis mounted, Red mobilized on 11 July and Blue did the same a week later. Red increased naval deployments in the Norwegian Sea and the Mediterranean. Concerns over the survivability of CVBGs led Blue to withdraw them from the Mediterranean to join with the two CVBGs that had recently left the East Coast and were then located north of the Azores.

Hostilities began with the invasion of Saudi Arabia by four Iraqi divisions and one Red airborne division. Simultaneously, an attack was launched by the Warsaw Pact on the Central Front (map 1). Worldwide, Blue and Red naval forces engaged in a series of intense battles. Red sought to isolate Blue and its allies with a diplomatic offensive. France, Japan, Pakistan, and Algeria were offered incentives to remain neutral. Israel was guaranteed security from her Arab neighbors and an uninterrupted supply of oil in return for neutrality. The Red invasion of Saudi Arabia could not be contained by indigenous forces and by in-theater Blue reinforcements. Therefore, Blue was compelled to withdraw to Israel.

Withdrawal of the CVBGs from the Mediterranean proved to be a political and military disaster. Red was able to overwhelm the remaining regional Blue forces. Deployed Red Soviet naval aviation/long range aviation (SNA/LRA) aircraft struck Blue and allied bases throughout the area with deadly effectiveness. The Naval Air Station, Sigonella, shelled by Red surface units and bombed by Red aircraft, was rendered totally unusable. Malta fell by the evening of the war's first day. Red land-based air superiority turned the central and eastern Mediterranean into a veritable Red lake. Politically, the NATO southern flank unraveled as Greece and Turkey were forced out of the war and Italy lay open to attack.

In the Atlantic, convoy operations were implemented, and two French CVBGs augmented the Blue forces that escorted shipping to Europe. A two CVBG force gained control of the Norwegian Sea, although the effort resulted in the loss of the USS *Vinson*.

An anti-SSBN campaign grew out of an overall Blue ASW effort. Red felt the need to respond to the depletion of part of its strategic nuclear reserve caused by this anti-SSBN campaign and did so by launching tactical nuclear weapons strikes against the Blue CVBGs. An SNA/LRA raid was launched from Luanda against Blue forces in the Atlantic and a second attack, out of Vladivostok, was directed against the two Blue CVBGs in the Pacific. These resulted in the loss of the USS *Kitty Hawk* battle group (BG) in the South Atlantic and the USS *Nimitz* BG in the Pacific. Blue had some

MAP 1
Central Region

difficulty in selecting a suitable Red target for retaliation, finally settled on a Red anti-carrier warfare (ACW) group in the Norwegian Sea. No other use of nuclear weapons occurred.

Due to the heavy commitment of Red forces to the Mediterranean theater, Blue elected to divert the four-carrier battle force (CVBF) from a planned re-entry into the Mediterranean to support of the Central Front. The land war in Europe was nationalized (pre-scripted) rather than played out in detail, and this allowed the players to extend their timelines beyond the first few days of war. The script postulated that NATO had managed to halt, at least temporarily, the Red advance, and, by game end, was conducting successful counterattacks.

As GWG '79 ended, Red sought a cease-fire that would recognize the gains made in Southwest Asia and the Eastern Mediterranean. Blue, while also seeking a cease-fire, refused to recognize Red gains and believed it held the advantage due to favorable momentum on the Central Front.

1980

The 1980 game delved into a broad range of unexplored topics. Blue was hard pressed throughout, because of the Red objective and aggressive employment of forces. However, as one game participant stated: "If the object of the game was to try out strategies, identify key issues, undergo concentrated learning experience, and, in the end, to come away with a much sharper focus on what global war might be like, then GWG '80 was a resounding success."

Largely because Red set domination of Eurasia as its objective and discriminately used nuclear and chemical weapons at the outset, this game was fundamentally about escalation control rather than ships at sea. By its demonstrated will to use nuclear weapons coupled with Blue pessimism about the strategic balance, Red was able to force Blue to choose between surrender and major escalation at succeeding levels.

The 1980 game was based on elaborate, detailed scenarios which covered multiple problem areas, worldwide. Once again the setting was the year 1985, and the scenario postulated serious unrest in Eastern Europe, with the loyalty of both East Germany and Poland to the Warsaw Pact increasingly in doubt.

Oil was a major factor in this game, which cast Red as a net importer. The combination of increased demand and the escalating crisis in Europe drove the price of gasoline in Blue to $4 per gallon. Further impacting the fuel situation was a coup in Nigeria, which then aligned itself with Red.

In the Far East, the People's Republic of China and Vietnam were at war, while in South Asia, Red, still involved in Afghanistan, was mounting sharp border attacks against Pakistan in reprisal for that nation's provision of sanctuary for Afghan "rebels." India had also begun to mobilize against Pakistan. Blue responded by sending five tactical air (TACAIR) squadrons, the 82nd airborne division, and a Marine amphibious brigade (MAB) to Pakistan. During this game, a bright spot for Blue was that relations with Israel, Egypt, Saudi Arabia, and Iraq had improved to the point that Blue could establish a major air base in the Sinai without adverse political consequences.

As the crisis became more acute, Blue withdrew the forces previously dispatched to Pakistan and repositioned them in Southern Iran and Northern Saudi Arabia with the aim of reducing the threat of confrontation with India and improving Blue ability to protect the Gulf oil fields.

In this scenario, war resulted from a deliberate, planned decision on the part of Red. Red leaders felt they were in a favorable military position vis-à-vis Blue, and this, coupled with increasing Warsaw Pact dissidence on the one hand and the growing need for oil on the other was sufficient motivation for the seizure of Eurasia. As in all these games, a primary tenet of Red strategy was to avoid risking the homelands. Therefore, Red did not open with nuclear weapons against Blue. Instead, the war began with a massive conventional attack on the Central Front, against Thrace, and through Austria. Smaller attacks were mounted in Norway and Iran. Red also planned to intimidate Japan and France into neutrality, while applying enough pressure in Southwest Asia to divert Blue. After victory in Europe, Red could then turn to the Persian Gulf and the Far East.

The Blue/NATO political objective was the restoration of the "status quo ante bellum," and Blue strategy was essentially reactive. The preservation of peace was attempted, and, once the war broke out, Blue moves were mainly in response to Red initiatives. Because Blue was not confident of success on the Central Front, the minimum Blue military objective was to hold on the northern and southern flanks, the GIUK (Greenland-Iceland–United Kingdom) gap and in the eastern Mediterranean and Persian Gulf.

Red launched the offensive only two days after Blue had begun to mobilize. In addition to extensive conventional attacks, Red used chemical weapons against Iceland, Guam, and the Azores. In an unusual but very effective move, Red detonated three nuclear air bursts off the east coast of Japan in an effort to intimidate that nation into neutrality.

Once nuclear weapons were used, the Blue National Command Authority (NCA) focus shifted from the tactical level to nuclear linkage. In the process, details such as the sensitivities of third parties, mobility problems, and even outcomes in specific theaters quickly became secondary.

Consequently, GWG 1980 became, almost immediately, an exercise in the control of nuclear escalation. Blue, in response to an SNA/LRA strike from Aden that destroyed a convoy of SL-7s (high-speed container ships) in the Indian Ocean and also to the Red nuclear salvo east of Japan, elected to launch a nuclear attack on Aden with B-52s. This decision was partially influenced by an erroneous report that Blue units had been destroyed in the Red nuclear demonstration off Japan. The Red response was immediate and devastating. Red aircraft utilized nuclear weapons to destroy three CVBGs in the

Indian Ocean and a fourth CVBG was lost to nuclear attack in the Pacific. After considerable thought about a suitable target for retaliation, Blue attempted to sink two *Kiev*-centered surface action groups (SAGs) in the Sea of Japan, with nuclear weapons. However, all the attacking aircraft were shot down prior to weapons release. Meanwhile, Blue eliminated all forward deployed Yankees by conventional means.

In Europe, the war on the Central Front was not going well for Blue. Cracks had begun to show in the battle line of the northern sector and France had not transferred full control of its army to Supreme Allied Commander Europe (SACEUR). Arrival of Blue reinforcements was slowed as forces could not be flown directly to the Federal Republic of Germany (FRG). Damage to many NATO airfields further hampered the airlift as well as the ability of TACAIR to support the battle.

Blue sought a "second front" to take the pressure off the central region, but lacking any readily available forces with which to mount a challenge in other areas, Blue recognized that it would only be "robbing Peter to pay Paul." Even aggressive PRC military operations, it appeared, would not put enough pressure on Red soon enough to make any difference.

The nuclear escalatory process attained a new dimension as the PRC, involved in a conventional war with Vietnam, sided with Blue and ordered Vietnam to cease assisting Red. Vietnam refused, and the PRC responded by exploding a nuclear weapon over Haiphong harbor. Vietnam replied with an attack using Red-supplied nuclear weapons against four targets in the PRC. In retaliation, the PRC struck Red sites with nuclear weapons, which precipitated a major nuclear strike against the PRC by Red.

The game reached temporary termination when Blue, desperately short of options, utilized the "hot line" to threaten an attack on Red at the SIOP (Single Integrated Operations Plan) level. This induced Red to cease hostilities, although Red calculated this was but a temporary pause. The game had reached D+5.

1981

Probably the most intriguing aspect of GWG '81 was the absence of combat on the Central Front. The primary Red objective was the historic goal of seizing the Turkish Straits. Secondly, Red sought control of the Persian Gulf and mid-east oil. While NATO and the Warsaw Pact were intact, their enthusiasm for joining this superpower conflict was minimal.

As with the two previous games, the scenario was set in 1985. The principal crisis governing events was a dispute between Red and Turkey over the interpretation of terms of the Montreux Convention, which regulates maritime passage through the Bosporus and the Dardanelles. A specific game objective was to study factors involved in nuclear escalation.

In Turkey, Red and its surrogates conducted a coordinated campaign to weaken and disrupt the Turkish government. This took the form of a propaganda campaign and demonstrations aimed at separating Turkey from NATO. In addition, Syria attempted to arouse Turkey's Sunni Moslem population. The Turkish government retaliated by threatening strict interpretation of the terms of the Montreux Convention. Red "escalated" with over-flights of Turkey, amphibious exercises in Libya, and Warsaw Pact force movements in the Black Sea, Bulgaria, and Romania.,

Southwest Asia was important in this scenario. Iraq moved toward the Red camp, leading to Blue concerns for the security of both Kuwait and Saudi Arabia. As the crisis deepened, tensions were raised by the discovery of a plan for a joint invasion of both Kuwait and Saudi Arabia by Iraq and Red.

Red commenced the war with an offensive against the secondary objective, Iran. Long-range aviation also struck targets in Saudi Arabia. Only when this campaign was well advanced did Red attempt to capture the Turkish Straits with an advance through Thrace, supported by an invasion of eastern Turkey.

Blue struck back against Red facilities in the Balkans and the Crimea with conventional air strikes from bases at Cairo and Izmir, and with carrier air. Red retaliation, while still at the conventional level, was effective, as two CVs in the Mediterranean were sunk.

Blue, perceiving that the military situation was deteriorating and its options reduced to strategic withdrawal or nuclear escalation, chose the latter and launched Tomahawk land attack missiles-nuclear (TLAM-N) attacks on Red bases in the Trans-Caucasus, Vladivostok, Alexandrovsk, and Petropavlovsk. Red responded immediately, firing intercontinental ballistic missiles (ICBMs) at Diego Garcia and Guam, and the *Nimitz* battle group was lost, also to nuclear attack. The Blue NCA released nuclear weapons to Turkey, which promptly used them against the advancing Red forces. Red responded with nuclear attacks on Turkish positions.

Shortly thereafter, a nuclear cease-fire was agreed to, although a conventional war continued in Turkey. All this occurred in five days.

The situation on the Central Front, though tense, never escalated to hostilities. Blue and Turkey were essentially alone in fighting Red. Indeed, there was a degree of resentment by other NATO members over the military forces committed to this crisis by Blue when a Red offensive into Western Europe threatened.

1982

GWG 1982 saw two major modifications from previous games. First, this game commenced with the war already in progress. The pre-hostilities phase, transition to war and initial fighting were gamed at the National Defense University (NDU) in Globex-82. This permitted GWG '82 to examine the contours of superpower conflict further into war than would have been possible otherwise.

Second, 1982 was the first year in which Army and Air Force participation was fully integrated into the game. This adjustment to joint play provided a richer context for the conduct of military play and the development of issues.

Again set in 1985, the scenario now shifted decisively to a European focus. As in previous games, unrest among the satellites was a problem for Red, particularly in Poland, where food shortages, increased food prices, and a slowdown by Solidarity precipitated a crisis. Further, Red concerns about the Blue relationship with Norway emerged as an important factor. Among points at issue in this relationship were pre-positioning of Blue rapid deployment force (RDF) equipment, fishing rights and territorial claims in the Barents Sea, mineral rights on the Svalbard continental shelf, and joint Blue, Canadian, Norwegian, and United Kingdom exercises in northern Norway.

Southwest Asia remained unsettled and a potential problem area for both Blue and Red. Relations between Israel and Syria had continued to deteriorate, resulting in open warfare in 1985. Red forces had intervened in Iran at the request of the post-Khomeini government (that leader having been assassinated) to put down civil strife. Red retained a presence in Iran through a subsequent grant of port facilities in the southern part of that nation. Saudi Arabia felt threatened by these developments, particularly so following an Iranian attack on a section of an Iraqi oil pipeline. A Saudi request for deployment of the RDF was granted.

Events in the Far East centered upon an agreement between the People's Republic of China and Japan for joint development of a large oil field in the Bohai Bay area. North Korea remained a threat that tended to divert Blue from other objectives.

The primary Red objective was the elimination of Blue political and military influence in Europe through a successful invasion of the Federal Republic of Germany and the consequent dismantling of NATO. The Red military strategy in support of this goal was a conventional offensive across the north German plain to cut off the Benelux countries (Belgium, the Netherlands, and Luxembourg) and seize the Channel ports. Red forces would hold in the center and south, while diplomatic initiatives were made to secure French neutrality. Red also planned to advance into northern Norway to gain a secure flank and to improve the tactical position in the event of a Blue naval initiative in the Norwegian Sea. A subsidiary ground thrust by Red into Thrace had similar objectives: to anchor the southern flank while increasing options for operations in the eastern and central Mediterranean.

The initial Red offensive in Europe commenced as planned but was stalemated at the Rhine. Similarly, the attack in Norway was checked at the Skibotn line by Norwegian units reinforced by a USMC MAB. Red, rather than violate Swedish or Finnish neutrality to outflank this position, struck the airfields at Bodo, Evenes, and Andoya with chemical munitions.

On the southern flank, Red did succeed in driving a corridor between Greece and Turkey. Initially, Blue had withdrawn the CVBGs from the eastern Mediterranean, but returned them as the front was stabilized to support an amphibious landing conducted to provide reinforcements to the NATO defenders in Thrace. While Blue naval forces suffered some loses, the exchange ratio was in their favor.

In the Atlantic, Blue established and maintained submarines in barriers from Greenland to Norway for the purpose of SLOC protection. Red sought to secure the SSBNs by placing them in "havens" at sea or under the ice in the north Norwegian and Barents. These Seas became an area of intense ASW conflict, with Blue doing well against Red. Two CVBGs were sent into the North Sea to help slow the Red advance in the FRG.

In the Far East and the Pacific, Red was on the political and military defensive. Red SSBNs were hidden in the northern Sea of Japan and in the Sea of Okhotsk. Blue concentrated on finding and destroying them as well as major Red surface combatants. While somewhat successful, Blue did incur heavy losses, particularly in the Sea of Okhotsk. Blue CVBGs initially moved back into the central Pacific, a maneuver similar to that undertaken in the Mediterranean. They subsequently were moved forward to engage Red surface units. In the Indian Ocean, a Red combined forces attack severely damaged both Blue carriers.

Blue adopted a forward, offensive strategy to sink the Red navy, and, though not without losses, it was successful. Red surface forces were virtually eliminated and the submarine component substantially depleted. However, the extent to which the Blue anti-SSBN campaign altered the strategic nuclear balance was unknown and did not play a significant role in respective NCA/VGK discussions on nuclear weapons use. Regarding the ground war on the Central Front, while Blue was able to upset the Red timeline and deny Red a quick victory, Red was still able to occupy substantial portions of the FRG.

No nuclear weapons were used in the 1982 game, though Red did make extensive use of chemicals, especially in north Norway and against Iceland. Heavy use of chemicals and the absence of any nuclear use was a factor that set this game apart from its predecessors, and was significant because of contemporary "real world" discussions on this very subject.

As the game progressed, Red sought to negotiate a cease-fire and to terminate the war. However, as in previous games, Blue maintained the position that the territorial "status quo ante bellum" in Europe was prerequisite to any cease-fire. Red refused to negotiate on this basis, and, at game's end, it appeared that a long war was in prospect.

1983

The scenario for the 1983 Global War Game postulated a series of crises in geographically separated parts of the world. As in 1982, however, the focus remained central Europe and the deteriorating relationships between Red and the satellites.

One of the major Red problems lay in East Germany and Poland. Worker unrest escalated due to government crackdowns. Riots occurred, mobs attacked police headquarters and indigenous troops sent to suppress the incipient rebellion mutinied.

Red, confused and taken by surprise, pulled troops back, leaving a power vacuum on the eastern side of the Inter German Border (IGB). With the insurrectionists in control in this area, talk of reunification became rampant and rumors of FRG military movement toward the east circulated.

Trends in the Middle East and Southwest Asia remained little changed from previous games of this series. Israel, nearly isolated politically due to continuing occupation of Lebanon, faced a possible invasion from Arab states led by Syria. Red had been involved in a massive military buildup in Syria and had stationed combat troops there. Although hostilities between Iran and Iraq had been terminated, the potential for instability in the Gulf remained high, as Iran maintained its policy of fostering Shiite agitation throughout the region.

In the Far East, major war was in progress in Southeast Asia. Vietnam had invaded Thailand, with success. In response, and after warning Hanoi of the consequences of continuing, the PRC launched an invasion of Laos and Vietnam. Although resistance was stiff, PRC troops were at the gates of Hanoi and Haiphong when GWG '83 commenced.

Central Europe was the focus of Red concern, as events in the German Democratic Republic (GDR) and Poland posed a threat to the Red "empire" and the Warsaw Pact that Red could not tolerate. Circumstances, however, forced Red to initiate hostilities before full mobilization had been achieved. Red military objectives, therefore, were the most limited of any game thus far. The goal, essentially, was to capture a significant amount of FRG territory and thereby lessen Blue influence on the Continent by demonstrating NATO's inability to defend a powerful member of that alliance, and then to negotiate a permanent solution to the "German Problem." While an offensive in North Norway was integral to the plan, Red had no other offensive aspirations on D-Day. As in the previous year, Red was anxious to avoid involvement in the Far East.

Blue sought to defend conventionally on the Central Front, to gain options from naval superiority gained through forward, aggressive attacks against all Red naval assets, and to shift the nuclear balance through an anti-SSBN campaign. The Blue strategy to achieve maritime supremacy was more coordinated than in previous games, and a part of it involved amphibious landings in the Kuriles.

The Red offensive on the Central Front was hampered by the short time that had been allowed for mobilization. Once launched, progress was relatively slow and a stalemate developed. Red sought negotiations almost from the outset, but Blue conditioned agreement to a cease-fire on restoration of the territorial "status quo ante-bellum" in Europe-terms unacceptable to Red.

Red, for a variety of reasons, decided to escalate the war horizontally. One means was to induce North Korea to move south, an endeavor in which Red was finally successful. Blue responded by supporting the ROK with forces previously detailed to the Kuriles invasion.

In Southwest Asia, Red mounted an attack into Iran and toward the Gulf. This decision resulted from a number of complex factors, including failure to succeed with several political initiatives with Arab governments. Red also reasoned that control of the region's oil supplies could be used as leverage against Blue. Blue had no effective counter in Southwest Asia, as the CVBG in the eastern Mediterranean had been moved west to augment Blue TACAIR on the Central Front.

For the first time in the global series, Red responded to Blue strikes on airfields in the homeland with attacks on North America. Red lost over 20 bombers while knocking out two distant early warning (DEW) line sites and damaging an SSBN installation in Washington State. Red also employed anti-satellite (ASAT) weapons to destroy Blue navigational space-based assets. Blue replied with Tomahawk land attack missile-conventional (TLAM-C) strikes against Red launch facilities.

Consistent with previous games, Blue launched an offensive against the Red SSBN force. The effort was relatively successful, sinking about half of that force by game end.

Neither nuclear nor chemical weapons were used in GWG-83. Although nuclear use was discussed by both NCA/VGK, Red saw no need for them and Blue could not find any employment that would be beneficial.

The 1983 Global War Game saw further development of the concept of prolonged, conventional war. When the game ended at D+30, the prospect was for continued hostilities as the stalemate on the Central Front had the potential to continue well into the future. In this connection, GWG-83 incorporated, for the first time, an economics panel to evaluate industrial/mobilization issues pertinent to general war. There was considerable activity on the diplomatic level, but negotiations foundered over Red demands to retain its Central Front gains and Blue insistence on return to the territorial "status quo ante."

Overview

The first five-year Global War Game series explored a broad range of significant issues. A number of new concepts and ideas evolved, many of which influenced the theater strategies for Blue and NATO forces. Others were re-examined or modified based on the lessons learned in the games.

Fully understanding the key issues requires that the reader be aware of how game dynamics interacted with scenario events and game analysis. This overview discusses the interplay among these aspects of the game and their impact on strategy development. While this section does provide a capsule examination of the games, the emphasis is on highlighting a selected number of the most significant themes and how they were analyzed.

The first year, the major emphasis was on naval play, and the roles of the Army and Air Force were essentially pre-scripted. Very early in the series, however, it became evident that events, particularly in Europe, could not be adequately gamed or the issues raised assessed properly without the full integration of Army and Air Force representatives, both in the play of the game and in the "study" part of the "game-study-game" cycle alluded to above. The use of both personnel and models these services developed to replicate outcomes of combat were critical to the realism of the game and the validity of the analytical process.

As the sister services became more involved in the game, Blue forces became more effective. Efforts to improve inter-service cooperation were continually emphasized, and a number of experiments were conducted to see how the forces of each service could work together to achieve common objectives. At the same time, the number of game participants, military and civilian, increased. Both these factors combined to raise both the quality and sophistication of game play.

Blue began with a strong, defensive mentality. The ability of forward deployed operating forces to survive in the face of intense Red air and naval attacks was a major concern. However, as the series progressed, Blue found not only that naval forces could operate in those forward positions, but that a more aggressive posture tended to produce greater success. True to the charter of the games, Blue experimented with a number of concepts in the deployment and use of naval forces. Throughout the series, these forces were employed innovatively and naval strategy was characterized by a willingness to explore different ideas.

The Red gaming approach also evolved significantly. Initially, Red operated tactically in a rigid, deterministic style, while at the levels of policy and strategy, several operations of questionable merit were attempted. This was due in part to a combination of the small number of players on the Red side and a limited amount of background and knowledge for realistically representing Red. An accurate simulation of the Red strategic thought process was also hampered by the use of U.S. military personnel who tended to "worst case" by concentrating known Blue weaknesses and ignoring the limitations of Red.

In order to better simulate Red, members of the intelligence and diplomatic communities were brought into the game to replicate Red thought processes and world outlook more accurately. These new participants defined Red objectives and strategy in terms of actual intelligence estimates rather than in terms of worst-case fears. Additionally, as the contingent of Red players expanded, sufficient numbers became available to allow the cell to interact fully with the game organization as opposed to being the more traditional, limited, opposition force cell. As a result, Red play became less dogmatic. These factors led to the formulation of Red goals that were less ambitious but probably more representative of "real world" Red policy. For example, the scope of Red military objectives diminished from "control of Western Europe" to a more attainable "neutralization of the Federal Republic of Germany," and the tendency too escalate across the nuclear threshold diminished.

This change in the Red cell also caused a shift in the way hostilities were initiated. During the first games, Red purposefully embarked on a planned war of conquest. Red began and used conflict as a tool to gain predetermined political objectives. This, in the 1980 and 1981 games, contributed to the rapid intensification of the crisis and a swift transition to war. While both these games involved relatively brief periods of diplomatic and military activity, Blue endeavored to negotiate its way out of crisis, on the one hand, while trying to position forces to gain advantage should war break out, on the other. Blue, in addition to trying to manage the confrontation with Red, had other problems. Blue tried to give direction to a NATO alliance whose members did not always concur on the proper response to a developing situation. Allies in other parts of the world had totally separate concerns. While participants found these problems difficult and occasionally frustrating, many insights were gained into factors that led to war.

Both Blue and Red learned it was most unlikely that one of the two superpowers would simply decide to go to war against the other. Both arrived at the conclusion that war was difficult to start, and would most likely occur as a result of a number of events largely outside the control of the eventual belligerents. Therefore, in later games, the "road to war" changed. Red, though still initiating hostilities, did so as the result of a chain of events that pushed Red beyond the ability to avoid war. In the '82 and '83 games, Red faced the prospect of a rebellious Eastern Europe and felt the need to act before things got totally out of control. This supports the premise that few rational leaders would intentionally start World War III.

Nevertheless, Red, as the aggressor gained substantial benefit. It allowed Red to choose the theater or region that fit its plans and then mass the required units. Elsewhere, Red generally practiced economy of force. Blue, in turn, had to concentrate forces in the geographic area of Red attack and found it difficult with what remained to build a force package strong enough to seriously distract Red from the main axis of attack.

Europe acted as a magnet for both Blue and Red. To Red, as a continental power, Western Europe was perceived as a threat and, therefore, a logical area for expansion of political and territorial influence. A successful Red offensive in this theater would weaken or destroy Red's primary global foe, the Blue/NATO coalition. Even the early attacks into Southwest Asia supported this goal, as control of Middle East oil would give Red enormous bargaining power.

Blue focus was also on Europe. The NATO alliance was the most important political/military link and the maintenance of the coalition was paramount in Blue strategy. Therefore, a Red offensive in Western Europe had to be countered at all costs.

The requirements of NATO decision-making had an impact on Blue policy. NATO was a defensive alliance with the goal of maintaining the political and territorial integrity of its members. It did not seek to seize territory from, or to overthrow the national governments of, the Warsaw Pact. Blue, as a member of NATO, adhered to that position, of necessity. This led to the articulation of war aims in terms of "restoration of the territorial status quo ante bellum."

The alliance relationship affected Blue in another aspect. As a maritime power, Blue was allied with what was, essentially, a continental coalition facing a continental foe. As Blue forces sought to support the European battle, they experienced the traditional problems a maritime nation encounters fighting a continental power. Most notably,

Blue had to find the most effective way to employ its naval power. Commanders realized that to use this strength placed Blue in a classic predicament; naval forces might not be able to win the war but a major naval defeat would significantly reduce Blue strategic flexibility. This situation was to profoundly affect Blue strategy and was largely responsible for the conservative mode of naval force employment in the early games of the series. Once Blue found that its forces could successfully defend themselves, its naval deployments became increasingly aggressive.

Although more aggressive force utilization produced increased success, the fundamental problem of how best to exploit maritime advantage against a continental opponent remained. While no definitive answers emerged from this series, the participants did gain a far better understanding of the role and value of maritime power in a global conflict.

The maritime/continental relationship presented Blue with yet another dilemma. Blue, as a maritime power, had to operate globally, if only to protect its interests. This caused substantial dispersal of forces, which tended to work to Red advantage. Thus, not only was Red able, as noted above, to mass at the point of offensive; the very orientation of Blue power worked to disperse its force even further.

Red was actually conducting two distinctly different wars in one. Within the Blue/Red context, Red was fighting a limited war. Red did not seek to destroy Blue. Within the context of the European theater—the Western Theater of Military Operation (TVD)—however, Red was waging an absolute war with the object of total victory. If it could achieve the neutralization of the FRG, this would, by Red estimation, lead to the emasculation and eventual dissolution of NATO and the concomitant reduction, if not elimination of Blue influence on the continent.

Escalation, both vertical and horizontal, was a topic that received considerable attention during the First Global War Game Series. Although theoretical issues regarding escalation had been studied in great detail elsewhere, these games explored the process within a global environment and utilized interactive techniques. As the sophistication of the games grew, year by year, knowledge and lessons learned increased proportionately. By the end of the five year series, a number of valuable insights into the range of complexities associated with the escalation process had been developed.

During the series, vertical escalation passed through the conventional war dimension and into the chemical and nuclear arenas. The nuclear aspect, as one might expect, attracted the most attention. Invariably, the players found that nuclear weapons' use overshadowed all other events and turned the game into an exercise in escalation control.

Through experience in the games, both sides came to the conclusion that nuclear weapons produced little tactical advantage. Blue, while essentially equal at the strategic level, suffered from a perceived inferiority at the theater and tactical levels. (Note: Both Blue and Red's view of the nuclear situation were based on estimated 1985 force balances.)

Red also came to this conclusion, though for different reasons. Use of nuclear weapons, in spite of Red theater/tactical advantages, proved to be counterproductive. Red had gone to considerable effort to build superiority in conventional arms. That advantage could be negated if the conflict escalated to the theater nuclear level, which could destroy the value of the territories gained as well as major Red forces. Additionally, nuclear use could put the homeland at risk, an outcome contrary to Red objectives.

Blue, however, faced a further disadvantage when contemplating nuclear escalation, and this was targeting. The vast majority of worthwhile targets for Blue were located within the Red continental homeland. A nuclear strike on the Red homeland was perceived to make escalation to the strategic nuclear level much more likely. Thus Blue found it difficult to select an isolated target that did not run the risk of precipitating nuclear disaster. An attack on the homeland with conventional weapons also had potential strategic implications, especially when the Red paranoia regarding homeland defense was taken into consideration. The inability to determine the nature—conventional or nuclear—of an inbound raid increased the risk of triggering a Red "launch on warning." All of these factors combined to make a Blue "graduated response" difficult.

In contrast, Blue, as a maritime power, offered Red a number of attractive and isolated targets, such as CVBGs and various island bases. Because Red believed that Blue had no symmetrical response to such attacks and that, in any event, the theater nuclear balance was in its favor, Red endeavored to use nuclear weapons to gain advantage in the first three games. Red was not without difficulties, however. Throughout the series, Red found it difficult to formulate a counter to the Blue anti-SSBN campaign. After several less successful efforts, Red accepted the losses as inevitable.

Chemical warfare was an area were Red was perceived to enjoy a distinct advantage. Red resources were thought to be superior, outnumbering those of Blue. When Red chose to employ chemicals, Blue again felt it lacked an adequate, symmetrical response. In fact, despite an avowed policy of nuclear retaliation for chemical attacks, Blue chose to do this on only one occasion.

The "theory" of horizontal escalation was that Blue initiatives away from the Central Front could either divert Red or lead to opportunities for offensive operations. Blue experimented with a number of approaches, but seemed unable to influence Red or to discover any significant Warsaw Pact vulnerability. Red remained wedded to a Central Front focus and refused to be diverted. For Blue, not only were areas of potential Red weakness difficult to reach geographically, efforts to do so could dilute valuable resources that were often needed elsewhere. If Blue chose to mass sufficient forces to be effective off the main axis of action, the availability of troops to support the primary theater could be adversely affected. Conversely, if Blue mounted an attack with a less favorable force ratio, effects were marginal.

While Blue did not achieve major success employing horizontal escalation strategies, analysis did show useful trends not readily apparent at first. Blue, hoping for a response that would produce immediate advantage, either looked in the wrong area or missed the initial indications of what could be significant, long-term benefits. Some of the more important results of horizontal escalation lay in actions that Red did not take. Blue, by positioning forces that had potential to harm Red, caused Red to maintain higher force levels in defensive positions. This was seen frequently in the maritime and air arenas, where Red maintained sizable forces in regions away from the primary area of combat to counter possible Blue offensive actions. As these forces were tied down, value for Blue ensued from their commitment for defensive purposes and their resulting non-availability for offensive efforts. Of equal significance were the instances where Red began a redeployment of forces to counter Blue. These actions showed the potential of achieving the desired dispersion of Red forces. However, many such redeployments were still in their initial stages at game end and did not become evident due to the short time span of the game. As the long war issue emerged, a link to horizontal escalation appeared to offer some attractive prospects.

Red found opportunities to use this same strategy. By lunching attacks into Southwest Asia, Red caused Blue to divert sizable forces away from other theaters. Additionally, through the use or threatened use of surrogates, such as North Korea, Red was also able to tie down Blue resources.

Initially, both sides envisioned a conflict of relatively short duration. However, over the course of the series, a number of factors became evident to indicate that Blue gained certain advantages from a long-war policy. Most notable was the opportunity to redirect superior Blue industrial, economic, technical, and agricultural resources to the battle. Once mobilized, these sectors placed Blue in a much more favorable position. By contrast, Red, with a larger portion of similar resources from a smaller economy already oriented to the defense sector, could achieve less, with Blue, therefore, gaining a relative advantage.

A key issue for Blue, then, was the ability to sustain itself and its allies through the early and intermediate stages of conflict to permit the benefits of full mobilization to accrue. Blue must, therefore, fight a potentially stronger Red force during these stages using only "on hand" resources. Red not only had a larger standing military force but also enjoyed a considerable advantage due to its greater arms stockpiles and "warm" production base.

From another aspect, Blue policy made a long war almost certain. Blue doggedly maintained a position that accepted no compromise from the negotiating condition that required restoration of the territorial "status quo ante bellum." However, the strong, initial Red conventional superiority made sizeable territorial gains virtually inevitable. Relinquishing these gains was clearly unpalatable for Red, and tactical/theater nuclear options did not appear to solve the impasse for either side. Red might achieve its political objective, but could not force Blue to agree to a cessation of hostilities on Red terms. Thus, a long war seemed in prospect.

For Blue, linking a long war strategy with horizontal escalation appeared to offer tangible benefits. Over a longer period, many Red vulnerabilities could be exploited effectively. For example, the Red ability to produce and distribute food, even during good times, was marginal at best. During wartime, much of the agricultural sector, manpower and equipment especially, would be mobilized. As he war lengthened, food availability would eventually drop. Food imports to augment suppies would not be an option. The extensive fishing fleet was vulnerable and would lose the freedom to operate. Blockade, combined with selective attacks against agricultural production and distribution systems and the commercial fishing fleet would exacerbate the problems. These actions, coupled with efforts to exploit the latent Red nationalities problem, had the potential to be an effective weapon. Much of the Red industrial complex was also exposed, and the effects of its attrition would be cumulative with the agricultural shortages.

A longer war would also provide Blue the opportunity to exploit fissures in the cohesiveness of the Red/Warsaw Pact coalition. Red ability to maintain alliance support appeared to vary with the military situation. A strong campaign with the objective of splintering the Warsaw Pact nations could produce favorable results.

The war termination issue presented a difficult problem that was never completely resolved. Neither side was willing to budge from their respective positions in order to end hostilities. As noted above, Blue insisted on the return to a territorial "status quo ante bellum" as a pre-condition to further moves. Red, on the other hand, offered a cease-fire in place with negotiations to follow.

Blue would not accept such art offer, believing that once a cease-fire occurred, Red would achieve a de facto legitimization of military gains, as NATO might find it extremely difficult to recommence hostilities if negotiations collapsed. Red, perceiving the military situation to be clearly in its favor, found it difficult to believe that Blue refused to enter into negotiations. The result was deadlock, as neither side was willing to budge from its position.

NOTES

1. This introduction to war gaming draws largely on two articles published *Naval War College Review* (Spring 2001, vol. 54, no. 2) by members of the College's wargaming faculty: Robert C. Rubel, "War-Gaming Network-centric Warfare," pp. 61–74, and Kenneth Watman, "Global 2000," pp. 75–88.

2. Bud Hay and Bob Gile, *Global War Game: The First Five Years,* Newport Paper 4 (Newport, R.I.: Naval War College Press, 1993), p. vii. Available at www.nwc.navy.mil/press/npapers/np4/np4.pdf. For the Maritime Strategy, see John B. Hattendorf, *The Evolution of the U.S. Navy's Maritime Strategy, 1977–1986* (Newport, R.I.: Naval War College Press, 2004), available at www.nwc.navy.mil/press/npapers/np19/NP19.pdf.

Introduction to the Second Global War Game Series

The Second Global War Game Series was conducted at the Naval War College from 1984 through 1988 to examine the nature and issues of a superpower conflict in a 1990s time frame. The second series built upon and extended the foundations laid by the first series (1979–1983), and the broad purposes were similar. The overarching objective was to gain insights into how naval campaigns might be conducted on a global scale in the event of war between the United States (Blue) and its allies and the Soviet Union (Red) and its allies. Specific objectives included the assessment of:

- The priorities of sequential operations.
- The adequacy and form of logistics systems to support extended, prolonged, and diverse naval operations.
- The impact of strategy and maneuver on force effectiveness.
- The impact of political and economic factors in developing strategies and the vulnerability of such strategies to international and regional constraints.
- The loci of nuclear thresholds in various theaters and concepts for escalation/de-escalation.
- The pattern and processes for control of military forces at national, headquarters, and tactical levels when combat activity is intensive and widespread.

A hypothesis that emerged from the first series and tended to shape Blue thinking about global war can be stated as follows:

- Due to Red holding the initiative, Blue seems unlikely to achieve a favorable position to successfully terminate a short, conventional war.
- Nuclear use tends to escalate and appears counter-productive for both Blue and Red.
- Therefore, Blue/NATO should plan to fight a protracted, conventional war.

Several other findings that emerged from the first series had substantial implications for the second game series. Among the most important was that while the Blue/NATO

Alliance had a defensive political orientation, offensive campaign options within the strategic defensive posture could be very effective in disrupting Red timelines and thus cause Red to revise original military objectives. Contrary to the belief then prevalent in some quarters, a Red offensive into Western Europe would not necessarily require a Blue/NATO nuclear response to halt that offensive short of the Channel.

The first series experience indicated that Blue/NATO naval forces would achieve dominance at sea. Indeed, as the series proceeded, it appeared that geographic areas, such as the north Norwegian Sea and the eastern Mediterranean, previously considered fraught with risk for surface units, could in fact serve as vital operating areas, given proper sequence of operations and tactics. Most important, maritime dominance permitted Blue/NATO to extend the war in time and expand the war in geographic scope.

A third point of interest dealt with war initiation and war termination. A conclusion of the first series was not only that a set of circumstances that would precipitate a NATO/WP war was very difficult to devise, but a negotiated settlement to such a war was virtually impossible to attain. A basic and necessary precondition for Blue/NATO to commence negotiations was a return to the territorial status quo ante, a position that Red rejected out of hand. Further, Blue was generally unwilling to enter substantive negotiations from a position of perceived military inferiority; Red, lacking any semblance of sea control, could not force a Blue capitulation. Consequently, war termination negotiations generally stalemated.

These factors and issues from the first series led to two questions that were pervasive in the games of the second series:

- What are the political, war-fighting, logistical, and mobilization issues that define the Blue/NATO capability to sustain a conventional war until the full military industrial and personnel resources of the free world can be mobilized to secure victory?
- How best can the maritime superiority of Blue/NATO be translated into strategic leverage useful in bringing the war to a successful conclusion?

Game Architecture

The games of the second global series were large both in terms of scope and number of participants. Generally, over 600 players were involved at any given time. All of the branches of the armed services were represented, as was the Coast Guard. Canada and the United Kingdom sent military and civilian players. The breadth of the game was also demonstrated by the numerous government departments and agencies involved. They ranged from those one might expect, such as the Departments of State and Defense, the Central Intelligence, and the Federal Emergency Management Agencies to some that one might not anticipate, such as the Bureau of Mines. Further, as the study of protracted conventional war was a major game objective, a large delegation of economic experts and specialists in manufacturing and industrial mobilization were included. Finally, the role in the game of nations other than Blue and Red required players with broad knowledge of the world in general as well as detailed experience in various specific geographical areas.

The game itself might be described as "three-sided," with a "Blue" team representing the United States, a "Red" team playing the Soviet Union, and a "Green" team for all other countries. The Blue and Red teams played on three levels: The National Command Authority (NCA) and the Supreme High Command (VGK), the Commanders-in-Chief (CINC), and Commanders of Theaters of Military Operations (TVD), and various corps and fleet levels for each side.

Considerable effort was devoted to ensuring the fidelity of game play. To this end, the Red team was composed of individuals thoroughly familiar with Soviet politics, military doctrine, and capabilities—selected from applicable government departments and agencies, the intelligence community, and the armed services. They were tasked to fight the Red order of battle as (to the best of their knowledge) the Soviet Union would, not as an American officer might.

Similarly, the Green team, composed mainly of retired State Department personnel, including some of ambassadorial rank, played both the respective allies of Blue and Red and all other nations as well. The following pages reflect not only diplomatic initiatives by individual states, nonaligned blocs, and nongovernmental agencies, but also demonstrate that allies did not always respond in the manner that Blue and Red expected.

Another important aspect of the game involved the mobilization of the Blue economy for a long, conventional war. Among the considerations that had to be addressed were the cost of the war and how it would be paid for, the potential need for rationing, and the control of anticipated inflation. Of prime importance was the conversion of factories to meet the needs of the battlefield and the concomitant problem of finding and training the workers to operate the expanded industrial base. A group working advanced technology issues considered means to ameliorate the shortfall in end items with long lead times and also considered several "Manhattan Project"–type proposals.

All of this required substantial support. Computers were used extensively for force movement and battle damage assessment, although the land table remained a manual operation. Models already in existence, such as the Naval Warfare Gaming System (NWGS) and the Army's Theater and Corps Operations and Training Simulation (TACOPS) continued to be utilized, augmented by new programs where required. For example, inability to assess some air combat interactions led to the creation of the Navy War College Air Model (NWCAM).

Logistics play was computer-supported, detailed, and of critical importance because of the concern over what was referred to as the "bathtub" effect. Consumption rates for munitions and major equipment such as aircraft and battle tanks in the intensity of modern war were not really known. However, because the validity of the concept of protracted conventional war depended on Blue/NATO sustainability, a large staff was necessary to track usage at the front with a high degree of accuracy.

There were a number of other tasks requisite to the proper functioning of the game. Battle damage assessment (BDA) was an involved process requiring separate teams to adjudicate the results of combat in the air, on land, and at sea. An intelligence cell monitored movements and engagements to determine what information would be available to Blue and Red based on game events; they then provided that information. A special weapons cell determined the effects of chemical weapons employment and was involved in off-line deliberations when one side or the other required an appraisal of the likely result of contemplated nuclear weapons use. A meteorological component was on hand to brief weather, worldwide, for every day of the war. A strong effort was made to create an environment that would, as realistically as possible, reflect some of the domestic pressures in the conduct of the war. A congressional cell was created with retired members of the U.S. House of Representatives reprising their former roles. They held hearings, offered policy suggestions, and were, on occasion, critical of the administration. An innovation introduced in this series was the Global News Network (GNN). The War College Public Affairs Office produced a morning TV show, *Good Morning Global*, in network format, as well as a daily newspaper. The televised news broadcast was delivered every morning and provided, in network format, interviews and descriptions of selected events from the previous game day. Normally, two game days were played in one real-time day, and this medium not only kept all players informed of the overall course of events but also became a well-used forum for the president of Blue and the general secretary of Red to set forth their views on the war and to try to sway "global" opinion.

Move Convention

The format of the first Global War Game was relatively simple and straightforward, but as the series progressed, the games became quite complex. The purpose of this section is to lay out some aspects regarding the structure and play of the series from 1984 through 1987 that may not be familiar to all readers. While there tended to be slight variations from game to game, the following descriptions are representative of what took place. The 1988 game will be considered separately. This section is not intended to

FIGURE 1
Blue

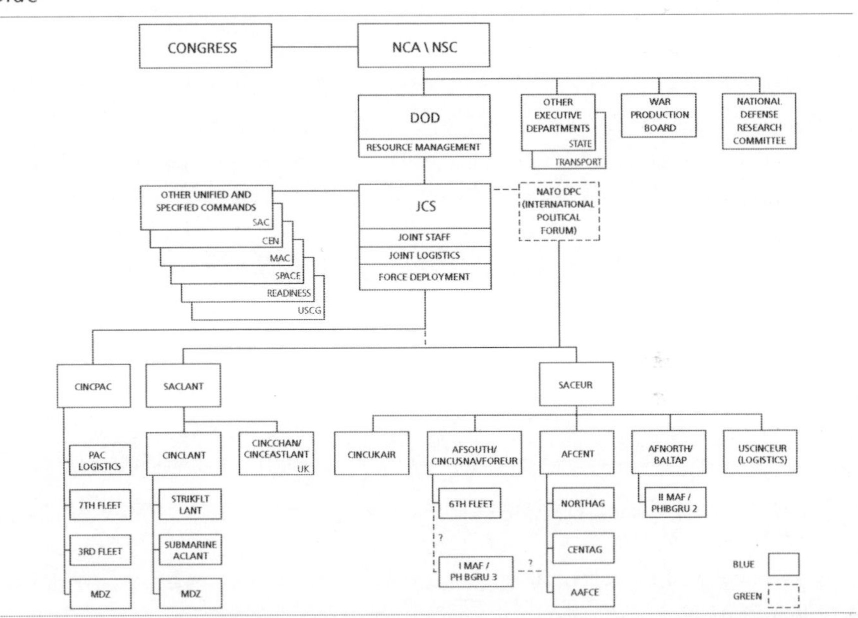

be an all-inclusive, detailed explanation of game mechanics, but it should provide a basic guide to the "flow" of the game.

Once the organizational framework of the game had been established in broad outline, a billet structure was required. For example, how would the Blue National Command Authority and Red Supreme High Command be staffed? (While by convention "Red" indicated specifically the Soviet Union and "Blue" the United States, in common usage the reference was usually to the Warsaw Pact and NATO more broadly. The color convention in this monograph is generally in the latter, broader sense; context makes clear when the more restrictive meaning is intended.) As has been noted above, the number of positions required expanded as the game progressed. Typically, the NCA had the following positions: President, Vice President, Secretary of State, Assistant Secretary of State (NATO Permanent Representative), Assistant Secretary of State, Secretary of Defense, Director, Central Intelligence Agency, National Security Advisor, Deputy National Security Advisor, Director of Mobilization, and, when required, the Chairman, Joint Chiefs of Staff (JCS), and a Press Secretary. Members of the VGK included the General Secretary of the Communist Party, Minister of Defense, Deputy Minister of Foreign Affairs (Ruling Communist Parties), Chairman, Council of Ministers, Chairman, State Security (KGB), Deputy Minister of Defense for Rear Services, and, when required, the Chief of the General Staff. It was then a process of selecting specific individuals to fill key positions

FIGURE 2
Red

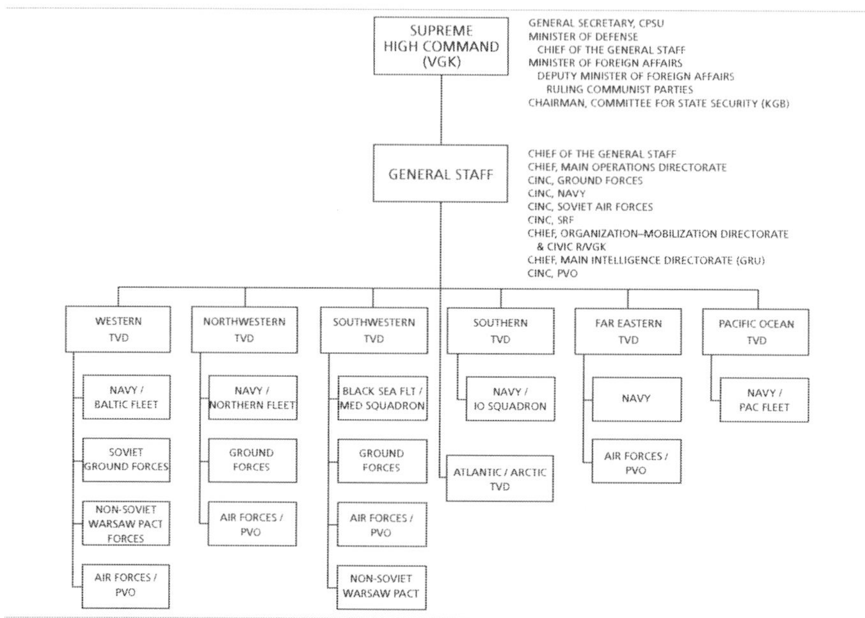

(the President of the United States was most often played by a retired U.S. congressman). Other organizations and military commands would be requested to select individuals to serve in various positions. The national laboratories, for example, were requested to send experts to staff the nuclear cell. A number of the organizations involved in providing players to the game also took part in the financial sponsorship of the game, and these dual contributions of manpower and money were both critically important in making the game as successful and important as it was.

The games of the second series all ran for three weeks, although not all players were in attendance for the entire game. Each participant "checked in" either on Sunday afternoon or early Monday morning and received an information packet that provided unclassified background information (the games were played at the SECRET level) and their specific cell assignment. The rest of Monday morning consisted of a briefings on general game information, such as scenario events, followed by adjournment to the assigned player cells for purposes of organization and additional briefings.

Tuesday morning saw game play begin in earnest. Players received situational briefs, including current intelligence estimates tailored to each side, Blue or Red. Because the focus on the games was on planning, the perspective at various levels of command was different. The NCA and JCS were looking out beyond 30 days and the theater CINCS, concerned with strategic decisions, focused on the seven to 30 day timeframe.

FIGURE 3
Control Group

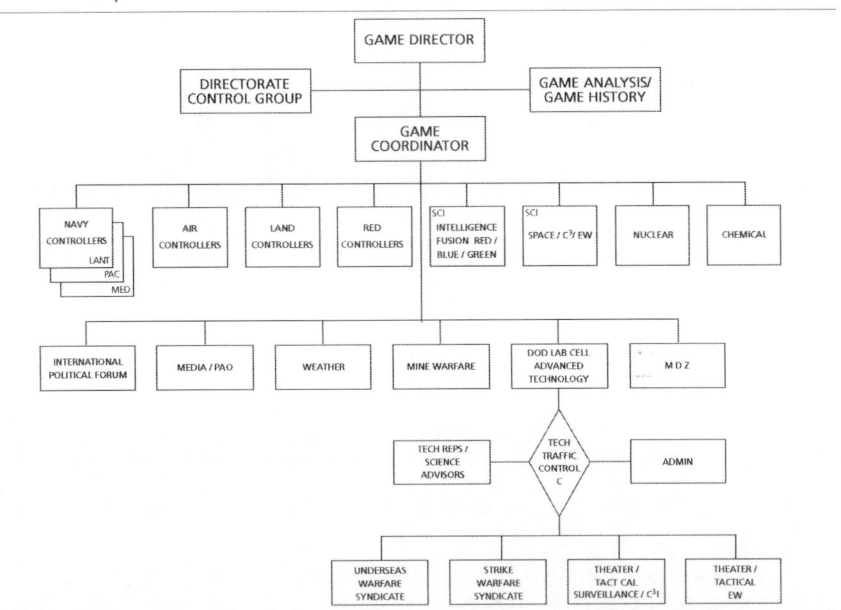

Campaign decisions at the fleet or regional command level were based on a three to seven day view, and the tactical level concerned itself with the next twenty-four to forty-eight hours. Therefore, CINCs (CINCPAC, SACEUR, etc.) and TVD commanders were provided with long-range guidance by the NCA or VGK. These theater commanders forwarded their strategic intentions to the various major command cells (CINCLANT, AFCENT, etc.) where campaign plans were drawn up, then detailed orders, or, in game parlance, "moves" were generated (6th Fleet, CENTAG, etc., level) for a two day planning cycle. These specified what units were to be moved and where, what targets were to be attacked, by which forces, with what weapons and when. Provisions for decoys, feints, or other special tactical procedures were included. These "moves" were in written form and presented to the umpires/controllers at 1100 and at 1530 each day to be assesseds on what was called the "game floor." The game floor was actually located in two places, in that the Army had a separate space for its "land table."

A war game can be described as a "manual" game or a "computer" game, depending on how the game is run. A manual game is one where virtually all operations are performed by hand. Maps of the geographic area of conflict would provide the basis for the game, and symbols representing the various forces would be moved from place to place in accordance with the "moves" ordered by the players. Battle damage assessment was done by rolling dice. Some of the complications of this method can be seen by

FIGURE 4
Game Floor/Table Layout

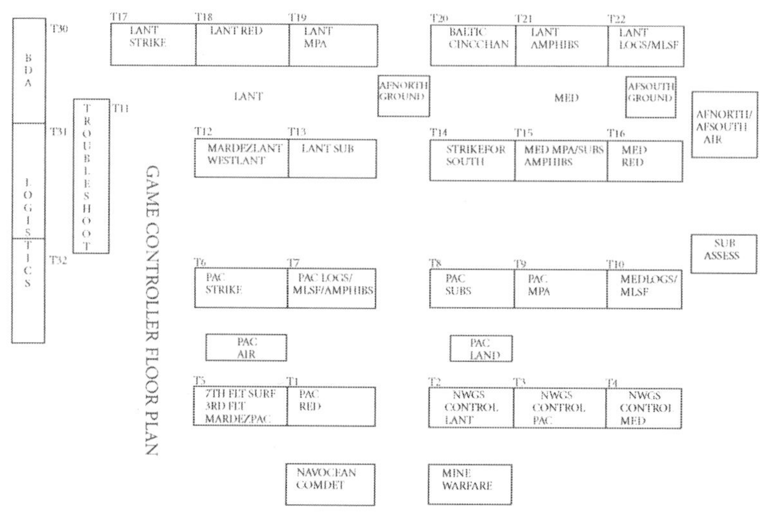

considering a launch of surface-to-surface missiles. The umpire would roll the dice once to determine the number of missiles that were actually launched successfully, once again to determine how many of those flew properly, again to ascertain the effect of enemy counter-measures, and once more to come up with the number which actually hit targets. This procedure was clearly unsuited to a game as complex as global.

A computer game relied substantially on those devices for all phases of the game. It had obvious advantages in the above example for determining battle damage assessment and was invaluable for keeping track of logistics consumption in general and ordinance expenditure in particular. (Sonobuoys were a case in point, as early games saw them utilized as if the supply was infinite.) Valuable as computers are, however, they could not replace totally the functions performed by a human umpire or eliminate the need for maps. For these reasons, the global game was a hybrid, incorporating features of both the manual and computer type games.

The "game floor" consisted of a number of "tables" to resolve the engagements that occurred because of the "moves" generated in the player cells. (Figure 4 shows the game floor schematic for the 1986 GWG) The personnel assigned to these tables, called "umpires" or "controllers," varied considerably in number, depending on the theater and command. All of the relevant services would be represented, so the "Pacific Strike" table would, of necessity, require several people. The "AFSOUTH Ground" and

"AFNORTH Ground" parts of the game, on the other hand, were played manually by a single individual. Further, controllers from Red were present at the major tables as well.

The duties of the "umpires/controllers" were a key part of the game. They functioned as all of the personnel, sensors, and weapons of the command that they represented. They maintained frequent liaison with other controllers to ensure the most accurate simulation of interactions considering the commander's directives, force disposition, EMCON policy, and environmental factors. They were also charged with defending their command's forces, if attacked, with all available assets, within the existing Rules of Engagement (ROE.)

Combat was initiated by a Blue or Red player through the game floor controller who received the written move ordering an attack. The defending controller would then respond. The attack plan and target defenses were then passed to the BDA table for adjudication. Naval engagements were generally assessed by the NWAGS, which took into consideration all of the variables involved in attack and defense, determined the ships that had been hit, how serious the damage was, and what had been sunk. NWAGS worked on a stochastic model, which was based on probabilities, random number draw, and single iteration. This process did not result in the most probable outcome, but one of any number of possible outcomes. Consequently, while a narrow band of the most probable outcomes would emerge from a number of iterations over time, the uncertainty inherent in war was preserved. The battle damage assessment process, therefore, provided random results within the realm on possibility, based on the best estimate of real world conditions. After review by the Game Director or his representative, the BDA results were forwarded to the appropriate controllers so that they could brief the players on the outcome of the engagements.

After combat resolution results had been approved, the Blue and Red umpires/controllers briefed their respective sides on the outcomes. These briefs were not 100% truth but presented to the players the information that would actually have been obtainable. These briefs took place both in the morning and afternoon immediately following the submission of the two-day move. The reason for briefing after move submission was to maintain focus on the planning purpose of the game as opposed to a continual reaction to the results of battle damage assessment. Events of particular significance that would affect the planning process, such as the loss of an aircraft carrier, would be reported immediately to permit plan modifications as necessary.

Further, a periodic intelligence brief would also take place. The Intelligence Fusion Cell would review the force movements that had taken place, along with other information that might have been gleaned through satellite surveillance or other forms of reconnaissance, and detail this information to the respective sides.

FIGURE 5

Move Convention Schedule

		TACTICAL ATAF TF	CAMPAIGN AFCENT/FLEET	THEATER USCINC/SACEUR	JCS/NCA
FIGHT COMBAT D+20	0800	SCENARIO RECAP/ADMIN/WX BRIEF ——————>			
	0830	PLAN NEXT MOVE D+21/D+22	ADJUSTMENTS TO CAMPAIGN PLAN <——	DELIVER 7–30 DAY PLAN	LONG TERM (30 DAY)
	1000	BRIEF <—— SUPERIORS ——>	DELIVER 7-DAY PLAN		FOCUS
	1100	DELIVER D+21/22 PLAN TO CONTROL IN WRITING	CONTINGENCY PLANNING	SEMINAR/BRIEFS AS DESIRED	
	1130	ASSESSMENT [D+20]	INTEL/FUSION UPDATE	——>	
FIGHT COMBAT D+21	1300	PLAN NEXT MOVE D+22/D+23	ADJUSTMENTS TO <—— CAMPAIGN PLAN	DELIVER 7–30 DAY PLAN	BRIEFS IN ACCORDANCE WITH PUBLISHED DAILY AGENDA
	1430	BRIEF <—— SUPERIORS ——>	DELIVER 7-DAY PLAN		
	1530	DELIVER D+22/23 PLAN TO CONTROL IN WRITING	CONTINGENCY PLANNING	SEMINAR/BRIEFS SKED PER CINCS DESIRE	
	1600	ASSESSMENT [D+21]/	INTEL/FUSION UPDATE	——>	

To summarize, the game day cycle began at 0800 with the Global Network News, then a scenario update and the weather forecast, which utilized actual weather that had occurred on the same day of the previous year. The two-day planning session commenced at 0830, and is shown in the illustration provided from the 1986 game (figure 5), for D+21 and D+22. During this period, the battles of D+20 were being fought and adjudicated on the game floor. The D+21 and D+22 plan was delivered to the controllers at 1100, followed by the assessment of the D+20 interactions. Planning for the D+22/23 move began at 1300 and was due at 1530. The assessment of D+21 events followed at 1600. This cycle permitted the play of two days of war for each calendar day.

The ground war in Europe was displayed on what was called the "land table." This consisted of a horizontally mounted map of the Central Region on which were placed "counters" representing the various Blue and Red units then engaged or moving toward the FLOT. The respective "moves" of land forces by Blue and Red were entered into the Army's TACOPS system, which determined casualties, remaining effective combat strength of units and the resulting geographic positions of units resulting from the engagements. Another system, TACLOGS, supported TACOPS by maintaining the status of major end items such as the loss of tanks, other armored vehicles, ammunition expenditure, etc.

Also of importance was the ongoing work of the logisticians. The inputs to the various computerized systems to resolve battle damage assessment provided an excellent basis for the tracking of equipment and munitions expenditure.

The game proceeded in this cycle until the Friday of each week. Normally, the morning would be a day of war-fighting, and the afternoon given over to what was called the "hot wash-up." This was an opportunity for some of the senior players in the game to address all the participants as to issues or events that had impressed them as being of particular significance. It also allowed for interplay among the principal representatives of Blue, Green and Red, for often the perceptions of what had happened and the importance of events or specific decisions varied substantially. This kind of discussion on the repercussions that could flow from misperceptions were often most enlightening, informative, and cautionary. This was particularly true of "signaling," a discrete action that was designed to convey a concern or threat to the opponent. More often that not, these signals were totally missed or wildly misinterpreted by the desired recipient. This led players to reflect that if such actions were either useless or harmful in a game in which players shared the same language and culture, what were the likely outcomes of attempts at "signaling" in the "real world"? Following the "hot-wash," the Analysis Group would begin preparing an in-brief summary of events for new players arriving for play the following Monday. This cycle was followed for each of the three weeks.

Overseeing and coordinating all of this activity was the Control Group. This organization was composed of the Game Director, other individuals selected by him, and representatives from major game cells. It met prior to the start of game play, at lunch, and again following the end of the game day. Its primary function was to ensure that the game ran smoothly. To this end, it was important to be certain that the head of each cell was running that cell efficiently, particularly if the person in charge had come into the game after the first week. It was also necessary to alert Battle Damage Assessment and the Analysis Group of a planned operation that might require special oversight. Further, with a game of this size, the possibility of discontinuities was always present, and Control, on occasion, had to resolve problems that arose from failure in game mechanics. Typical of this would be a situation where Blue or Red made a questionable decision without information that should have been available to them.

A large Analysis Group, staffed mainly by reserve officers, collected data on the game. Every major cell had at least one analyst present, who took notes on what occurred. This group held meetings on a schedule similar to that of the Control Group, so that all members could be informed of potentially significant events before they occurred. This was important so that the responses to and perceptions of a particular initiative could be chronicled from the Blue, Red and Green perspective. The leaders of the Analysis

Group generally stayed for a week after the game to put into final form the reports of events in specific cells, for example the Red VGK, Blue Joint Chiefs of Staff, Green, Blue CINCPAC, Red Southwestern TVD, etc. This served as the basis for the final game report, composed by the staff of the Game Director and War Gaming Center and then distributed to the participating organizations and commands.

As a seminar type of planning simulation, the mechanics of the 1988 game were considerably different, although the fundamental, three-sided (Blue, Red, Green) construct remained the same. Game time was frozen at D+75, which corresponded to 3 February 1991. The game functioned at three levels:

GAME LEVEL	GAME RESPONSIBILITY
NCA/VGK	National Planning/Negotiations
JCS/General Staff	National Strategic Planning
CINCs/TVD Commanders	Theater/Campaign Planning

Instead of umpires/controllers, Theater Advisory Teams were established as part of a Military Assessment Group to act as a source of information so that plans could be properly formulated. These teams—there were two, one for Europe/Atlantic and another for the Pacific—also assessed the theater commander's war plans for feasibility and potential weakness. Traditional assessment models were available for this purpose, and the teams provided the same services to Blue and to Red.

Other simulated organizations that were utilized on the Blue side in this game were:

> The National Security Policy Group (NSPG) focused on overall national policy formulation and was comprised of the Vice President (chairman), National Security Advisor, the Secretaries of State and Defense, the Chairman, Joint Chiefs of Staff, the Director of Central Intelligence (DCI) and the Director of the War Resources Board.
>
> The Negotiators Cell was headed by the State Department, with additional membership drawn from the Office of the Secretary of Defense (OSD), the Joint Chiefs of Staff, the CIA and NATO.
>
> The purpose of the Inter-Agency Mobilization Group (IG/MOB) was to advise the NSPG concerning broad issues associated with the mobilization of the nation to support the war effort. Participants included representation from the Department of Defense, the Federal Emergency Management Agency (FEMA), the Department to Energy (DOE), and the Department of Transportation (DOT). Members of other cells, such as the NSPG and the War Resources Board, joined meetings as required.
>
> The War Resources Board/National Defense Research Council (WRB/NDRC) addressed industrial mobilization and force structure planning issues. Its membership

FIGURE 6
Organization

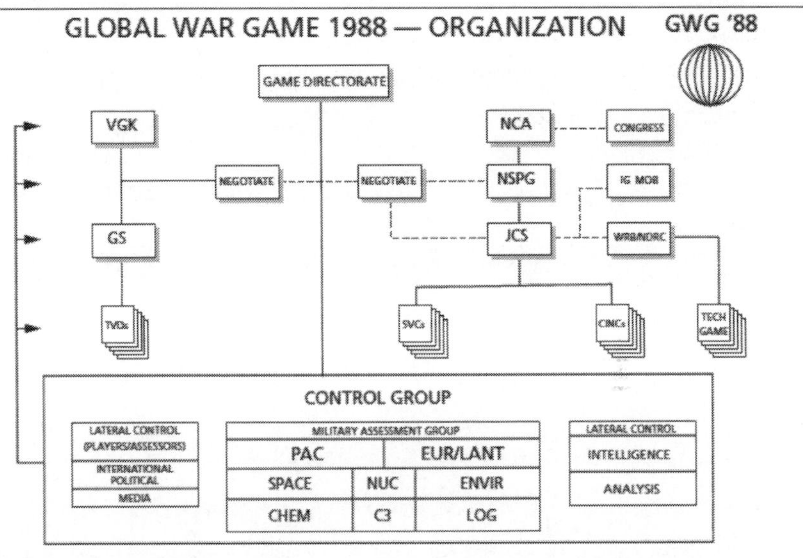

was designed to replicate the interactions that would occur between the DOD, various federal agencies, including regulatory, and private industry.

The remainder of the cells, control, nuclear, space, environment, logistics, analysis etc. performed, essentially, as in previous games. An outline of the cells and their inter-relationship is provided in figure 6.

The flow of activity in this game differed considerably from that of its predecessors because the five major game drivers, the NCA, negotiators, JCS, CINCs, and NATO were doing different things at different times. Their respective timelines are displayed in figures 7 through 11. These charts permit one to follow the sequence of the game. The CINCs prepared plans for regional strategies and campaigns that were presented to the JCS. The JCS then went into the "tank" to come to a conclusion as to the course(s) of action they would recommend to the NCA. While this was going on, the National Security Policy Group was determining the broader aspects of national policy, negotiations were ongoing as were discussions among the NATO allies.

All the strands of the game began to come together on Wednesday afternoon, with the negotiators report to the NCA. Success or failure on that front laid the basis for the refining of the Blue political position Thursday morning. The military recommendations of the JCS were available early Thursday afternoon, enabling the President to set fourth to the NATO Council of Ministers the alliance options, political and military, as Blue saw them. (At the same time, a session similar to the "hot wash" was taking place, in which the assessment teams met with Blue, Red, and Green players to discuss respective plans and possible outcomes.) Finally, with consultations among allies complete, the President finalized his decisions and delivered them to the "country" in a Friday morning "State of the Nation" address.

This cycle was followed for each of the three weeks of Global '88.

FIGURE 7
National Command Authority Schedule

NCA	MON	TUE	WED	THU	FRI
0800	ADMIN/ CHECK-IN	DEVELOP INITIAL POL POSITION (WITH/NEG)	INTERACT WITH IG/MOB WRB, CONGRESS, NDRC, ETC.	REFINE POLITICAL POSITION	FINALIZE PRES. DECISIONS
0900	GENERAL BRIEFS				
1000				↓	STATE OF THE NATION ADDRESS
1100	SCENARIO OVERVIEW				
1300	ORG/ADMIN			RCV JCS BRIEF	
1400	REVIEW GLOBAL SITUATION (WITH/NEG)	VISIT SCIENCE GAME			
1500			RCV NEG BRIEF	NATO MINISTERIAL MTG	
1600					

FIGURE 8
Negotiation Time Schedule

NEG	MON	TUE	WED	THU	FRI
0800	ADMIN/ CHECK-IN	DEVELOP INITIAL POL POSITION (WITH/NCA)	NEGOTIATION SESSION #3	SUPPORT NCA	↓
0900	GENERAL BRIEFS				
1000			MODIFY INITIAL POL POSI (AS REQUIRED)	↓	STATE OF THE NATION ADDRESS
1100	SCENARIO OVERVIEW	NEGOTIATION SESSION #1			
1300	ORG/ADMIN		BRIEF PREPS	↓	
1400	REVIEW GLOBAL SITUATION (WITH/NCA)	NEGOTIATION SESSION #2			
1500			BRIEF NCA	NEGOTIATION SESSION (AS REQUIRED)	
1600					

FIGURE 9
Joint Chiefs of Staff Schedule

JCS	MON	TUE	WED	THU	FRI
0800	ADMIN/ CHECK-IN	DEVELOP GLOBAL MILITARY PLANS & OPTIONS	↓	TANK SESSION	↓
0900	GENERAL BRIEFS				
1000			RCV CINC's BRIEFS	BRIEF PREPS	STATE OF THE NATION ADDRESS
1100	SCENARIO OVERVIEW	↓			
1300	ORG/ADMIN	↓	REFINE GLOBAL MILITARY POSITION	BRIEF NCA	
1400	REVIEW GLOBAL SITUATION				
1500		↓ VISIT SCIENCE GAME		SUPPORT NCA	
1600					

FIGURE 10
Commanders in Chief Schedule

CINCS	MON	TUE	WED	THU	FRI
0800	ADMIN/ CHECK-IN	DEVELOP REGIONAL STRATEGIES AND CAMPAIGN OPTIONS	COORD. WITH ALLIES	ATTEND JCS TANK SESSION	
0900	GENERAL BRIEFS				
1000			BRIEF JCS	OUT BRIEF PAC ALLIES	STATE OF THE NATION ADDRESS
1100	SCENARIO OVERVIEW				
1300	ORG/ADMIN	↓			
1400			SUPPORT JCS	OPEN SESSION WITH RED, GRN & ASSESS.	
1500	REVIEW REGIONAL SITUATION	↓			
1600					

FIGURE 11
North Atlantic Treaty Organization Overview

NATO MC/ DPC/NAC	MON	TUE	WED	THU	FRI
0800	ADMIN/ CHECK-IN	DEVELOP NATO POLITICAL POSITION AND WAR TERMINATION OPTIONS	RECEIVE MNC BRIEFS*	REFINE POLITICAL POSITION	
0900	GENERAL BRIEFS				
1000			COORD. WITH NCA	↓	STATE OF THE NATION ADDRESS
1100	SCENARIO OVERVIEW				
1300	ORG/ADMIN	↓	↓	↓	
1400					
1500	REVIEW WAR SITUATION	↓	↓	NATO MINISTERIAL MEETING	
1600					

*MNC = Ministerial Counselors

CHAPTER ONE

The 1984 Global War Game

Introduction

The 1984 Global War Game was the initial game of the second Global War Game series (1984–1988). Consequently, there were some characteristics of this game that made it unique. Aside from the overall purposes of the series stated above, this first game had other specific objectives:

- To provide an initial estimate of the world of the 1990s that would serve as a basis for the next four games.
- To explore evolving technologies that would influence military operations in that decade.
- To explore the nature of protracted, conventional war.
- To provide a baseline reference in such things as the respective orders of battle for the following games in the series.
- To serve as a test bed for specific areas of interest that had emerged from the analysis of the First Global War Game Series, 1979–1983.

GWG 1984 also initiated a shift in focus from the games of the first series. Those games had been primarily operational in nature, while the games of the second series would emphasize a planning format supported by campaign analysis and operations gaming techniques. The game book for 1984 emphasized this shift toward strategy:

> The Global War Game is a research game designed to explore US global war fighting capabilities. The main emphasis is placed on identifying issues that require attention in planning global strategy. Particular attention is given to where and how naval forces can make the greatest contribution to combined arms strategy. . . . The Global War Game (GWG) is a test bed of current strategic wisdom. It is a forum to assess the state of what we have and design the shape of what we want.

Operational decisions continued to play a prominent part in the game. Indeed, Global, as played in 1984 and successive years of this series, consisted of four complementary games. The first aspect was that of a research game, which cut players loose from established plans and doctrine and gave them the flexibility to explore. The planning aspect of the game forced players to think in terms of a global, combined-arms strategy. The operational game provided a time sequence of events that tested strategy and confronted players with the necessity of making choices. Finally, the seminar portion of the game presented an opportunity to develop topics of major importance in detail. Aside from the overarching series objectives, the players in the 1984 Global War Game were asked to do two specific tasks:

- Explore the characteristics of crisis and war in the early 1990s, and
- Increase the understanding of a long-war strategy.

Scenario

The scenario for the 1984 Global War Game postulated a world with many problems. The crucial one, however, was the deteriorating economic situation in Poland and Eastern Europe. It envisioned a situation where, by the late 1980s, economic conditions in Eastern Europe had worsened and worker unrest reached such levels that it hampered government efforts to meet even normal demands for goods and services. In the spring of 1990, the disruption in Poland had grown to nationwide proportions. General strikes had paralyzed the economy on several occasions. The government was under extreme pressure, both from its own citizens and from its Warsaw Pact allies, to restore order. Consequently, Red mobilized seven divisions; in June those units, in conjunction with the entire Polish army, two East German divisions, and one division each from Czechoslovakia and Hungary, reimposed government control.

In the German Democratic Republic (GDR), similar discontent was augmented by a strong peace movement. In July 1990, harsh repressive measures on the part of the government intensified the opposition. During the third week of that month, security forces opened fire on mass demonstrations, and 20 protesters were reported killed. Attacks on Communist Party headquarters followed in five cities, and troops sent to restore order were met with barricades. Skirmishes between government forces and dissidents continued, and by the end of July, some GDR military units had mutinied. As mobs began to gather in areas where Red troop garrisons were present, those forces began to pull back to the east. By the end of July, the western GDR was in the hands of the pro-Western rebels, while the eastern part of the country was in the hands of the loyal East German and Red forces. The rebels in the west began to set up democratic city councils and were in contact with both the press and officials of the government of the Federal Republic of Germany (FRG).

As August began, the GDR insurgents resisted all efforts to restore order, and some utilized the FRG as a haven from which to conduct minor but violent attacks into the

GDR. The FRG had mobilized selected military units to maintain order at the Inter-German Border (IGB) on 30 July. On 1 August (D-12), the Politburo, gravely concerned about the continued deterioration of stability in the GDR, mobilized ground, air, and naval forces to restore the IGB and the East German government by conventional military action. Blue mobilized five days later (D-7). Although neither Blue nor Red had desired war, circumstances beyond the control of both precipitated a situation in which neither believed an alternative existed.

Political Objectives and Military Strategy

Blue Objectives

The most basic of the Blue political objectives was to maintain NATO and other alliances around the world and to protect, or restore as necessary, the territorial integrity of those allies. Blue sought to attain these primary goals without recourse to nuclear weapons. Further, Blue believed that hostilities offered the opportunity to neutralize Red influence over non-European surrogates. Indeed, achievement of these objectives could well result in the fragmentation or dissolution of the Warsaw Pact.

Blue Strategy

The strategy devised by Blue to attain the political goals is best considered by geographic region.

Central Europe

- Meet any Warsaw Pact attack as far forward as possible.
- Establish reserves to block penetrations and to exploit opportunities.
- Effectively use Blue air power to blunt Red air operations and to retain key command, control, and communications (C3), air defense, and nuclear capabilities.
- Establish and maintain local air superiority and provide air support to ground forces.

Atlantic and Norway

- Conduct a vigorous, forward anti-submarine warfare (ASW) campaign to quickly destroy the Red strategic nuclear reserve.
- Insert Blue/UK/Netherlands marines in North Norway to block deep Red penetration.
- Hold aircraft carriers and additional marines in reserve for use as necessary.
- Protect sea lines of communication (SLOCs) and lines of communication (LOCs).

Mediterranean

- Destroy deployed Red naval forces.
- Provide support to NATO southern flank, if attacked.
- Conduct offensive operations in the Balkans to relieve Red pressure on the Central Front in Germany.

Indian Ocean

- Destroy Red Indian Ocean Squadron.
- Retain USN Middle East Force (MIDEASTFOR) plus one SSN for regional contingencies.
- Move the only Indian Ocean carrier battle group (CVBG) to the Pacific.

Pacific

- Conduct vigorous ASW campaign.
- Thwart any Red attacks on Japan.
- Pressure Red by threat to southern Kurile Islands.

Red Objectives

The primary political objective of Red was the neutralization of the FRG. If all or even a substantial part of West Germany could be occupied, NATO would probably collapse due to the Alliance's inability to protect its most important Continental member. The dissolution of NATO would achieve a Red political goal—the diminution or elimination of Blue influence on the Continent. Another Red objective was to keep the war short and nonnuclear by quick attainment of military objectives to be followed by initiatives for a prompt cease-fire.

Red Strategy

Central Europe

- Restore the IGB.
- Occupy all or substantial parts of the FRG.
- Capture West German ports on the North Sea.
- Conduct an offensive into Jutland to force Denmark to capitulate and thus fragment NATO.

Norway and Atlantic

- Establish air superiority over northern Norway.
- Eliminate Blue early warning capability in North Norway.
- Control coast and interior of North Norway.
- Posture nuclear-powered ballistic missile submarines (SSBN) in Atlantic and Arctic and protect their bastions.
- Control, if possible; otherwise, deny Blue use of Norwegian and Barents Seas.
- Position fleet submarines (SSN) for anti-SSBN operations.

Southwest Asia

- Minimize Blue capability to attack Red homeland.
- Block NATO access to Black Sea.
- Execute holding operations in Thrace and eastern Turkey.

Indian Ocean

- Deter/conduct holding operation against Iran and Iraq.
- Destroy Blue forces.
- Refrain from offensive operations to deny Blue a basing excuse.

Pacific

- Neutralize Japan and strip away Blue air defense capability.
- Attack targets in Aleutians, Alaska, and Hawaii.
- Destroy Blue forces, establish sea control, especially in the Seas of Japan and Okhotsk.

The Central Front

The war began on 16 August 1990 with a major Warsaw Pact (WP) offensive against NATO forces. The primary weight of the Red attack was in the Northern Army Group (NORTHAG) sector, and the advance carried 50 kilometers in the first two days and 70 in the first three. NATO forces attempted a counterattack against this penetration on D+4, striking northeast from the Fulda area to try to turn the southern flank of the Red salient. NATO air was surged in support of this offensive, and while it did serve to divert some WP reinforcements, the advance across the north German Plain continued and this limited counterattack was withdrawn on D+6. NATO reserves and air power, including the use of B-52s, blunted the Red advance by D+7. In NORTHAG, the forward line of troops (FLOT) was in the outskirts of Hamburg and Hanover on D+10 when the Red Second Operational Echelon closed.

The Red buildup and consolidation continued on D+11, and two Polish armies pushed into Schleswig-Holstein, cutting off Denmark from the rest of NATO. The Warsaw Pact offensive in NORTHAG resumed on D+12. Red staged an airborne attack on Bremerhaven as part of this renewed drive that soon carried across the Elbe. Bremerhaven fell on D+13, while, to the south, Red commenced a thrust toward Munich. That city fell, along with Augsburg, on D+15, and the Red advance continued on toward Stuttgart. In NORTHAG, NATO had formed and was holding, with the aid of massive air support, a new defensive line anchored on the Weser River. At D+19, relative combat power in NORTHAG was about even, and to the south, NATO reinforcements caused Red to hold up the advance on Stuttgart.

By D+20, however, Blue was confronted with two major problems on the Central Front. First, the Red Second Strategic Echelon had closed and begun a strong attack that threatened Frankfurt. Second, Red units had reinforced the Polish forces in Jutland and renewed the offensive into Denmark. The political ramifications of the fall of a NATO member were such that the Alliance decided on an amphibious operation that went ashore on the western side of the Danish peninsula on D+22. A marine amphibious force (MAF) and one army division, supported by five aircraft carriers (CV) and about 250 other ships, were augmented by an assault by the 82nd Airborne Division. The Weser line continued to hold, while, to the south, a second defensive belt contained the Red thrust on Frankfurt, although the city was within range of Red divisional artillery. On D+23 this attack had been spent, and Red terminated offensive operations to await developments.

NATO seized the initiative with a six-division offensive toward Hamburg, which, if successful, would force the withdrawal of the Warsaw Pact forces in Jutland that were opposing the Blue beachhead. The 101st Airborne Division had been added to the original force, but a breakout had not been achieved. This attack was to be followed by a three-phase NATO counterattack.

- Allied Forces Central Europe (AFCENT) was to launch 13 French divisions between Kassel and Fulda toward Halle, to rupture Red LOCs and form a southern pincer to cut off WP forces in North Germany.
- NORTHAG to attack in the direction of Magdeburg, forcing a breach south of Hamburg, to form the northern pincer.
- AFCENT was also to attack toward the Oder River, with objective and direction to be determined based on the deployment of the Red Third Strategic Echelon.

Phases one and two commenced on D+26 with the French forces breaking through and advancing to the northeast, while the NORTHAG units moved against light opposition. In conjunction with these attacks, Rangers were employed in a deep penetration mission against airfields in the Berlin area. Meanwhile, Red was moving up reinforcements composed of nine divisions from the Leningrad military district (MD) and 25 from the Kiev and Caucasus MDs. By D+29, the French southern pincer had linked up in Halle with two airborne divisions that had taken the city on D+27. However, the northern arm of the pincer was held up at Luneburg by stiffening Red resistance. The Jutland beachhead was stable, but efforts at breaking out had failed. The third phase of the NATO counteroffensive began on D+29 in the direction of Brunswick (Braunschweig) for the purpose of supporting the north shoulder of the French salient. However, Central Army Group (CENTAG) was becoming concerned over increasing Red pressure on the French in the vicinity of Mannheim.

D+30 found the NATO counteroffensives continuing in the face of strong Red opposition occasioned by the more rapid than expected arrival of the Third Strategic Echelon. The French drove on beyond Halle toward Magdeburg and Leipzig and, supported on their left by the CENTAG forces moving on Brunswick, crossed the inter-German border (IGB) into East Germany. However, the open right flank of the French penetration was coming under increasing pressure. To the north, the check at Luneburg led NORTHAG to redefine objectives, and the northern pincer swung south on an axis Uelzen/Wolfsburg. In south Germany, the Red offensive toward Stuttgart was resumed, and NATO forces were suffering heavy casualties. By D+33, the NATO offensive operations reached their limit with a link-up of the two pincers at Celle. Mounting Red pressure, however, forced the withdrawal of the forces involved in all three phases on D+34/35. This counterattack, however, had thrown Red off timeline and necessitated diversion of forces destined for Norway and the Balkans, leaving Red vulnerable in both regions.

By D+35/36, the 34 divisions of the Third Strategic Echelon had restored the initiative to Red, and D+37/38 found NATO on the defensive on all fronts. The first of the Army Reserve and National Guard units from the Continental United States (CONUS) arrived in theater on D+38 and were immediately pressed into action to hold three Warsaw Pact offensives aimed at Bremen, Frankfurt, and Stuttgart. The Blue contingent in Jutland remained confined to their beachhead. This, then, was the situation when play went to a seminar format at D+48 (map 2).

Norway

Red attacked Norway on D-Day, moving across the Finnmark with two motorized rifle divisions (MRD) and conducting an amphibious landing of a Soviet naval infantry

MAP 2
The Central Front 1984 Game D+48

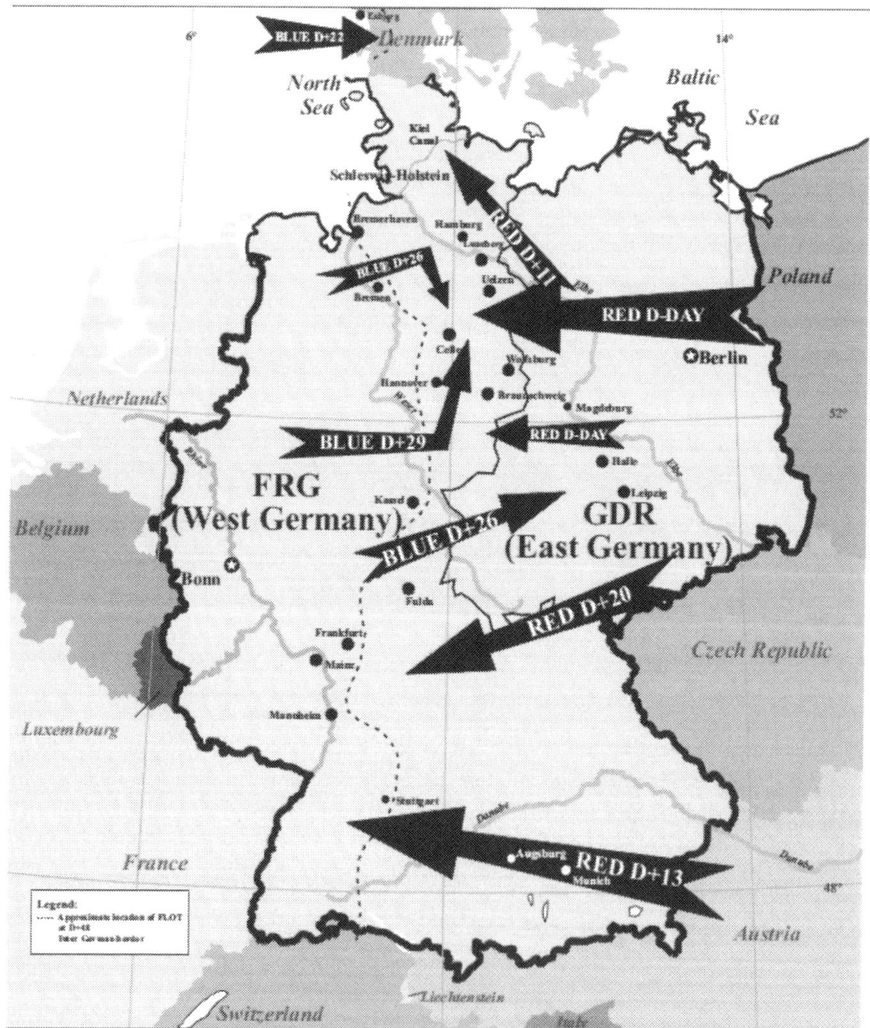

(SNI) regiment in Porsangen Fjord. The airfield at Banak was captured, and four Norwegian early warning posts were closed. The Red advance continued toward the Skibotn valley, slowed both by bad weather and strong resistance of combined Blue, Norwegian, and UK forces. The Blue components—a Marine Amphibious Brigade (MAB) and Maritime Prepositioning Ships (MPS)—had arrived in Norway between D-9 and D-7. NATO Improved Hawk batteries and tactical air forces were able to effectively counter Red air, and Blue air strikes helped force Red to go over to the defensive at Alta, short of their Skibotn objective.

Balkans

After the initial "shootout" in the Mediterranean, Blue naval forces were well positioned. With the exception of a few submarines and numerous mines, there were few Red forces left to oppose Blue, and the swiftness and completeness of the Blue victory had cowed Red surrogates into neutrality. Further, Red Soviet Naval Aviation and Long-Range Aviation (SNA/LRA), bereft of targeting information, chose not to commit to offensive action after D-Day. This left NATO forces free to launch a massive tactical air campaign into Bulgaria to delay or disrupt any plans Red might have for invading Thrace. This campaign essentially destroyed Red combat air patrol (CAP) capability in the area, slowed the Red buildup for an invasion of Thrace, and laid the basis for the NATO offensive of D+47. This attack involved six Greek/Turkish divisions backed by two Blue army divisions and a MAB. Red responded by shifting two divisions from Hungary, and the battle was continuing at game end.

The Atlantic

Red moves toward war became evident during the prehostility period of Global '84 when, on D-15, 80 percent of Red submarine and maritime combatants sortied and the Black Sea Fleet surged. Between that date and D-10, Warsaw Pact fleets in the Baltic also left port. NATO took prompt advantage of this warning, and by D-Day had 16 SSNs on station in the Norwegian, Kara, and Barents Seas. Blue also deployed other forces to areas of potential conflict as a show of force. The *America*, *Saratoga*, and *Wisconsin* Battle Groups were tasked to cover Cuba, the *Roosevelt*, *Coral Sea*, and *Lincoln* Battle Groups moved to positions south of the Iceland–United Kingdom Gap and the *Independence* steamed to join the Sixth Fleet. Between D-10 and D-5, Blue marines arrived in Norway, 10 guided missile frigates (FFG) were put on Eastern Atlantic (EASTLANT) patrol, and Western Atlantic (WESTLANT) amphibious ships, including the *Nassau* and *Guam*, were ordered to load out and proceed to the UK. Because of these actions, D-Day found Blue naval forces well disposed, with SSNs forward, three CVBGs just south of the Greenland-Iceland-Norway (GIN) Gap, and three others off the UK. FFGs supported by Ocean Surveillance (T-AGOS) ships had assumed ASW positions, the four Yankees in the Atlantic were being tailed, and two converted SSBNs were on station to lay CapTor minefields in the Barents. Protective minefields were in place off the Blue coast. At D-4, five Norwegian patrol submarines (SS) formed a barrier off the North Cape and the French SSN/SSBNs were in safe haven in the Bay of Biscay.

When hostilities commenced, the converted SSBNs laid a 96-unit CapTor field in the Barents and Mk-57 fields along expected Red SSN/SSBN transit routes. The Shetlands and Faeroes were also mined, utilizing surface, subsurface, and air platforms. These operations used 290 mines or 80 percent of assets. The Yankees in the Atlantic were promptly sunk, two by SSNs and two by maritime patrol aircraft (MPA). In the Norwegian, Barents, and Kara Seas, Blue SSNs sought targets in the following priorities: SSBNs, SSNs, and surface ASW platforms. During the first week of the war, Blue sank 7 Red SSBNs, 24 SSNs, 2 SSs and nuclear-powered cruise missile submarines (SSGNs), the only operational CV, and one *Kiev*, with another *Kiev* so badly damaged as to be out of action. During this period, Blue lost ten SSNs. During the entire game, Blue SSNs sank 19 SSBNs, 38 SSNs, 6 SSGNs, 7 SS, and 23 major surface ships at a cost of 26 SSNs.

On D-Day, Blue surface forces moved initially to sink Red AGIs and then to support ASW operations. Intensive air operations were conducted north of the GIN Gap coordinated with surface forces. One CV was moved close to southern Norway to support the land campaign, if necessary. Red sabotage of the Sound Surveillance System (SOSUS) in Norway hampered the ASW effort, but the capabilities of thin line arrays and the SQR-19 compensated. Aside from operations in support of the amphibious operations in Jutland and an abortive Red anti-SLOC campaign (both of which will be discussed separately), the naval war proceeded with Red forces suffering heavy attrition. By D+48, surviving Red naval units had been driven into ports of safety, and, while this remnant did constitute a fleet in being, only one Oscar-class SSGN remained at sea. Specific events of interest are as follows:

- D+3, Danes and Swedes mine Baltic choke points.
- D+7, UK reports initial clearing of Red SS/SSN from North Sea.
- D+8, three CVBGs south of GIN Gap release support SSNs to replace those lost.
- D+10, two CVBGs off Cuba deployed to UK, leaving *Wisconsin* BG in position.
- D+23/25, two SSN-launched TLAM(C) strikes against Olenegorsk petroleum, oil, and lubricants (POL) facilities and on Murmansk.
- D+25, Blue reviews SSN patrol areas. Decision made to pull units out of Kara Sea and reduce those operating in the Barents.
- D+30, Blue SSNs attack Red amphibious force in the vicinity of Norway's North Cape, sinking the majority of Red surface units involved in an attempt to outflank Skibotn defense line.
- D+35, Red sorties 11 diesel SS against Blue CVBGs operating in North Sea. *Invincible* and *Hermes* attacked unsuccessfully; diesel submarine threat caused Blue considerable alarm.
- D+38, only remaining Oscar SSGN launches sole successful antiship cruise missile (ASCM) attack of war. *Invincible* and *Hermes* damaged, but not put out of action.

At D+30, Red, sensing the probability of a longer war, embarked on an anti-SLOC campaign. Fourteen SSN/SSGNs were sortied via the Kara Sea, North Spitsbergen, and the Denmark Strait. Blue was caught unprepared, and Red was not detected until exiting the Denmark Strait. Of the 14 boats involved, all were sunk by D+40, two by the CapTor minefield in the Denmark Strait, eight by Blue SSN, and four by maritime patrol aircraft (MPA). They did, however, sink one SL-7, four Ro/Ro (fast), and four Ro/Ro (slow) transports.

At D+22, Blue forces conducted an amphibious landing near the FRG-Danish border on the western side of the Jutland Peninsula to prevent that NATO member from being totally occupied by Warsaw Pact forces. Five CVs and 250 other ships were involved in landing a Marine Amphibious Force (MAF), MPS equipment, and one infantry division. The 82nd Airborne was also utilized, and the 101st Airborne put ashore later. The amphibious fleet and supporting ships were attacked by five regiments of Backfires. The attack initially concentrated on the amphibious ships and resulted in a loss of about 25 percent of available ground strength.

Following the landing, Blue maintained substantial CV assets in the North Sea to provide tactical air support to NORTHAG in general and the Jutland beachhead in particular. This concentration attracted the attention of Red and resulted in the SS/SSGN attacks noted above. While the Blue forces were still pinned in their beachhead at game end, Red had not knocked Denmark out of either the war or the NATO Alliance, and Red forces that might have been employed elsewhere to NATO disadvantage had to be diverted to Denmark.

At the end of the game, then, Red had been driven from the Atlantic and neighboring seas, the SLOCs were secure, Cuba was not a factor, and Blue naval assets were assisting in the land battle on the Central Front.

The Mediterranean and Southwestern TVD

Red actions prior to D-Day involved Spetsnaz operations and covert minelaying. Beginning at D-12, Red began the insertion of Spetsnaz teams to sabotage nuclear storage sites, nuclear attack–capable airfields, and command, control, communications, and intelligence (C3I), in that order of priority. Also prior to D-Day, Red sortied eight Ro/Ro ships with an estimated 1,000 mines per ship. One was assigned the Straits of Sicily and Messina, another the Suez Canal, and the other six to the Aegean. The ship assigned to the Suez was detected on D-2 and sunk in the Canal, blocking it. A Foxtrot laid 12 mines in Souda Bay and a Tango laid 12 more in Augusta Bay on D-2, neither being detected.

On D-Day, Blue promptly destroyed Red AGIs and other tattletales as the expected "shoot-out" began. The Soviet Mediterranean Squadron (SOVMEDRON) ships and submarines struck two Sixth Fleet CVBGs in the vicinity of Rhodes, sinking three ships but leaving the CVs undamaged. The Red forces were essentially destroyed, incapacitated or forced into ports of Red surrogates. Red also launched an SNA/LRA attack with three regiments of Black Sea Fleet (BLKSEAFLT) Backfire and one regiment of Blinders. Red prepared for this attack with SS-22 attacks on six Turkish airfields, and only four Backfires and six Blinders were shot down over Turkey. The attack against Sixth Fleet was made with AS-4s; no CVs were damaged, and Red lost 36 Backfires and nine Blinders. Blinders also hit the airfield at Souda Bay, cutting the runway for three days. These attacks were the last air attacks launched against Sixth Fleet, as Red did not wish to risk assets without targeting intelligence.

By D+25, NATO had completed mine-clearing operations in the Mediterranean, interred 89 of an estimated 250 Warsaw Pact merchant ships in the area when hostilities commenced, and forced the others into ports in Libya, Morocco, and Syria. The three CVBGs now present, *Independence, John F. Kennedy,* and *Eisenhower,* became involved in a successful air campaign against Red air assets and other targets in Bulgaria. A number of Tomahawk land-attack missile (conventional) (TLAM(C)) attacks were launched, the most notable being a strike on a new CV and a *Slava* fitting out at Nikolayev, based on intelligence obtained from a remotely piloted vehicle (RPV). An effort was also made to insert four SSNs into the Black Sea, but two were sunk and one damaged by minefields.

Game's end found NATO in control of the Mediterranean, with the CVBGs employed in supporting an Allied ground offensive toward Bulgaria.

The Far East

While previous Global War Games had found Red essentially passive in the Pacific Theater, it seized the initiative in 1984. Perceiving that it would be unable through diplomatic pressure and military threat to keep Japan neutral, Red launched a large-scale air attack on Blue/Japanese air defense assets, using both aircraft and SS-22s. These attacks were so successful that Japan was left with essentially no air defense capability. An example of this effectiveness was the D+2 attack on airfields at Chitose and Misawa, which put both out of action for 48 hours and destroyed 85 percent of their POL supplies.

Red also struck at Blue targets throughout the Pacific. Adak, Shemya, and Amchitka were hit on D+1, 2, and 5. Further, key installations in Guam and Hawaii were attacked by Red unconventional warfare forces, which were also employed against Japan. These included high frequency direction finder (HFDF) sites and a super-high-frequency (SHF) station. Diego Garcia was also bombed and put out of action for three days, with 50 percent of all POL, hangars, and port facilities destroyed. These "worldwide" strikes were conducted not because Red sought to expand the war, but because Red reckoned it could not tolerate potential threats to its flanks and wanted to preempt them to the extent possible. Red attempted to accomplish the same goal by offering bilateral treaties of nonbelligerency.

Red had flushed a large number of SSN/SSGN to the east of Hokkaido and the Kuriles prior to D-Day for anti-CVBG operations. The remainder of the Red navy was retained in the Seas of Japan and Okhotsk.

Blue, acting on warning given by Red deployments, surged SSNs prior to hostilities to be in a position to wage intensive ASW campaigns in the Bering Sea and the Seas of Japan and Okhotsk. Initial Red SSBN losses were heavy, but ceased after D+16 as Red drew the remaining assets back into the well-protected shallow water bastions in the northern Sea of Okhotsk. A Blue USN/USAF attack destroyed Red bombers, sank several small combatants, and damaged repair facilities at Cam Ranh Bay.

There was a small-scale "shoot-out" in the Indian Ocean, where the *Kitty Hawk* battle group was en route to join the other Pacific Fleet CVBGs in the vicinity of the Philippines. A Charlie-class SSGN attacked the *Kitty Hawk*, but its missiles were shot down by an escorting Aegis cruiser, and the Charlie was sunk by the support SSN. This CVBG also sank a Krivak by air-launched Harpoon and destroyed an AGI (auxiliary vessel general intelligence purposes) with gunfire. A *Kara* and another Krivak were dispatched in the Arabian Sea by air-launched Harpoon shortly after D-Day. Although these actions were the only major ones to take place in the Indian Ocean, Red did its best to harass Blue/NATO/Japan energy supplies. Periodic bombing raids were undertaken against oil production facilities; Ras Tanurah was heavily bombed, and a desultory anti-SLOC campaign in the Indian Ocean claimed 12 super tankers. However, the Middle East in general and the energy situation in particular never became a major concern to Blue.

Blue held six CVBGs, including the *Kitty Hawk*, in the Philippine Sea during the early days of the war, awaiting the destruction of Red submarines in the waters east of Hokkaido and the Kuriles. This positioning of the CVBGs, combined with a protracted period of extremely bad weather, which hampered Blue air operations, provided Red with a "window" to invade Hokkaido. On D+11, Red initiated a large amphibious assault led by two SNI regiments followed by motorized infantry units transported in Ro/Ro ships. Eighteen amphibious and merchant ships were lost in this assault, and both *Kiev*s in the Red Pacific Fleet sustained severe damage. However, the Red forces did get ashore and established two large salients, one on the Wakkanai peninsula and the other in the Sapporo area. Noting this Red success, the Democratic People's Republic of Korea (DPRK) commenced mobilization and invaded South Korea on D+15.

As the weather cleared and Blue antisubmarine operations proceeded, the CVBGs were able to move north and pound the Red forces ashore on Hokkaido. By D+30, the five divisions of Red troops then ashore were unable to make further progress and a decision was made to withdraw them, which was accomplished on D+32/33. Partially to cover this withdrawal, Red launched a massive air attack on the Blue CVBGs force operating southeast of Tokyo. Red lost 182 planes in a raid that included Backfire, Badger, Bear, Foxhound, Fulcrum, Flanker, and Fencer. Blue lost 101 aircraft; several escorts and auxiliaries were sunk; *Lincoln* and *Midway*, heavily damaged, were towed to Japanese yards for repair.

Blue planned to continue the Pacific war by invading the southern Kurile island of Kunashir, with follow-on landings to take place on Simushir and Iturup. This decision was taken in spite of urgent pleas from the Republic of Korea (ROK), which, while holding its own against the North Korean invasion, wanted the CVBGs to provide additional air support. As Blue naval forces maneuvered for the attack on Kunashir, Red launched another massive air attack on the CVBGs, now positioned east of Hokkaido. The *Ranger* sustained six hits, was on fire and dead in the water. The estimated time of repair (ETR) was 10 months; seven escorts were also sunk. Blue bombing of the Kuriles, including a number of B-52 strikes, appeared to have neutralized any military utility the islands might have had for Red. With Red threatening to place atomic demolition mines (ADM) on the islands, Blue and Japan seemed to independently reach the conclusion that there was no military necessity to invade.

The situation on the Korean peninsula had become stalemated. Initial DPRK success in the East had been blunted by a South Korean counterattack, and Seoul remained in ROK possession. Little change had occurred since D+40 or so, and Blue continued to refuse ROK requests for CVBG support. At game end, however, Red had agreed to provide MiG-21s to Pyongyang, which appeared to threaten a shift of air superiority to the north.

The PRC had mobilized early in the war, but had taken no aggressive action against Red. Nonetheless, Red had felt it necessary to maintain its regular defensive deployments against possible contingencies, and had not drawn down its forces employed for that purpose.

Although these were the events of principal importance in the Pacific, there were ongoing submarine operations against Red forces that put to sea. Further, both the Blue air force and naval air assets attacked the Belkin coast, and TLAM(C) missiles were utilized in attacks on Vladivostok and Sakhalin.

Insights

The major issues of the 1984 Global War Game can be considered to fall under three broad topics:

- Looking at longer war—out to D+60.
- Developing insights into unified global strategy.
- Implications of fighting with 1990s equipment and tactical innovations.

One of the questions of concern over the "long war" hypothesis involved the ability of Blue and NATO to successfully wage protracted, conventional war as well as the effect that Blue willingness and capability to do so would have on deterrence.

As far as the latter point is concerned, it appeared that the Blue ability to deter by adopting a long war strategy might be scenario-dependent. While such a prospect would give Red cause for concern, it seemed that Red, if faced with the prospect of the loss of East Germany or the unification of Germany, would choose to fight, even if a protracted war was in prospect. Once the battle was joined, it appeared that Red, if confronted with limited resources and potential trouble on the flanks, would scale back the original objectives and settle for more modest goals, such as an intact Warsaw Pact alliance and, possibly, a demilitarized Germany. However, should Red be thrown off its early timelines and hit with a strong Blue counteroffensive, the use of weapons of mass destruction was a very real possibility.

As the Global Game progressed in 1984, it appeared that with reasonable mobilization lead time and effective use of warning, Commander-in-Chief Europe/Supreme Allied Commander Europe (CINCEUR/SACEUR) had stronger defensive fighting power than many had perceived. A "flexible defense" that employed maneuver and flanking attacks had succeeded in slowing Pact offensive. The air/land battle concept appeared to be working well, and Blue (as distinct from NATO) had logistic and ordnance stocks that were generally adequate. Thus, at D+48, Blue, though hard-pressed, was holding out, in spite of Red's commitment of all forces west of the Urals. Virtually all theaters except the border with the PRC had been stripped of Red troops, a situation deemed unlikely in a "real world" circumstance.

The game results tended to show that a long-war strategy did have some deterrent features and was a valid war-fighting option for Blue/NATO. However, while successful execution of the strategy avoided Blue selection of the nuclear option, it did have the effect of pushing Red in exactly that direction. Red, at game's end, was determined to secure a cease-fire and satisfactory war termination, even if weapons of mass destruction had to be used. If the war continued, Red saw their long-term (two to three years) situation as untenable.

The development of a global strategy linking offensive operations to overall war objectives had been recognized in the first global series as an issue of critical importance. While maritime superiority gave Blue multiple options to put both military and political pressure on Red, there was no "Big Game Plan" to coordinate Navy, Army, and Air Force assets for combined and joint land operations, nor was there any pre-hostilities planning to provide for follow-on campaigns and logistical support. In the event, it appeared as though AFNORTH, AFCENT, and AFSOUTH were waging separate wars.

If Blue could implement an overall strategy, Red would be forced to react to it as the initial offensive plan was upset and timelines began to slide. Without such a strategy, both sides tended to remain in a reactive mode until Red built enough force to press toward either original or modified objectives.

Blue had identified four major points of leverage:

- North Norway.
- Baltic Approaches.
- Western Mediterranean (Ligurian Sea).
- Eastern Mediterranean.

The western Mediterranean and the Baltic Approaches provided the opportunity for direct support of the Central Front, while attacks from North Norway and the eastern Mediterranean could threaten the Red homeland.

In Global '84, Blue attempted to exploit offensive operations at three levels:

- Operational—A major double envelopment in AFCENT using NORTHAG and CENTAG reserves.
- At the theater level, with an attempt to create pressure in the Balkans by AFSOUTH.
- By the planned use of the Strategic Reserve for invading Jutland and threatening the Baltic coast.

If operations in North Norway to thwart the Red advance that began on D-Day were considered, Blue/NATO was thus exercising three out of the four points of leverage identified above.

Blue/NATO forces in North Norway were successful in halting the Red attack short of its objective, the Skibotn Valley. However, there was no appreciable augmentation of Allied forces in Norway after the very early stages of the war. Essentially, the CVBGs never entered the Norwegian Sea. Consequently, there was only a token TLAM attack on the Kola and no buildup of force of any kind to seriously threaten the Red homeland with attack, let alone mount a ground offensive. Red felt free to reinforce the Central Front with forces from the Leningrad MD and could rationalize that the minimum objective in North Norway had been attained.

The Blue landing in Jutland was not planned as a counteroffensive, but was initiated for the political reason of keeping Denmark from being knocked out of the war. While Blue was never able to break out from a beachhead that became more tenuous as the game progressed, the operation did demonstrate several potential advantages:

- A number of Red divisions were diverted from offensive operations on the Central Front.
- The ability to support the operation with CVBG air allowed concentration of land-based aircraft further south.
- If adequate force levels could be attained, the Central Front campaign could be directly supported, with the offensive continuing east along the Baltic littoral or moving directly south against the flank of the Red advance.

The decisive victory attained by Blue in the D-Day shoot-out in the Mediterranean Sea opened the SLOC to Greece and Turkey and promoted regional stability, particularly among the Muslim countries in the area. Blue wanted to exploit this situation, but was unable to do so, in part because the Alliance had no plans for an offensive in this theater. Therefore, both land forces and logistics sustainment were absent. While Blue utilized air and TLAM assets to attack Bulgaria and the Black Sea ports, land operations in Thrace were not begun until D+47.

While these events were taking place in Europe, Blue was endeavoring to seize the initiative in the Northwestern Pacific with the goal of invading the Kuriles. Although this operation was finally shelved due to a Red threat to place ADMs on these islands and to detonate them if Blue invaded (and then accuse Blue of initiating nuclear war), a larger question arose as to whether it was better policy just to neutralize the islands rather than occupy them.

These operations suggested that there were military criteria that should be considered when actions about the Red periphery were contemplated and that these criteria had applicability to air and naval as well as land operations:

- Is the leverage that may be gained from the operation worth the cost? and
- Can a large enough force package be built to exploit opportunities maritime superiority creates?

The importance of a coherent strategy that brings all available assets into play is an imperative if a long-war strategy is to succeed. Such a strategy may not depend on a "knockout punch," and one probably does not exist in any event. The overarching strategy appeared to be to stall the Red land offensive, constitute reserve forces, and then push the counteroffensive. Barring the use of nuclear weapons, the war would probably end when one belligerent decided the price was too high and victory too far away.

Fighting with 1990s equipment and tactical innovations led to a number of valuable insights. Some of the most important are discussed briefly below.

- Antisubmarine Warfare—The Blue submarine thin line arrays and SQR-19 appeared to have achieved a quantum leap in Blue capability. While it had been anticipated that Red efforts in quieting their SSNs would diminish the Blue advantage, this did not prove to be the case. Blue did find it difficult to come to a conclusion on one tactical issue. As Red losses mounted and Red units moved deeper into bastions, Blue approached a point of diminishing returns. It is important to formulate parameters as to when to reduce or suspend the anti-SSBN campaign.
- While tactical aircraft (TACAIR) attrition continued to be very high, 60 percent for Blue and 70 percent for Red, the Blue technological advantage appeared to be shrinking. While Blue held a 2.5-to-1 ratio at D-43, the capability of Red fourth generation aircraft, particularly when integrated with Mainstay, was a cause for concern. While further experience and intelligence may result in a downgrade of current performance estimates, these airframes are clearly superior to their immediate predecessors.
- Red utilized SS-22s with conventional warheads in their attacks on air bases in Japan and Turkey. They proved extremely effective in the role, and both their use and effectiveness came as a surprise to Blue.
- The possible use of chemical weapons by Red was a concern to Blue. As the outbreak of hostilities seemed imminent, Blue pondered the question of whether or not Red would use chemical weapons (CW) at the beginning of the war and, if so, how. Blue considered what response to make if Red did attack with CW, the principal issue being a perceived lack of symmetrical response due to the lack of a deep strike capability. The possibility of a tactical nuclear weapons (TACNUC) retaliation was discussed. Overall, the use of weapons of mass destruction was initially unattractive to both Blue and Red, primarily because both sides feared that the response of the other side could lead to loss of control and unintended escalation. However, by D+48, Red had determined that massive chemical use was necessary. Red did not believe there was any significance to the scope of their attack; that if Blue was going to respond with nuclear weapons, they would do so regardless of the scale of chemical use by Red. Blue, on the other hand, had decided on principle that a nuclear response would be appropriate if the use of CW by Red was massive and devastating. It should be noted that Red decided not to use chemical weapons against France because of fear of nuclear retaliation by the French Independent Nuclear Force (INF).

CHAPTER TWO

The 1985, 1986, and 1987 Global War Games

Scenario—The Road to War

The scenario for the 1985 Global War Game was based upon possible events, worldwide, that culminated in the outbreak of war on 20 November 1990. As with the 1984 game, this scenario portrayed two superpowers not totally in control of events or their allies and an evolving situation in which both Blue and Red finally found themselves in a war that neither sought but which neither could avoid.

In Europe, the basic issue involved an apparent trend toward German reunification. Dissident elements in the German Democratic Republic (GDR) had established contacts within the Federal Republic of Germany (FRG), and as these contacts expanded, they were condemned by Red. For its part, the East German government restricted access to West Berlin. This caused West Germany to insist that all Germans should have access to Berlin, and the FRG government demanded a tripartite demarche to Red.

In early November, the situation worsened. On 5 November, the GDR placed further restrictions on the air and ground corridors to Berlin, but implementation was hampered as some East German border guards deserted their posts and a tide of refugees began to flow westward. This action precipitated a border firefight, and the GDR authorities took steps to ban all Western news reporting of the border chaos. Further, West German National Television carried reports of Red frigates (FF) ramming open boats crowded with refugees fleeing the GDR. The NATO refugee agency was ordered into operational readiness.

Red also had troubles along the southern flank. The war in Afghanistan dragged on, with support for the rebels provided by Blue and the People's Republic of China (PRC) being funneled through Pakistan. Further, chaos in Iran followed the death of the Ayatollah Khomeini in 1985. The council that replaced him was incompetent, and no single faction was able to assert control. In October of 1990, the National Front for the Liberation of Azerbaijan declared independence and requested recognition and military support from Red. Red mobilized four divisions from the Transcaucasus Military

District (MD) and three regiments of Soviet Naval Aviation (SNA), recognized the Republic of Azerbaijan on 20 October, and invaded on 4 November with seven divisions plus elements of an airborne division from the Odessa MD. Resistance was light, and Red anticipated that ten days would be required to "consolidate" the situation.

Blue was having problems to its south, as well. The situation in Central America was festering as Red vastly increased aid to the communist government of Nicaragua. "Contra" strength and activity had continued to grow, and when Blue army engineers were killed inside Honduras by Nicaraguan government forces attacking the "contras," Congress acted. A joint resolution called on the President to define the roles and missions of all Blue forces in or close to Central America within 90 days.

Red activity in Cuba was also of concern to Blue. Military aid had been increased to include Nanuchka missile corvettes and Koni-class frigates, Fulcrum aircraft and SA-6 missiles. Further, deployment visits by Red surface action groups (SAGs) and fleet submarines (SSN) had become more frequent, as had reconnaissance flights.

Elsewhere, NATO's southern flank was in disarray. The Greek government had permitted Blue basing agreements to lapse, requiring redeployment of assets to Italy and Turkey. Red naval units had begun Greek port visits, and anti-American and anti-NATO demonstrations had become commonplace. Athens not only reasserted Aegean claims but also threatened "unilateral" resolution of the Cyprus problem. The situation was exacerbated when the Blue Secretary of Defense visited Ankara at Turkey's request.

Red intervention in Azerbaijan was of immediate concern to the Turkish government. Further, Red and Bulgarian complicity was suspected in a wave of terrorist bombings and the assassination of diplomats, both at home and abroad. The Turks sought Blue aid and reassurance.

In Asia, the Blue perspective was mixed. The Secretary of State visit to the PRC had been productive. Agreements had been reached on Blue military aid, both for domestic purposes and for forwarding to the Afghan rebels, and a port visit to Shanghai by an Aegis cruiser emphasized the warming of relations.

Elsewhere in the Eastern Hemisphere, things were not promising. The death of Marcos had plunged the Philippines into chaos and virtual civil war. The economy was in shambles and the "New People's Army" was on the march. American military installations were being attacked or sabotaged.

On the Indian subcontinent, fear of a Pakistan nuclear program led India to attack the Islamabad reactor facility and airfields as well. Pakistan retaliated against Indian airfields. Further, both these countries suffered from serious internal problems. Political, economic, and social difficulties raised questions of Pakistan's internal cohesion, while

Prime Minister Rajiv Ghandi had placed India under martial law to try to control internal strife. India's relationship with Red remained solid, while the PRC supported Pakistan.

On 10 November 1990, Blue Special Operation Forces (SOF) became engaged with Red forces in Afghanistan. Casualties were heavy on both sides. Surviving Blue personnel were captured, tried by a field court martial, found guilty of being "mercenaries," and executed.

Key Events on the Road to War, October–November 1990

15 October	National Security Council (NSC) meets and decides to call up 100,000 reserves to deter Red. Other agenda items included possible retaliation against Nicaragua, a demarche to Cuba, and the state of Blue public opinion with regard to possible war.
16 October	NATO "REFORGER" exercise begins.
1–9 November	Major Red exercise in Sakhalin concludes, but a residue of the forces remains, raising concerns in Tokyo about a potential threat to Hokkaido. Various Red air defense and Soviet Naval Infantry (SNI) exercises take place in the Far Eastern Theater of Military Operations (FETVD).
	Red western military districts and Pacific military districts go to "increased combat readiness" as do Non-Soviet Warsaw Pact (NSWP) forces. Two divisions from the Leningrad MD in the Kola mobilize.
10 November	Blue receives indications that Red and NSWP are conducting widespread mobilization. Red SSBNs leave port and ASW groups put to sea. NSWP naval units marshal under Red control. Mobile missile units depart their garrisons and the Strategic Rocket Forces (SRF) go to "increased combat readiness." Moscow issues a demarche to Norway and informs Paris that a neutral France will not be attacked in the event of a European war.
12 November	Warsaw Pact (WP) forces in the WTVD move to a "threat of war" readiness level.
	The President of Blue requests and receives from Congress a Declaration of National Emergency and orders full mobilization. NATO declares a "simple alert," and the Rapid Reinforcement Plan (RRP) is implemented on SACEUR recommendation, with approval of the Military Council and the DPC.
15 November	NATO plan of operations (OPLAN) established.

16 November	Red declares a maritime exclusion zone around SSBN bastions and orders naval forces to attack any intruders.
17 November	Blue/NATO concludes that Red/WP forces have moved to "full combat readiness."
18 November	NATO declares "reinforced alert."
20 November	Warsaw Pact offensive begins at 0600. NATO declares "general alert."

Political Objectives and Military Strategy

Blue

Hostilities in the 1985 Global War Game commenced on 20 November 1990, when Red and other Warsaw Pact combined arms forces launched a massive, multifront offensive into the FRG, and on D+3 through Austria toward Bavaria. The Red decision to go to war against NATO in Europe culminated over a year of increasing East-West tensions stemming mainly from political and economic difficulties within Eastern Europe. Red anxiety over the possibility of German reunification, fueled by incidents along the inter-German border (IGB) and in Berlin, all contributed to the Red conclusion that its fundamental security interests in Europe were at risk and that a resolution of the crisis on terms favorable to Moscow was not likely through means short of direct military action.

Of interest and worthy of examination are the original political objectives of Blue and Red and how those objectives were modified and changed as the war progressed. Blue/NATO political objectives in GWG '85 were, essentially, the same as those cited for the 1984 game. There was, however, an expansion of Blue goals implied by the wording "to protect Blue and Western vital interests worldwide."

Red, on the other hand, tended toward more specificity, vowing to "Solve the 'German Problem' once and for all on Red terms through demilitarization and/or neutralization of the Federal Republic of Germany."

In the 1986 game, Blue political objectives were enunciated in an essentially European perspective that reflected the concerns and realities of the war in progress. By and large consistent with prior games, they were stated as follows:

- Restoration of NATO territorial integrity and the restoration of status quo ante for Austria, West Berlin, and Azerbaijan.
- Reduction of the status and influence of Red and the Warsaw Pact and a diminution of Red "global reach."

- Attrition of Red nuclear assets to the point that Blue finishes the war with a favorable nuclear balance.

The Blue strategy for achieving these goals emphasized three objectives:

- Stabilize the military situation in the central region as first priority. Use "economy of force" in other theaters, as necessary, to accomplish this.
- When the front is stabilized, bring maximum coordinated military, political, diplomatic, and economic pressure to bear to convince Red that a nonnuclear, negotiated settlement is in Red's best interest.
- Blue would make clear to Red that it did not intend to challenge its territorial integrity of Red or its political leadership.

Blue acknowledged that the success of this strategy required that Red be convinced that Blue was militarily, politically, and psychologically prepared for a protracted, conventional war.

Red

Red political objectives were also generally consistent but tended to emphasize increasing concern for the immediate safety of the homeland and the future security of Red and its political leadership. While Red still viewed the neutralization of the FRG as paramount, and sought to roll back Blue influence, Red did not want the war to escalate. Red wished to minimize damage to the homeland and reserve military forces, to sustain Communist Party control, and to shore up the system of political and military alliances in Eastern Europe. Red also wanted to retain strategic and theater nuclear deterrence and, hopefully, dominance.

Red strategy in the ongoing war rested primarily on concentrating military forces to consolidate the territorial gains achieved on the Central Front. Red believed that this could be accomplished with a force deployment that achieved sufficient concentration but retained enough strength to tie down Blue/NATO forces elsewhere and limit damage to the homeland. Red also wanted to maneuver France out of the war. In total, Red was determined to:

> Make Blue realize that the war in Central Europe will be so long and costly to Blue that they will feel compelled to negotiate with Red to regain the FRG on terms that would be favorable to Red in reestablishing order in the Eastern Bloc countries—East Germany and Poland in particular.

In summary, then, the postwar status of Germany, particularly the FRG, was central to both Blue and Red. While substantial symmetry seemed to exist in the respective objectives and strategies, there was a growing Red concern for the physical and political safety of the homeland and for the future of the "Eastern Empire."

Part of this elevated Red concern dealt with a rethinking of the nuclear conundrum. If Blue defeat was to be defined as Red military victory in Europe and Blue being pushed off the Continent, then Blue, with the rest of the free world at its disposal, would have a number of long-term military, political, and economic options vis-à-vis Red. If, on the other hand, the Red Army could not deliver victory, Red faced unmitigated disaster. The "Eastern Empire" would almost certainly be gone, and the strain of war on Red manufacturing and agriculture would wreak such devastation on the Red economy that the primacy of the Communist Party of the Soviet Union (CPSU) would be under dire threat. In what represented a dramatic change in perceived conventional wisdom, it now appeared that Red might be more likely to initiate nuclear war than Blue.

The Central Front

The size and timing of the initial WP onslaught was determined as much by the tempo and nature of the North Atlantic Treaty Organization (NATO) military response to the indications and warnings (I and W) of war in the central region as by the overall military readiness posture of the Pact forces. NATO forces in the European Theater had attained high states of readiness well in advance of D-Day. Indeed, NATO had conducted its largest Return of Forces to Germany (REFORGER) exercise, and those troops, particularly the Blue III Corps, were available in theater. As a consequence, the WP decided to begin its offensive with only those forces in the Western Theater of Military Operations (WTVD) that had attained full combat readiness. Pact forces in other areas lagged behind in preparedness and did not begin offensive actions until several days after the war started. The Pact had, however, mobilized the Second Strategic Echelon, and the initial correlation of ground forces was about even.

At 0600, 20 November 1990, Red attacked along the length of the IGB with its First Operational Echelon of 37 divisions. Supreme Allied Commander Europe (SACEUR) military objectives were:

- To hold the Red attack as far forward as possible.
- To constitute reserves and reconstruct units as conditions permitted.
- To conduct counteroffensives to restore the territorial integrity of NATO members.

In conducting these operations, SACEUR was prohibited from attacking Red territory. The major axis of the WP assault appeared to be against the Belgian Corps posted along the Northern Army Group/Central Army Group (NORTHAG/CENTAG) boundary. On D+3 (23 November), Red invaded neutral Austria in order to broaden the front into the southern part of the FRG. On D+1, France had mobilized. Lead elements were promptly dispatched to the FRG, as the main French units concentrated at their assembly areas. On 24 November (D+4), Austrian forces came under NATO command.

At the end of the first week of the war, NATO had lost but little ground. While the front was stabilized in the north and center, pact forces had made gains in the south, advancing to within 50 km of Munich. The Belgian Corps had been badly mauled, and SACEUR planned a counterattack by the Blue III Corps in the direction of the Fulda Gap to relieve the pressure and to break up the Red salient that had been created at the NORTHAG/CENTAG boundary. The southern situation also caused SACEUR concern, where it appeared that Red was about to break through. Austrian losses had been heavy and their resistance effectively broken. Red was moving on Munich with seven divisions, and the 1st French Army was advancing to try to hold Red on a line from Nuremberg to Stuttgart on 27 November (D+7). At the northern end of the front, Polish forces had attacked into Schleswig-Holstein, but NATO was holding the line of the Kiel Canal, although Hamburg had been abandoned on 26 November (D+6). It was on that date that the NATO Defense Planning Committee (DPC) authorized Allied Forces Northern Europe (AFNORTH) to attack the Red homeland.

Air action was heavy from the start of the war, with Red concentrating on Blue airfields with known or suspected nuclear assets. Blue air attacks centered on WP airfields and on battlefield air interdiction (BAI). By D+3, both sides had lost about 960 aircraft and the use of eight to ten airfields. On that date, Blue shifted the bulk of its air operations to close air support (CAS). After D+4, SACEUR made the decision to utilize all air assets available, including aircraft carrier battle groups (CVBG), to interdict the closing Second Strategic Echelon.

On 27 November (D+7), Red fully committed the Second Operational Echelon and achieved a major breakthrough in the vicinity of Kassel, which the Blue III Corps was tasked to contain. In the south, in spite of stubborn French resistance, the Red drive on Munich continued. On 30 November (D+10), the French 2nd Army went into line with the 1st in the vicinity of Nuremberg. At the same time, Italian units began an advance toward Innsbruck against battalion-strength opposition.

On 1 December (D+11), the II Marine Amphibious Force (MAF) staged an amphibious landing at Esbjerg on the western coast of Denmark. The landing was successful, but the *Coral Sea* was lost in an eight-regiment Badger/Blinder/Backfire Soviet Naval Aviation/Long-Range Aviation (SNA/LRA) raid utilizing AS-4 and AS-6 missiles launched at a range of 150 miles. In concert with this attack, Red forces crossed the Kiel Canal and the Danish border and attempted a coordinated attack with airborne forces to destroy the beachhead at Esbjerg. The Red airborne units sustained about 60 percent casualties; the Blue marines stabilized their position and linked with two Danish mechanized battalions from Zealand and FRG elements that had retreated up the peninsula.

While Red forces in the south continued their advance toward the Rhine, the main Red effort on 2 December (D+12) seemed to be along the Göttingen/Paderborn/Giessen/Fulda line. The Blue III Corps counterattack against the Red salient had attained its objective in relieving the pressure on the Belgian Corps, but that unit and the Netherlands Corps had to fall back as supplies were expended. As this gradual and orderly retreat was conducted from an almost equally exhausted Red, Blue continued the III Corps counterattack while the 8th Blue division attacked to the northeast on 5 December (D+15).

In Denmark, Red continued efforts to oust the Blue/NATO forces from the peninsula. On 3 December (D+13), Red attempted an amphibious landing on the east coast of Jutland. Twenty-five hundred SNI suffered 50 percent casualties, two guided missile destroyers (DDGs) and seven amphibs were sunk, and another two DDGs and nine amphibs were damaged. Red endeavored to suppress Blue air defense capability in Jutland, but an offensive by II MAF reached the western part of the Danish-German border on 7 December (D+17). At the southern end of the front, Italian forces entered Innsbruck the next day.

8 December 1990 (D+18) marked the end of GWG 1985 (map 3). SACEUR saw the period 12–16 December as the next period of crisis; that was the expected closure date of the five armies that constituted the Second Strategic Echelon. This force was augmented by Red divisions pulled out of Bulgaria. The Central Front had lapsed into a state of relative inactivity, and SACEUR utilized the respite to reconstitute units to the extent possible while Red awaited the arrival of the Second Echelon. The Third Strategic Echelon was moving through Poland.

The Blue III Corps counteroffensive was continuing as GWG 1986 commenced (map 4). The objective of this attack was to wear down the Red and Polish armies north of Kassel and, by so doing, force Red to use significant portions of the Second Strategic Echelon as "gap fillers." The attack succeeded in destroying seven WP divisions, but had to be halted when the Second Echelon, delayed for four days by intensive air interdiction, finally closed.

Coincident with this counteroffensive was a deterioration of the situation on the southern flank. The badly battered French forces, now reinforced by the 3rd French Army, attempted to withdraw to protect their national frontier. Red massed 29 divisions between Stuttgart and the French border and attacked on 11 December (D+21). Four divisions of the 1st French army were trapped in Stuttgart. Red forced a crossing of the Rhine at Mannheim on D+22, and the momentum of the assault carried Red across the Rhine and into the hills of Eifel, where terrain and Blue reinforcements stemmed the advance. Red had conserved and reconstituted air power during the bad

MAP 3
The Central Front 1985 Game D+18

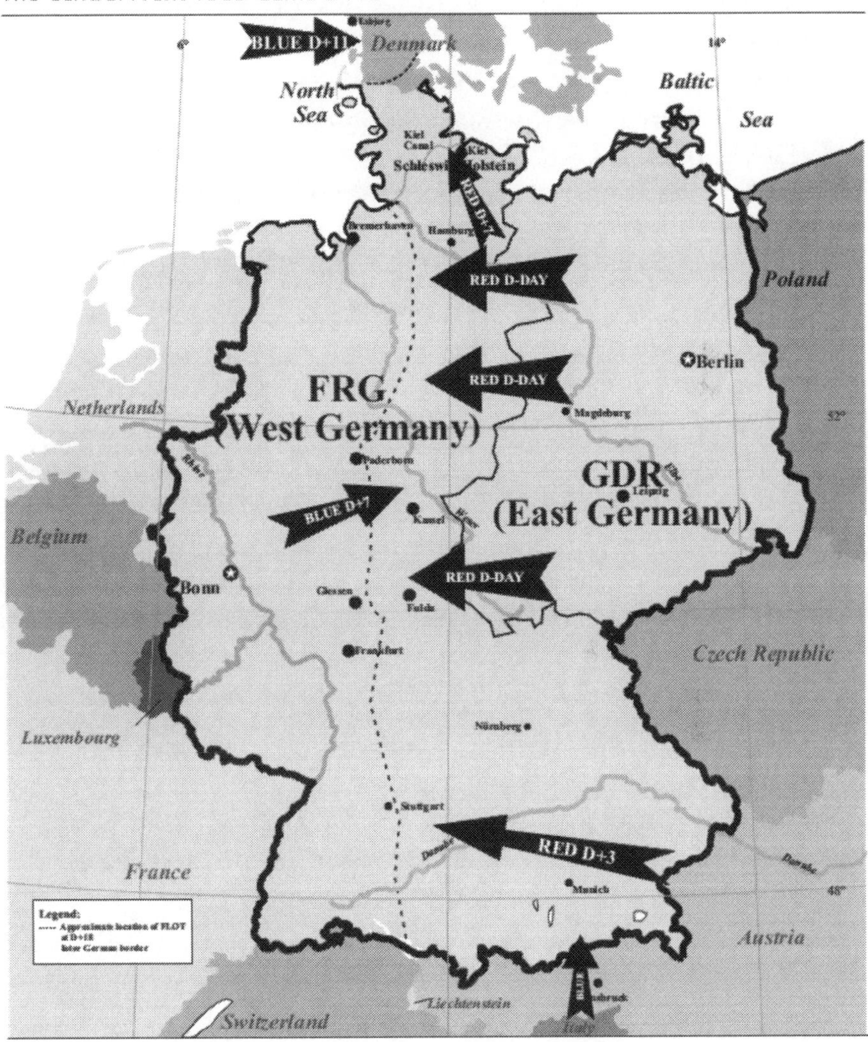

weather that preceded this offensive and was thus able to support it with seven divisions of tactical aircraft (TACAIR) for battlefield air interdiction/close air support (BAI/CAS) operations. The four divisions encircled at Stuttgart had been allowed by Red to withdraw as part of their effort to detach France from the Western Alliance. To the east, the Italians maintained a slow advance in the direction of Munich, opposed by two Hungarian divisions.

The closure of the Second Strategic Echelon definitively restored the initiative to Red. Five divisions were allotted to the southern pincer where the principal effort was to be made. Five were sent north to take advantage of opportunities that might arise, and three were retained in the center as a strategic reserve. The "opportunity" in the north did eventuate as SACEUR rushed all available mobile reserves south to try to retrieve the situation there.

On 16 December (D+26), a Red offensive shattered the Netherlands Corps, seriously depleted by the early frontier battles. As the Dutch fell back, SACEUR tried but failed to hold the line of the Weser. Remnants of the NATO force fell back behind the Ems Canal. In an effort to counter Alliance air and to retard Blue reinforcements, Red launched conventional missiles on NATO airfields and on Netherlands and FRG port cities.

A third Red initiative involved an attempt to destroy the Blue III Corps in the vicinity of Siegen/Giessen. Fixed by a Red frontal attack and outflanked by Third Echelon forces that closed on 23 December (D+33), III Corps and a United Kingdom corps were unable to disengage. Outnumbered and facing fresh divisions from both the Second and Third Echelons, these units held the Red advance for three days before being destroyed. This gave NATO time to forge new defensive lines in the north and center.

Thus, on 25 December (D+35), the infusion of the Third Strategic Echelon had enabled Red to attain deep penetrations at both ends of the Central Front. Red reached the borders of Luxembourg and the Netherlands and drove on into the Benelux. On 30 December (D+40), dikes were opened and the lowlands east of Amsterdam were flooded to slow the Red advance.

In the south, Red continued to try to turn the NATO flank in the Vosges and along the Moselle by making a "tactical incursion" into France. Red calculated, correctly, that France would not resort to the use of nuclear weapons unless national survival was threatened, and Red made certain that such was not perceived as the intention. France committed its forces to NATO command on 25 December (D+35).

By 30 December (D+40), SACEUR was defending a line running from Amsterdam through Düsseldorf to the vicinity of Verdun. Little of the FRG remained under Alliance control, and NATO had grave concerns about possible political repercussions should all of it be occupied by Red. On the other hand, the Red southern flank was "in the air," and the line on air parity ran approximately south from the Jutland Peninsula. Consequently, NATO had superiority over the forward edge of the battle area (FEBA), while Red held sway to the east.

As the military situation had deteriorated following the commitment of the Third Strategic Echelon (D+33), deployment of Blue army combat units was accelerated at the expense of sustainment forces in order to meet the threat. By 1 January 1991 (D+42), this accelerated deployment was essentially complete with the equivalent of a

MAP 4
The Central Front 1986 Game D+19 to D+42

reinforced corps expected to arrive on D+48. This would move the correlation of forces to about 1.3 to 1.0 in favor of NATO. However, the anticipated arrival of the Fourth and Fifth Strategic Echelons, anticipated about 5 January (D+46) and 13 January (D+54), would alter this ratio to 1.56 to 1.0 in favor of the WP.

However, on 30 December (D+40), increasing and unequal rates of aircraft attrition caused the WTVD commander to substantially reduce the tempo of operations to conserve aircraft. This decision gave NATO control of the air over the FRG, and the unopposed CAS, BAI, and air intercept (AI) missions resulted in the heavy attrition and substantial slowing of the closure of the Fourth and Fifth Strategic Echelons. Further, it greatly assisted the NATO defense against WP forces attempting to breach the Rhine River line.

This was the situation that confronted NATO at the commencement of GWG 1987, 2 January 1991 (D+43). SACEUR faced a decision regarding the utilization of the arriving reserves: to strengthen the defenses along the Rhine or to initiate a counteroffensive. Given NATO air superiority, the Red force concentration along the Rhine in the vicinity of Bonn, the weariness of Red forces opposite CENTAG, and the extended and unanchored Red southern flank, SACEUR planned a five-phase offensive:

- Attack in CENTAG to occupy territory from the Moselle to the Rhine.
- Assemble a major force (the First Allied Army) for the counterattack.
- Break through Red positions on a Frankfurt/Karlsruhe axis.
- Continue the attack toward Magdeburg and Leipzig.
- Maneuver to prevent breakout of encircled Red forces and then, if feasible, open ground access to Berlin (see map 5).

The first phase of the operation began on 30 December (D+40) with CENTAG forces attacking from the Moselle to attain the left bank of the Rhine. The attacking force was composed of one Blue and one French corps, and as it advanced, AFCENT was forming 16 divisions from Blue, France, Germany, and the United Kingdom into the First Allied Army. On 5 January (D+46), with the arrival of the Fourth Strategic Echelon delayed and the WTVD commander concerned about the Blue advance toward the Rhine, the Supreme High Command (VGK) delegated authority to employ chemical weapons (CW).

D+48, 7 January, saw the arrival on the Rhine of lead elements of the VII Blue and French Corps in the vicinity of Karlsruhe. Just to the north of the army group (AG) boundary, the advance of I UK Corps toward Frankfurt, though heavily opposed, threatened the encirclement of four Red divisions.

To the north, NATO forces were hard-pressed in holding the Rotterdam-Essen line. Efforts to break out of the Jutland Peninsula had been repulsed. SACEUR was concerned about this lack of success because it was believed that the northern pincer was necessary to distract the Fifth Strategic Echelon.

On 8 January (D+49), Red used persistent and nonpersistent CW in Jutland, but winter weather limited its effectiveness. The CW use was an indication of lack of Red combat power, caused in part by the delay of the Fourth Strategic Echelon, which had finally begun to arrive, albeit in a piecemeal and attrited state. Chemicals were used again on 9 January (D+50), and while the I UK Corps was forced back across the

MAP 5
The Central Front 1987 Game D+43 to D+64

Rhine, the VII Blue and I French Corps continued to advance. In the confusion caused by the Red CW attack on I UK Corps, two Red divisions crossed the Rhine and became established in what was to become known as the "Bonn pocket."

On 11 January (D+52), Blue responded to the Red CW use with similar attacks against WP forces along the Kiel Canal, and against two airfields in Czechoslovakia. The VGK, concerned about escalation, had previously withdrawn discretionary authority from the WTVD commander.

SACEUR launched Phase Three of its offensive, code-named Operation GOLDEN SWORD, on 12 January (D+53). The 16 Allied divisions massed at Luneville attacked with VII Blue Corps to the north, I French Corps in the center, and German III Corps to the south. The geographic objective was Magdeburg and a linkup there with forces attacking southeast out of Jutland and the Italians moving north from the Munich-Salzburg area. NORTHAG concentrated on the containment of the "Bonn pocket," which now had six divisions in it, as Fourth Echelon troops were fed in as they arrived.

GOLDEN SWORD made excellent progress: Fulda was reached on 13 January (D+54) and Frankfurt taken by helicopter assault. On 15 January (D+56), a unit of the First Allied Army crossed the IGB. Red reserves destined for the "Bonn pocket" had to be diverted to try to stem the three-pronged NATO attack: the Italians had crossed the Danube, and I and II MAF along with the Sixth FRG Panzer were breaking out of Jutland.

On 16 January (D+57), Red concern became obvious when CW was again utilized. Three persistent CW "barriers" were laid: along the IGB to stop the First Allied Army; near Munich to impede the Italians; and along the Kiel Canal to slow the northern pincer. Despite these attacks, the First Allied Army was advancing 50 km per day, and the Italians, having passed through Regensburg, were under Allied Forces Central Europe (AFCENT) operational control. The Jutland attack, however, was stalled by strong Red resistance.

The Red WTVD commander recommended heavy CW use as the situation continued to deteriorate. In addition to the progress of GOLDEN SWORD, NATO forces had seized the initiative at the northern end of the line. Allied forces were advancing on Amsterdam, and the French were in the process of surrounding several Red divisions in the vicinity of Strasbourg. Red was focusing on trying to build a force to counterattack the First Allied Army, which now took precedence over reinforcing the Bonn pocket.

By 20 January (D+61), nine Allied divisions had entered the GDR, and on 22 January, Leipzig fell and the southern bank of the Elbe was reached. To the south, the Italians had pushed Red out of Bavaria and entered Czechoslovakia and the GDR. Link-up with AFCENT southern pincer had occurred near Ansbach on 19 January (D+60). The northern pincer out of Jutland had regained the initiative and was moving on Hamburg.

D+64 (23 January) found Blue digging in along the Elbe. The Rapid Reinforcement Plan (RRP) was complete, and no additional reinforcements could be expected. GOLDEN SWORD had reached its culminating point and could stretch the thin line of ground forces no further. Another vital consideration was that the Elbe represented the limit of Blue air cover. Red was pinning its hopes on the Sixth Strategic Echelon, made up of 23 divisions from the Far Eastern Theater of Military Operations (FETVD), then approaching the Elbe.

The Atlantic

Commander-in-Chief Atlantic's (CINCLANT) broad objectives at the outset of the war were to establish and maintain sea control while denying the same to Red. The first concern, however, was to ensure the safety of the SLOCs. Beyond that, Blue intended to mount an early and sustained antiballistic missile submarine (SSBN) campaign against both the Yankees in the Atlantic and the bastioned "boomers" of the Northern Fleet.

Further, the Blue concept of operations went beyond maritime-based support of NATO's northern flank. While the importance of holding North Norway remained an important goal, Blue planned to secure conditions that would permit CVBG air, in coordination with Tomahawk land attack missiles (conventional) (TLAM(C)), to make direct attacks on the Red homeland, particularly the Kola Peninsula area. As a part of the Blue "long war" strategy, it was considered important to develop strategic leverage by demonstrating the ability both to strike Red itself and to destroy "targets that matter," facilities that would have an impact on Red ability to wage a protracted war. A necessary prerequisite to the execution of this strategy required the clearing of the Norwegian Sea, and as much of the Barents as possible, of Red surface and submarine threats and maintaining sanitization of the Norwegian littoral. Red diesel SSs were a particular concern in this regard.

Red, on the other hand, endeavored to protect the bastioned SSBNs by geographic location, heavy mining, and a defense in-depth provided by surface action groups (SAG) and SS/SSN/SSGN deployed in the Norwegian and Barents Seas. While Red did not plan to mount a classic anti-SLOC campaign, it did utilize a Cuban-based SAG, clandestine mining, sabotage, and special operations forces to introduce uncertainty into Blue operations and slow the flow of reinforcements to Europe. Countering these Red initiatives was one of CINCLANT's first tasks.

The bulk of military action in the Western Atlantic (WESTLANT) took place during the first week of the war. On D+2, a Red SAG consisting of a Kresta II guided missile cruiser (CG), a Krivak I guided missile frigate (FFG) and a Krivak II FFG attacked the Panama Canal, closing it for one week. This force was then promptly sunk by a Blue air attack. The other major military threat in the hemisphere, Nicaragua-based IL-38s, were taken out by Blue, and a coalition of Blue, Colombia, and Venezuela served to preempt any attempts at aggression on the ground. A strong Blue demarche to Cuba had the desired effect as that country's Foxtrot submarine (SS) remained in port.

Red utilized submarines to mine the ports of New Orleans, Houston, and Galveston. These efforts had minimal success, with only two merchant ships sunk out of 150 sailing during the first days of the war. Both ports were closed briefly, and on D+7, Red recalled all but two of the SS/SSN stationed in WESTLANT.

Blue immediately attacked the three Yankee class on station in the Atlantic, and all were dispatched by D+2. The actions of the first few days of the war left Red with three cruise missile submarines (SSGNs) and eight SSNs in the Atlantic. In the Norwegian Sea and the Barents, Blue attacked with forward-deployed SSNs against Red Northern Fleet assets and the bastioned SSBNs. Red had deployed three SAGs, centered on BLKCON 5, and including several *Kiev* aircraft carriers (CV) in the Barents Sea. Blue found the bastions well protected and lost two SSNs on the third day of the war.

By D+7, Blue had marshaled a four-CVBG strike force consisting of *America*, *Independence*, *Roosevelt*, and *Saratoga*. Anti-submarine warfare (ASW) protection was provided by the *Illustrious* and *Invincible* groups, and the *Coral Sea* had been ordered to the vicinity of Jutland. On D+8, the CVBG strike force and supporting ASW groups moved into the Norwegian Sea. This coincided with a general pullback of Red SS/SSN, with those in the vicinity of the Greenland-Iceland-United Kingdom (GIUK) gap moving north and those in WESTLANT withdrawing to the east. A strike against the Kola was launched on D+9, after which the *Roosevelt* and *Saratoga* headed south (belatedly) to support the Jutland amphibious landing while the *America* and *Independence* sheltered in the Norwegian fjords.

After two weeks of war and frequent attacks, the Northern Fleet SAGs had sustained heavy damage. Blue SSNs and P-3 Harpoon strikes had sunk one *Kiev* CV, two Kresta I CGs, one Krivak FFG, and one *Sovremenny* destroyer (DD), and gained a 50 percent mobility kill on a *Kirov* battle cruiser. This result was attained at the cost of two Blue SSNs and six P-3s. The SAGs were attacked again on D+15 as they were attempting to withdraw. Blue launched a coordinated attack with SSNs, carrier-based air, Tomahawk antiship missiles (TASM), and Harpoon. The damaged *Kirov* was sunk, as were a second *Kiev*, one Krivak I, one Krivak II, one *Udaloy* DD, and three auxiliaries. Red lost 27 aircraft, Blue 14. Blue continued to assault the bastioned SSBNs and lost SSNs primarily in minefields that Red continually expanded and thickened and also to minefields laid by the SAGs across transit routes in the Barents.

On D+14, the *Independence* was torpedoed by a Foxtrot SS in Vestfjord. Dead in the water (DIW), the ship was taken under tow only to be hit again on D+15 by two torpedoes from two Foxtrots. As GWG '85 ended, *Independence* was en route Trondheim for shipyard repairs. This event had a strong influence on force mobility for the rest of the war, as Commander Striking Force (COMSTRIKEFOR) could never be certain of being free of the diesel threat.

As GWG '86 began on D+19 (9 December), the aircraft carrier battle force (CVBF) was in Vestfjord. *Roosevelt* and *Saratoga* had rejoined, and aircraft from the damaged *Independence* and *Coral Sea* (sunk supporting amphibious operations at Jutland) were being consolidated ashore to provide a replacement pool and for utilization in support of the land battle. Battle force ASW suffered a loss on D+21, when *Ark Royal* was torpedoed and departed to Bergen for shipyard repair. The battered Red SAGs, now consolidated from three to two, one with BLKCON 5 and the other a *Kiev*, were trying to withdraw to the eastern Barents.

Poor weather restricted air operations for most of the first week of Global '86. However, on D+25 both SAGs were attacked by TASMs launched from the *Dallas* and *Providence*. The BLKCON 5 SAG lost a *Kirov* and had two other ships damaged. A planned air strike on the BLKCON 5 SAG, scheduled for D+27, had to be delayed because the CVBF lacked targeting intelligence and the CVBGs remained in Vestfjord. Red gained information about the planned departure of the *Forrestal* from Norfolk and ordered an Akula to take station northeast of the Virginia Capes (VACAPES).

In Washington, the subject of Cuba continued to be discussed. While the D-Day demarche by Blue had thus far been effective, concern still existed that Cuba might become a problem. The JCS addressed the question on D+27 and laid out the following options:

- Form a CVBG based on *Forrestal* for air strikes in support of CJTF 140.
- Put *Wisconsin* in the Caribbean to strike selected targets.
- Institute a blockade of Cuba.

The JCS recommendation was that no forces be diverted to Cuba.

However, on D+29, Fidel Castro delivered a two-hour speech during which he ordered mobilization of Cuba's guard and militia units, and placed the naval forces on full alert. The following day, the JCS sent a message to CINCLANT declaring that Cuba was a threat to Blue military and civilian assets in the Caribbean, Blue southeast coastal areas, and regional SLOCs. CINCLANT was ordered to take immediate action to neutralize military installations, forces, equipment, and naval/aircraft/military and civilian communications facilities. CINCLANT responded that a blockade was not feasible because it would require a diversion of assets from the Norwegian Sea campaign. On D+31, the battleship (BB) *Wisconsin* and the *Kidd* were ordered to proceed at best speed and take station 50 miles south of Guantánamo. This was the start of a buildup that, by D+42, would include the FFGs *Truett*, *Simpson*, and *Groves* as well.

While the majority of military action in WESTLANT occurred during the first week of the war, Blue had worked diligently to maintain the security of the SLOCs and the safety of the continental United States (CONUS), which were not without threat. On D+16, for example, Red had attempted to bomb the Panama Canal and Kennedy Space Center with two Bear aircraft, and on D+14 the Coast Guard had captured a Red merchant ship flying the Spanish flag that had 300 mines aboard.

Commander Maritime Defense Zone Atlantic (COMMARDEZLANT) had four task units operating from Galveston to the Canadian border for ASW protection of the coastal SLOCs. Mine countermeasure (MCM) operations were ongoing along the Q routes, and the Coast Guard was stopping and inspecting vessels off Norfolk, Wilmington, and Charleston. Protective minefields had been laid off Norfolk, New York City, New Orleans, Galveston, Charleston, Morehead City, Kings Bay, and Mayport.

Hemispheric allies were providing assistance as well. On D+29, Argentina began continuous patrols of the Beagle Channel, Strait of Magellan, and Cape Horn to assure the safety of Blue and Allied shipping. Chile also joined in, establishing a continuous patrol of its waters at the continent's southern tip.

On D+30, the *Forrestal* chopped to COMSECONDFLT to sortie on D+31 for the vicinity of the Irish Sea and further assignment. She sank in the VACAPES op-area from multiple torpedo hits and an escorting guided missile destroyer (DDG), struck by a single torpedo, sustained a 50 percent mobility kill. The Red SSN was destroyed by MPA based at Patuxent River Naval Air Station.

At the time of the *Forrestal* sinking, both Blue and Red were reassessing their respective submarine campaigns. While Red surface forces capable of enfilading the SLOCs appeared to have been neutralized, the Blue ASW campaign was intensifying. Submarine Allied Commander Atlantic (SUBACLANT) assets were disposed as follows: 14 SSN under the ice, 4 in the Barents, 13 in the Norwegian Sea, 4 in the Greenland Sea, and 5 in the GIUK gap. Seven French and Portuguese SS/SSN were postured in the Bay of Biscay and near the coast of Portugal, seven Norwegian and three UK SS were operating in the Skagerrak. Three Canadian SS were on station south of Greenland. There were no Red SSBN west of the line from Spitsbergen to North Cape. By D+35, Blue saw a diminishing return from the anti-SSBN operations. The boomers that remained were further east—around Nova Zemlya—and better protected as Red continuously strengthened minefields. Therefore, Blue began a pullback of SSNs to form a nine-boat barrier from Spitsbergen to North Cape.

Red was beginning to consider a limited anti-SLOC campaign, and to that end was doing a "roll call" to determine the number of general-purpose submarines that might be dedicated to that operation. Red was also evaluating the mine situation. While Red mines had proved successful against Blue SSN trying to penetrate the bastions, usage was running at 300 mines per day, and supply was a problem. Inventories would be exhausted by D+36, with no remaining mines due in theater.

At D+35, Blue had gained control of the Norwegian Sea and western Baltic approaches. While COMSTRIKEFOR complained about lack of information on Red SSN/SS/SSGN, the fact was that there were extremely few in the area. Blue losses had been substantial, but offensive air and missile operations continued against surviving Red Northern Fleet units and against the Red homeland. One of the two remaining SAGs was attacked on D+35, and the BLKCON 5 was disabled and her aircraft reassigned to the Northwestern Theater of Military Operations (NWTVD).

On D+36, Blue planned for a coordinated strike into the Kola Peninsula. The Blue objective was to try to influence the strategic balance by demonstrating that Blue had the ability to attack the Red homeland. The attack was planned with the realization that heavy losses were to be anticipated, as the DPC refusal to authorize overflight of Finland severely restricted routes on ingress/egress. Targets selected for attack included:

- Red aircraft, early warning and ground control intercept (EW/GCI) sites, command and control facilities, and airfields.
- A nuclear power plant.
- The mining of Murmansk harbor.

The attack was elaborately planned in an effort to minimize casualties. Signals intelligence (SIGINT), obtained on D+25, indicated that Red would launch combat air patrol (CAP) whenever Blue aircraft flew east of 27 degrees east longitude. Consequently, while the plan of attack called for 103 aircraft, only 32 would actually be for strike purposes. Most of the other aircraft involved would endeavor to overwhelm the Red air defense system by penetration and feints.

Several other coincidental operations were staged to deceive and distract. One CG and two DDs were stationed at 71 degrees 35 minutes north and 27 degrees 30 minutes east to lure Red interceptors into a missile trap. Also, a TLAM(C) attack would supplement an AFNORTH strike on the 77th MRD at Banak.

The attack was conducted on D+37, with aircraft launched from the *America* and *Roosevelt* in Vestfjord and *Saratoga* in Andfjord. Red lost 23 aircraft (Foxhound, Flanker, Fulcrum, and Flogger), one combatant and one auxiliary sunk, and an airfield was rendered inoperable for several days. Blue lost 24 aircraft; the CG and two DDs were targeted by an Oscar and later sunk by multiple torpedo hits while returning to the CVBG.

The strike on the nuclear power plant was one of the most controversial events of the game. While the plant was disabled, the damage inflicted was greater than that at Chernobyl, and the resultant release of radioactive material precipitated massive diplomatic "fallout" from neutrals and allies alike.

D+43, 2 January, marked the start of Global '87. The positioning of the CVBGs remained the same with *Independence* and *Ark Royal* still under repair and HMS *Illustrious* conducting ASW northwest of Vestfjord. COMSTRIKEFLT defined the missions of the CVBF as follows:

- Strategic ASW.
- Air superiority.
- Support to ground forces.
- Strategic power projection.
- Denial to Red of the use of the airfields at Alta and Banak.

The request for permission to overfly Finland was reiterated and denied by the DPC on D+46.

As SACEUR began the counteroffensive on the Central Front, the naval war in the Baltic became more intense. After massive air attacks to defeat the Blue amphibious landings and early efforts to reinforce Jutland directly, the buildup of Blue forces on that peninsula and the efforts by Blue to break out across the Lubeck Canal led to a fierce struggle to control the western and central Baltic.

The main Blue effort in early January was against Warsaw Pact convoys transiting from the eastern Baltic to support the Red units trying to contain the Blue salient south of the Kiel Canal. NATO SSs faced increasing opposition from Red mining operations, and surface ships were utilized extensively to keep the transit lanes clear. As Red mining efforts intensified, FRG Tornados took over some of the interdiction efforts.

On D+50, as a result of losses to mines, Blue moved both an MCM and a fast-patrol boat (FPB) squadron along the coast of Sweden to clear the SS transit routes. These forces were withdrawn as Red countered by moving 40 small combatants in their direction. Red left part of this force in the area for the remainder of the game to discourage future Blue incursions. Because neither side was able to establish definitive air control over the west-central Baltic, advantage tended to ebb and flow depending on which side held the temporary edge in assets.

For this reason, the struggle for supremacy continued throughout Global '87, with neither side able to fully exploit the potential geography offered. Blue would have used area control to secure the northern flank of an eastward offensive, Red as an avenue to supply and reinforce divisions west of Rostock. A major effort to achieve this aim led to a three-day running battle. On D+59, Red began to sail a 30-ship convoy from Kaliningrad to Rostock with elements of the Sixth Echelon. This convoy came under sustained air and submarine attack from Blue/NATO forces. It limped into Rostock on D+61, having lost ten escorts and a number of troop and supply ships.

Red continued throughout Global '87 to interfere with Blue logistical support for the Central Front. A success was achieved on D+54 when a Spetsnaz unit sank a merchant ship in the Miraflores locks, shutting down the Panama Canal for three weeks.

Other initiatives were not so successful, primarily because of the reluctance of Fidel Castro to do what Moscow wanted him to do. There were signs of Cuba's lack of cooperation as far back as D+24, when both that country and Nicaragua abstained from a Red request that both nations cooperate in mining the approaches to the Panama Canal, using Red equipment and with their personnel clad in Red uniforms.

By early January (D+44), Blue suspected a Red plot to rearm at least one SSGN utilizing a Cuban base for that purpose. Blue instituted intensified MPA/ASW operations off the island, but with strict instructions not to violate Cuban air space or territorial waters. While this anticipated operation concerned Blue, no evidence that it occurred was discovered. The fact that the operation did not come about was not for want of effort on the part of Red. Indeed, continued inaction on Castro's part led to a plan by Red to accomplish the rearming without his permission, utilizing an Air India flight to transport conventional warheads sufficient to replace 50 percent of the SSGNs' normal nuclear load out. Blue learned of this plan, and it was not attempted. Finally, a thoroughly frustrated Red suggested on D+61 that Castro consider a trip to Moscow for "consultations," an invitation that the Cuban leader felt it wise to decline.

Following the submarine "roll call" described earlier, the VGK decided to initiate a limited anti-SLOC campaign. This decision was taken on D+44 with the following assets detailed to the operation:

- A northern Fleet Akula was dispatched to the southwestern approaches to the English Channel (SWAPS) .
- A Sierra in the Mediterranean was to out-chop on D+47.
- A Mod Kashin in Luanda was ordered to participate as well.

The following summarizes the results of this:

- D+45—Akula sinks merchant ship in SWAPS
    - Mod Kashin sinks Japanese tanker.
- D+47—Akula sunk in SWAPS
    - Sierra exits Mediterranean.
- D+49—Sierra sinks four merchant ships off Spain/Portugal.
- D+50—Mod Kashin sinks two merchant ships off Angola.
- D+53—Sierra sinks merchant ship in Iberian Basin.

- D+54—Sierra sinks merchant ship off Spain.
- D+58—Sierra sinks French SSN.
- D+60—Mod Kashin sinks two tankers.
- D+63—Sierra sinks two merchant ships.

As the game ended, the Mod Kashin was still at large, and Blue was dedicating substantial assets to an intensive ASW campaign in the Iberian Basin. The widely dispersed sinkings had convinced Blue that several Red SSNs were still operating in that area instead of the single Sierra that was in fact responsible for the attacks.

As GWG '87 progressed, both Blue and Red commanders gave thought to the possibility of nuclear escalation. Supreme Allied Commander Atlantic (SACLANT) and Commander Striking Fleet Atlantic (COMSTRIKEFLTLANT) feared that Red might use such weapons against the CVBF to gain a more favorable correlation of forces. Therefore, a request was made to the DPC for tactical nuclear release authority when there was clear I and W of imminent Red escalation. This request was denied. Almost simultaneously, on D+48, the NWTVD commander asked the VGK for permission to use nuclear weapons against the CVBG. This request was also denied, as the VGK was generally satisfied with the situation in theater, and further, was unsure of the Blue response.

The nuclear issue arose again at D+50. COMSTRIKEFLTLANT concluded that Red use of chemical weapons had lowered the nuclear threshold and renewed the request to the DPC for "conditional" tactical nuclear release and for permission to overfly Finland. The nuclear request was again denied, but the long-sought over-flight permission was granted subject to three conditions:

- The strikes be "surgical" against specific targets.
- There be no reattack until the DPC evaluated Finnish reaction.
- Finnish aircraft to be attacked only in self-defense.

However, on D+53, a planned strike into the Kola across Finnish air space was delayed by the Blue National Command Authority (NCA) and on D+54, concerns over possible diplomatic repercussions led Blue higher authority to deny permission for the attack.

The nuclear issue was raised again in another context on D+57. COMSTRIKEFLTLANT expressed concern that a mass SNA raid on the CVBF would overwhelm the available defensive assets of fifty F-14s, and four SM-1 and seven SM-2 shooters. Believing that a three-regiment attack would succeed, that commander requested authorization to use SM-1-ER BTNs (nuclear warheads) as a "weapon of last resort." This request was denied.

Throughout Global '87, the primary utilization of the CVBF air assets was in support of ground operations. At D+54, for example, the Strike Force was averaging 80 sorties per day against the Red MRDs. An important adjunct of this air campaign was to prevent Red from utilizing Norwegian airfields captured in their advance. Blue losses, especially in attacks on these captured air facilities, were substantial, and on D+58 COMSTRIKEFLTLANT limited Allied Forces Northern Europe (AFNORTH) to 30 sorties per day to conserve pilots and aircraft, A-6s in particular. That commander also had to husband resources to provide cover and support for Operation ICE PICK, whose amphibious component was scheduled to go ashore on D+62.

Red made two significant moves to reduce the power of the strike force. The first of these was a deception operation using the hulk of the *Leonid Brezhnev* (BLKCON 5) as a decoy to lure Blue strike air into a trap. The "trap" was baited on D+50 when the *Brezhnev* was towed into a position where a Blue attack could be intercepted by Red air, and a Mainstay orbit was moved to attract Blue attention. Forgers flying out of the Kola simulated air operations, and auxiliary power was provided to operate radar and generate other emissions. Towed barges were used to replicate escorts.

On D+54, Blue misidentified the decoy as the remaining *Kiev* SAG and decided on an SSN attack rather than air. This strike was conducted with TASM on D+56, and it was only after that that Blue began to believe they were dealing with a Red feint. The decoy force remained in position at game end, ignored by Blue.

The other Red move against the CVBF was a multiregiment SNA/SAF attack spearheaded by two Backfire regiments flown into Archangel from outside the theater. Changed conditions on the Central Front led to a different perception of the CVBF by the VGK. On D+45, Red had gone through an elaborate deception to keep the CVBF north. Three MRDs had maneuvered in the "Finnish Wedge," and an amphibious force embarked and put to sea to try to persuade Blue that the strike assets would be necessary to counter a massive invasion of Norway. However, the success of GOLDEN SWORD caused a shift on the part of the VGK. As the Red position in Germany deteriorated, the CVBF was seen as a potential strategic threat, regardless of its current tasking. On D+60, the VGK ordered that plans be formulated for the destruction of the Battle Force, and did not rule out the use of nuclear weapons. The result of this order was the attack of D+62.

This was another of the Red multiregiment attacks flown directly against the CVBF through Finnish air space. Losses in the air were heavy to both sides, but effective air defense, coupled with terrain shielding provided by the topography of the fjords, left Blue with two escorts sunk and superficial damage to several other units. Carrier air operations continued unimpaired.

Perhaps the most significant result of this Red attack was that it brought at least temporary closure to the long-debated question of Blue overflights of Finland. COMSTRIKEFLTLANT had consistently believed that his force effectiveness was substantially reduced by the tactical complications imposed by the prohibition on the use of Finnish air space. He thus had renewed his request for overflight on D+60, stating in the process that the inability to do so was responsible for what was termed a "semi-stalemate." The Red attack on D+62 led to a granting of the desired permission on D+63, and, as the game ended, planning was underway for a combined TLAM(C) and air strike against railroad marshalling yards and a power plant in the Kola on D+64. Finland was to be advised of the operation when the aircraft were en route, and it was hoped that the government would do no more than issue a mild public protest.

Discussion over the best utilization of COMSTRIKEFLTLANT CVBGs had been ongoing throughout Global. It was suggested that if both Blue and Red wanted to see the CVBF remain in Vestfjord and environs, someone was wrong. Others observed that "strategic ASW," stated as the CVBF commander's first priority for the 1987 game, did not require three CVBGs. Orders from the NCA to use part of this force to support the Esbjerg landing in the 1985 game were not complied with; finally two CVBGs were sent south, but too late to provide assistance. Similarly, toward the end of GWG '87, a request by SACEUR for one carrier to aid in averting impending disaster in the eastern Mediterranean was rejected.

Tactically, COMSTRIKEFLTLANT was concerned about the Red submarine threat, particularly diesel SSs that might be lurking along the Norwegian littoral waiting for a CV to emerge from the protection of the fjords. Further, and as noted above, the prohibition on use of Finnish air space was viewed as preventing the full exploitation of the CVBF strike capability. Strategically, the situation on D+56 was seen by the CVBF commander as follows: Red will shortly realize that Red alone cannot terminate hostilities. It follows that Red will adopt a protracted war strategy, and, without the CVBF to the north, Red would be able to target the UK and that such action could result in serious limitations on Blue strategy and prospects.

The Mediterranean

AFSOUTH's basic objective at the beginning of the war was to gain control of the Mediterranean for Blue and to deny it to Red. The *John F. Kennedy* CVBG and the *Iowa* SAG were initially positioned just south of the Aegean with the *Eisenhower* battle group located south of Turkey. The overall plan of operations was to immediately strike all Red units that could be attacked, to lay minefields to channel Red SS/SSN movements, and to prepare for air and missile strikes into the southern tier of the NSWP states and against targets in the Crimea and the Black Sea. Red planned to do what it could to reduce Blue striking power in the region, to maintain forces there as long as possible, and to restrict Blue mobility. Preparations, particularly for the latter, had begun before the start of hostilities, with clandestine mining of choke points and preparations to close the Suez Canal. Red did achieve this objective on D-Day by sinking a merchant ship in the Canal, closing it until 2 January (D+43).

The war in the Mediterranean began with the expected D-Day "shoot-out," and by D+10, Red surface forces had been eliminated or driven to seek shelter in "neutral" ports. Blue success, however, had not been attained without substantial cost, particularly from Red SS/SSN/SSGN:

- D-Day—*Eisenhower*, hit by three torpedoes from a Red SS, was unable to launch aircraft for 24 hours. Ultimately the effects of this damage forced the ship into Piraeus for non–dry dock repairs on D+27.
- D+1—*Clemenceau* sunk; *Foch* damaged and en route port after attack by Sierra SSN.
- D+2—Red sub attack on Blue amphibious group off Crete sinks LST-1179 with heavy loss of embarked marines; *Wasp* (LHD-1) put out of action and arriving Naples for repair on D+9.
- D+3—*Kennedy* hit by torpedo from Foxtrot SS and put out of action for six hours.
- D+5—AOE *Detroit* sunk by Foxtrot SS.

This early damage to CV assets turned out to be most significant in two aspects:

- The loss of the *Clemenceau* and *Foch* left the western Mediterranean bereft of NATO naval strike capability and a bare minimum of two operational CVs in theater. This concerned CINCSOUTH because it limited ability to support planned offensive operations.
- When a major crisis did develop with the Red counteroffensive in the Balkans and into Turkey in Europe, *Kennedy* was the only in-theater strike asset available to CINCSOUTH, but accumulated battle damage and attrition to planes and personnel severely reduced that ship's capability.

Submarine assets aside, the major Red forces in the Mediterranean consisted of two SAGs, one centered on a *Moskva*, the other on a *Slava*. Blue waged a running battle with these two forces, and by D+6, they had consolidated into a single SAG that was positioned off Libya. On that day, these forces launched an SS-N-12 missile attack on the *Kennedy* CVBG and the *Iowa* BBBG. The *Kennedy* was put out of action for six hours, and the *Iowa* received superficial damage. Almost simultaneously, the combined Red SAG was attacked by Blue SSNs *Phoenix* and *Newport News*. While the *Phoenix* was lost, a *Slava* CG and *Udaloy* DD were sunk, reducing the Red Eskadra to two Kara CGs, three Krivak FFGs, and ten auxiliaries. The last Red surface combatant was eliminated on D+10. In spite of these successes, there was discussion of the relative merits of early CV air strikes into the Balkans as opposed to the prompt and complete destruction of all Red surface assets. Illustrative of this argument was the fact that a strike planned on D+7 against the SAG off Libya had to be conducted by land-based air from Greece because of a shortage of CV-based attack aircraft.

A second operation was an ongoing offensive against Red forces in the Black Sea. On D-Day, a *Slava/Sverdlov* SAG was positioned in the western Black Sea, 21 FFGs were dispersed in seven different groups, 14 SSs were deployed, and a convoy was en route to Bulgaria. These units came under immediate Blue/Allied attack, with a Turkish SS sinking a Kara CG on D+4. On D+8, the Red SAG was struck by Blue air and at a cost of 38 aircraft sank a Krivak II FFG and a *Sovremenny*, damaged a CG, a light frigate (FFL), a *Udaloy* DD, and an AOR. On D+10, Blue attacked this SAG again and, using TASM, sank a *Slava* CG and another *Udaloy*. A Blue air strike the following day destroyed five of the Black Sea FFLs and a Turkish SS took out an AGI.

As Global '85 ended, Blue objectives in the Mediterranean had been accomplished. The Red naval forces there had been essentially eliminated, and with no ability to target the CVBGs, Red was reluctant to commit SNA/SAF. On D+13/14, the VGK ordered the SWTVD commander to go on the defensive and transfer all attack aircraft to the WTVD. Then, on D+24, Red withdrew all remaining surface units from the Black Sea while continuing submarine activity therein. From then until the Red counteroffensive described elsewhere, activity in the Black Sea was essentially confined to an endeavor of Allied SSs to sink their opponents and vice versa. Blue carrier-based air operated principally in support of the Greek/Turkish offensive in Bulgaria, and TLAM attacks were launched against targets in the Crimea and against the Red space facilities at Tyuratam.

The deteriorating situation on the ground in Bulgaria was a factor in the decision to introduce Blue/NATO surface forces into the Black Sea. With the *Eisenhower* in Piraeus for repairs (D+27), nineteen Blue/NATO ships began entry into the Black Sea. Three were sunk by mines, but the remaining sixteen hugged the Bulgarian coast and proceeded toward Burgas, and preparations began for the movement of the *Iowa* BBBG through the straits to bolster the Turkish army's seaward flank.

On D+36, 200 decoy vessels—various hulks and old merchant ships—were moved from the Sea of Marmara through the Bosporus and into the Black Sea. At the same time, Allied forces were massing in the Aegean: the *Kennedy* CVBG, the *Iowa* BBBG, and various French, Spanish, Italian, and Greek task groups. Although some involved expressed extreme reluctance to hazard naval units in the Black Sea, that movement began on D+40, with escorts taken from the *Eisenhower* BG establishing a screen with

MODLOC 50 nautical miles from the Bosporus. The *Iowa* BBBG arrived in the Sea of Marmara, and the hulks and barges were placed in position five to ten nautical miles off the Black Sea coasts of Turkey and Bulgaria. On D+41, 4 Greek and 2 Turkish ships established naval gunfire support (NGFS) positions off Burgas, and the arrival of two Italian submarines raised the total of NATO SS in the Black Sea to twelve.

The *Iowa* entered the Black Sea on D+42 preceded by the *Hawes* (FFG-53), which moved toward the central portion of that body of water operating a deception device to simulate the *Iowa*. *Iowa*, meanwhile, took station off Burgas for NGFS missions, with 50 hulks to seaward to decoy missiles as well as a heavy ASW screen. A Kilo was sunk by these forces, but a Foxtrot hidden among the hulks torpedoed *Iowa*. Dead in the water, *Iowa* was taken under tow and was halfway back to the Bosporus at the end of Global '86.

On 9 January (D+40), Red began to consider the prospect of targeting the *Eisenhower*, pier side at Pireaus, and on D+43, the planning for Operation APOLLO was complete. The next day, using HUMINT for targeting, twelve SS-12 missiles were launched and five hit the *Eisenhower*. The carrier, about to return to active operations, departed for CONUS; estimated time of repair six to eight months. This left the *Kennedy* as the only theater strike asset available to oppose the Red counteroffensive.

From this point on to the end of Global '87, Commander-in-Chief South (CINCSOUTH) desperately endeavored to obtain air assets to halt the Red advance. Appeals for a CBVG from another theater failed, and while B-52s were occasionally available, the brunt of stemming the Red counteroffensive had to be borne by the diminishing air crews and aircraft of the consolidated *Kennedy* and *Eisenhower* air wings. Maritime success had come at a heavy cost to Blue/NATO: *Clemenceau* sunk; *Foch*, *Eisenhower*, and *Iowa* out of action; and *Kennedy* resources so depleted that Blue's ability to stop Red was in serious doubt. Red occupation of the Turkish Straits appeared likely at game's end.

The Far East

Considering the Far East a secondary theater, Red objectives were limited. Because Red did not want a two-front war, a primary objective was not to do anything that would stir up historical animosities. Further, Red hoped through diplomatic and economic means to secure the neutrality of Japan. Virtually any offensive action directed against any forces but those of Blue would place those overarching goals at risk. The primacy of these objectives led Red to restrain the DPRK, initially at least, from attacking the ROK. Essentially, Red objectives in the FETVD can be summarized as follows:

- Protect the Red homeland.
- Preserve the Red strategic nuclear reserve (SSBNs).

- Neutralize Blue nuclear strike capabilities.
- Keep the People's Republic of China (PRC) and Japan from actively aiding Blue combat or combat support operations.

Blue objectives and concerns, in a geopolitical sense, were directed toward Japan as an active ally and as an economic center whose productive capacity could be critical in a protracted conventional war. Indeed, there were some who argued that these two goals were in conflict; to the extent that Japan was active in the war against Red, the more likely that the potentially vital plants and factories would be placed at risk of attack.

Further, Blue sought for some means to "play the China card," to involve the PRC as a clear potential threat to Red. Commander-in-Chief Pacific (CINCPAC) objectives can be outlined as follows:

- Maintain control of the Pacific Basin and the SLOCs therein.
- Maintain pressure on Red to prevent the shift of forces to Europe.
- Destroy Red forces in the Far East.
- Maintain Japanese alignment with Blue and preserve Japanese economic power.
- Influence the PRC, at a minimum, to remain uncooperative with Red.

While a stated objective was to maintain pressure on Red to prevent the transfer of forces to Europe, there were several other initiatives undertaken that were important in a long war perspective. The 1982 and 1983 Globals had demonstrated the difficulty of accomplishing this by simply launching air and missile attacks against Vladivostok, the Belkin Coast, Sakhalin, and Petropavlovsk. However, there were targets which, if effectively threatened, should give Red pause in shifting assets and, even if this was unsuccessful, place Blue in a better position to fight a protracted conventional war. For example, there were important Red manufacturing facilities at Komsomol'sk on Amur: airframes for the fourth generation Flanker were produced there, as were Akula-class submarines. The metal fabricating facilities at Khabarovsk were another valuable target. Further, amphibious operations against the Kurile Islands appeared valid. From a strategic perspective, they could ease the task of attacking Red SSBNs bastioned in the Sea of Okhotsk and pose a threat to Sakhalin; politically, a wavering Japanese government might be steadied by the promise of the Kuriles' return. These actions in the Pacific can be viewed as a corollary to the shift in emphasis in the horizontal escalation strategy in Europe—away from merely distracting Red and toward the development of strategic leverage that could be critical in prosecuting a long war.

The war in the Pacific began with relatively limited activity. Red, as noted above, had little to gain from offensive initiatives, and Blue was in the process of marshalling forces. The

Ranger and *Vinson* battle groups had been ordered out of the Indian Ocean by the NCA on D-Day and were en route to join the *Kitty Hawk*, *Lincoln*, *Midway*, and *Nimitz* battle groups in the Philippine Sea. *Missouri* and *New Jersey* BBBGs were also present.

The *Ranger* and *Vinson* CVBGs were not engaged by units of the Soviet Indian Ocean Squadron (SOVINDRON) during their eastern transit. Indeed, this theater saw little activity during the game. On D+2 a Krivak I was sunk in the Indian Ocean by a P-3 launched Harpoon, and on D+4, a Krivak II was sunk in the North Arabian Sea, again by a Harpoon from a P-3. This left Red with a Juliett SSG, a Foxtrot SS, an Echo SSGN, and a November SSN in theater. Red used these assets in a desultory and ineffective anti-SLOC campaign before withdrawing them for more important functions. Red also tried to interdict energy resources with a brief ground incursion into northern Iran on 11 and 12 December and with a D+10 air strike against that country's oil facilities by two regiments of Badgers transferred from the Crimea and staged out of Kabul. In the final analysis, Red actions in Southwest Asia and the Indian Ocean were neither concerted nor coordinated and, therefore, not of lasting concern or consequence to Blue.

The position of the Japanese government tended to retard the pace of offensive operations. During the first week of hostilities, Blue conducted air operations with units based in Japan against Red SAGs operating in the Sea of Japan and against Bear reconnaissance flights. When Red protested that this was not in keeping with Japan's professed neutrality, the Japanese government condemned the Blue actions and forbade the future use of Japanese soil as a base for Blue attacks on Red forces. Efforts to resolve this issue were brought to a standstill by the death of the Emperor.

While Blue was consolidating forces, Red spent the first week of the war putting all its units on alert except for those on the PRC border. Air assets were dispersed, SSBNs deployed to bastions in the Seas of Japan and Okhotsk, and SSNs positioned seaward of the Kuriles. Red mining activity concentrated on the bastions, the Kurile passages and the Strait of Malacca. Operational plans were developed for air and missile strikes on Japan if diplomatic measures failed to secure that nation's neutrality.

In addition to generating the CVBF out of SNA range, CINCPAC mined the Strait of Tsushima and the Kuriles and, for defensive purposes, Guam and the approaches to Tokyo Bay. The sanitation of the operating area of Red SSNs was begun as was the anti-SSBN campaign. The results of these actions during the first week were heavily in favor of Blue, with the exception of the torpedoing of the *Nimitz* by a Red SSN on 3 November (D+3). The *Nimitz*, DIW, was taken under tow for Hawaii and repair. On D+6, Red again attacked the *Nimitz*, utilizing Bear aircraft and air-to-surface missiles. One hit was obtained, and *Nimitz* rerouted to Guam for emergency repairs before proceeding to Pearl Harbor. Red lost three aircraft.

While ASW and ASUW operations continued, Blue began an aggressive campaign against Red air defense assets that was to continue throughout the war. Because of the position of the government of Japan, land-based strikes had to be flown out of Korea and losses were substantial. TLAM(C) augmented these Pacific Air Force (PACAF) attacks and the CVBG forces joined when the submarine sanitation campaign permitted. The principal targets were the airfields, over-the-horizon radar (OTHR), ground control intercept (GCI), and other facilities critical to Red air defense. Special Operations Forces (SOF) units took part in these operations as well. Vladivostok, the Belkin Coast, Petropavlovsk, the Kuriles, and Sakhalin were the geographic areas of concentration.

While the necessity of flying out of Korea increased Blue losses as noted above, Blue was also confronted with a very capable Red air defense. Mainstay, combined with fourth generation interceptors, gave Red a truly formidable air defense capability. The importance of defeating this capability lay in the fact that offensive operations in the Kuriles and the prosecution of attacks against the Komsomol'sk and Khabarovsk facilities could not take place until they were overcome.

Early in December, CINCPAC moved the CVBGs and BBBGs north toward Japan in an effort to draw out Red SSNs and SNA. Blue believed that most of the Red SSN threat had been eliminated, but was aware that two of three Red SSGNs were not accounted for. Red responded with a coordinated SSGN and SNA/SAF attack on 6 December (D+16). The Red objective was to eliminate as much of the Blue threat as possible with one massive strike. An Oscar SSGN launched 32 SS-N-19 missiles at the CVBF, scoring hits on the *Kitty Hawk* and *Lincoln*; several escorts were also damaged. One hour later, the force was hit by a 10–12 regiment SNA/SAF air-to-surface cruise missile (ASCM) attack, with the missile launchers escorted by Flanker and Foxhound. Airborne Warning and Control Systems (AWACS) based in Japan were able to give warning of this attack, and counter-targeting devices were used to generate an 8 to 1 false/real target ratio. An average of 84 missiles per CV were fired, but *Kitty Hawk*, hit again, was the only carrier to sustain damage. Little attrition was inflicted on the attacking force, primarily because of the effectiveness of the escorts. The *Kitty Hawk* went to Osaka for repairs, the *Lincoln* to Yokosuka.

Red viewed Japanese willingness to take the two CVs into port as a serious violation of neutrality, and attacked Japan at 0730 on 16 December (D+26). SS-12s were used for air defense suppression in strikes on Chitose, Atsugi, Misawa, and selected South Korean bases as well. Bombers struck Komatsu to destroy the F-111s based there and the *Kitty Hawk* in dry dock at Osaka. That CV, hit again, was put out of action for at least one year. *Lincoln* was not targeted.

Diplomatic reaction was swift. The following day the government of Japan:

- Reaffirmed its dedication to Alliance obligations and pledged to use its self-defense forces to protect Blue forces in Japan.
- Recalled all reservists to active duty and appealed to all able-bodied Japanese to volunteer for military service.
- Stated that Blue forces in Japan would be given permission to retaliate against Red.

Nor was this all. The PRC also denounced the Red attack, called up 200,000 reserves, and ordered an additional five divisions to reinforce the border with Red.

The war against Red air defenses and the response by Red were mentioned above as a key factor in the Pacific campaign. From D+20 to D+30 (10 December to 20 December), Blue lost 100 aircraft despite improved tactics and more support from Japan. From D+30 to D+40 (20 December to 30 December), Blue lost an additional 70 planes. Red attacks on Japan often utilized SS-12s as on D+30 when Chitose, Misawa, and Komatsu were hit. Red air struck Chitose and Misawa on D+42, losing 83 aircraft against 30 for Blue. Mining operations were continued by both sides through the month of December. Blue also pressed attacks against Red SAGs off Vladivostok and the Belkin Coast as well as continuing the ASW and anti-SSBN efforts.

The last week of Global '86 saw renewed offensive initiatives by Blue. Efforts to roll back the Red air defense continued with strikes against the Kuriles and southern Sakhalin and the use of SOF against early warning (EW) and GCI sites. The airfield on Iturup was a frequent target.

The Marines commenced offensive operations on 29 December, when the 1st MAB conducted a heliborne assault on the island of Shikotan, which was taken with the loss of two helicopters and 72 killed. The island was secured in two days, with Red losing 32 KIA and 568 prisoners of war. As Global '86 ended, the remainder of the 1st MAB was loading out at Tomakomai for an amphibious assault on the island of Kunashir in the Kuriles, and Blue withdrew the marines from Shikotan and turned the island over to Japan.

The commencement of Global '87 found both Blue and Red appraising their positions, and both were influenced by events in Europe. The position of the Blue NCA had been that when the Blue interests in the Far East were secure, then transfer of some assets to the European theater would be in order. Red had in fact begun to do this as of D+28, when ten seasoned divisions were moved westward and replaced by a similar number of new recruits. On D+44, the Blue NCA directed that CINCPAC transfer 48 F-16s and 50 F-15s from Japan and Korea and 24 aircraft of various types from Alaska to SACEUR.

CINCPAC objected and sought to evade the directive. CINCPAC's intentions were as follows:

- Continue to degrade the Red air defense by attacks on airfields, OTHR, SAM, and GCI sites.
- Take out the remaining Red SAGs.

The CINC estimated that 50 percent of the Vladivostok air defense and sortie generation capacity had been destroyed and, although losses had been heavy, wanted to pursue the offensive. Three of the CVBGs were near the Aleutians, the other two were southeast of Japan, and CINCPAC believed the remaining Red submarine threat was manageable.

The Red view of the situation was conditioned by the failure of the Western TVD commander to secure victory on the Central Front. As had been the case in previous games, Red sought solution to the strategic problem through horizontal escalation. Regardless of warnings from the PRC, emphasized by the call-up of another 500,000 PLA reserves on D+43, Red authorized an attack by the DPRK on South Korea on 5 January (D+46). Red saw this as a no-lose situation vs. Blue, as it would force the latter to keep forces and supplies in the Far East and might even pressure Japan out of the war. Moscow discounted the likelihood of offensive action by the PRC. Further, Red felt that the relentless Blue air campaign was gaining superiority.

The question of transfer of assets as directed by the NCA now became a major issue, as CINCPAC continued to evade and allies weighed in as well. On D+47, CINCPAC agreed to the shift of aircraft and supplies to Europe, but airlift arrangements had to be finalized first. The Republic of Korea protested the pull-out of these aircraft and supplies, and the government of Japan expressed concern as well. D+48 found CINCPAC informing the NCA that the transfer of aircraft would have to be delayed, because outside tanker support was required to avoid sacrificing the offensive counter-air (OCA) campaign now showing evident signs of success. On D+49, the Blue NCA ordered CINCPAC to use Pacific Command (PACOM) tanker assets to "swing" the aircraft to Europe, even if it meant sacrificing the OCA campaign. CINCPAC responded that the three CVBGs off the Aleutians were within several days of neutralizing Petropavlovsk, promised to bring them south to aid PACAF on the Belkin Coast, and asked the JCS to intercede with the NCA to delay the transfer of the PACAF assets. The JCS refused to help. The issue surfaced again on D+50, with CINCPAC informing the NCA that SACEUR had no "bed-down" facilities for the fighters to be transferred, and therefore they would not be sent. On D+51, Allied Forces Command Europe (AFCE) agreed to provide tankers the transfer, with an estimated time of arrival (ETA) of D+56.

While these "negotiations" were going on, the air offensive against Red continued, and with growing success. Red endeavored to blunt this success with an attack against the CVBF operating off the Aleutians. On D+48, a combined air and submarine attack was launched against this force. Four regiments of Badger and Backfire made a feint to draw off Blue air as five Red SSN staged a torpedo attack. One Aegis cruiser, one FFG, and two supply ships were lost. There was no damage to any of the CVs, and one of the Red SSNs was sunk.

In spite of Blue progress, Red began the transfer of older aircraft to the FETVD on D+50 in preparation for the move of fourth generation aircraft to the WTVD. The progress of GOLDEN SWORD required this action, although the VGK viewed the situation in the Far East with mounting concern. The air defenses in Kamchatka were down by 50 percent and the Blue kill ratio had risen to four-to-one as half of the FETVD's fourth generation aircraft had been sent to Europe. Of particular concern to Moscow was the effect that apparent Red impotence in the face of Blue attacks might have in Beijing. By D+53, the General Secretary was pondering the use of tactical nuclear weapons against the three CVBG battle force that was attacking the Belkin Coast. From his point of view, such an attack was not escalatory. Blue did not have a comparable target and, Red believed, would not use weapons of mass destruction (WMD) against the Red homeland. Further, it would probably take Japan out of the war, and it would send an unmistakable signal to the PRC as to the seriousness of Red intent. Red decided to let things play out further, but did resume SS-12 attacks on Japan, hitting Chitose and Misawa with four weapons each on D-55. Further, Red deployed two SSGNs with conventional warheads to the West coast of Blue on D+61 and attacked Blue bases in Alaska the following day. On D+57, Blue began to reduce the air sortie rate because of the transfer of assets referred to above, and by D+59 it was down to 65 percent of the levels attained prior to the "swing." Planning continued for a helicopter-borne invasion on Uturup.

The DPRK launched an invasion of the ROK on D+62, assisted by Red aircraft. They later attacked bases at Osan, Kunsan, and Taegu, all of which were put out of action. Blue lost 78 aircraft on the ground and 77 in the air. Red lost 99. Misawa was struck again by SS-12s. The PRC reacted immediately, closing the Yellow Sea to Red and DPRK ships and aircraft, and offering the use of airfields to Blue for attacks on the DPRK. On D+64, Japan, with Komatsu, struck again by SS-12s, offered to finance the estimated $2.3 trillion for the first two years of the war.

CINCPAC proceeded with the invasion of Uturup, Operation PISTOL PETE, on D+62. Following that success, he began to address the Korean situation and was doing so when the 1987 Global Game ended at D+64. The three years of continuous play had had a result similar to other games in the Global series: CINCPAC had clearly accomplished the mission assigned and protected the interests of Blue and its allies. This particular game highlighted the potential conflict between the NCA and theater commander and drew a very clear contrast between theater and global priorities in prosecuting a long, conventional war.

CHAPTER THREE

The Campaigns on the Flanks

Overview

The first Global series had examined the concept of "horizontal escalation," or actions away from the Central Front, as a means to deflect the Red focus and precipitate dispersal of forces away from Germany. Referred to by one participant as the "let's go thump on Cuba syndrome," most perceived the concept as more harmful to Blue than to Red. While the games of the first series were generally too short to completely analyze the effects of these operations, it did appear to be a common Red tactic to practice "horizontal escalation" against Blue if the Central Front offensive bogged down.

The second Global series, while continuing these peripheral operations, saw them as offensive initiatives that had the potential to develop strategic leverage against Red. Four geographical avenues were identified in GWG '84:

- North Norway.
- Baltic Approaches.
- Western Mediterranean.
- Eastern Mediterranean.

While three of these four areas had seen play in previous games, Blue had then perceived that strategic imperatives dictated a response that was essentially defensive.

- Blue always prepared to defend North Norway against a predictable Red offensive that sought, by degrading NATO air defense and SOSUS capabilities, to facilitate Red control of the Norwegian and Barents Seas.
- Blue had become sensitive, particularly in the 1984 game, to the possible political repercussions if Denmark were occupied or forced into a separate peace, thus breaking the political cohesion of NATO.

- Blue was always concerned that a Red offensive through the Balkans toward the Turkish Straits would have adverse military and political consequences, especially given the friction between Greece and Turkey.

The second global series, particularly the '85, '86, and '87 games, saw the shift in Blue approach from defense to offense. A successful offensive would not only secure the objectives that Blue required, it could also pose a threat to Red forces/homeland. Some of the possibilities were as follows:

- While an overland offensive by Blue in North Norway appeared to have limited prospects, could an effective joint air offensive be mounted against the Kola?
- Although political considerations required a robust defense of Denmark, could NATO open an air corridor down the Baltic toward Leningrad? Could NATO ground forces break out of Jutland and attack east into the GDR or thrust south into the flank of the Warsaw Pact offensive?
- What was the potential of an attack north from Italy toward Munich? From a military perspective, it could threaten Red LOCs; from the political, might it not succeed in destabilizing Hungary?
- The potential rewards of a Balkan offensive also appeared attractive. Could an invasion of Bulgaria be successful in knocking that country out of the Warsaw Pact and thus putting pressure on even less reliable Romania? From a military perspective, the occupation of a portion of the Western Black Sea littoral could facilitate Blue sea and air operations against the Red homeland.

The second global series, in exploring all of these options, sought to develop answers to questions such as the following:

- Can large enough force packages be built to exploit the opportunities maritime superiority creates?
- Can sufficient leverage be attained or advantage gained to compensate for the cost or offset alternative use of assets involved?

This section will examine these four campaign options as they were played out in Global '85, '86, and '87. It should be noted that the supporting naval force deployments did not change to reflect the shift from a defensive to an offensive orientation. This led to a game situation where a great deal was being attempted without a reallocation of assets commensurate with a "risk/reward" type of analysis for each of the four campaigns.

A further aspect of this shift to an offensive strategy was a conscious effort to identify targets that matter. Previous offensive air activity, particularly in the Far East, had been judged as less than successful, because the objective had been the essentially negative one of preventing Red from shifting forces from the FETVD to the West. A long-war strategy, on the other hand, suggested that there were key targets, the destruction of which would impinge on the ability of an adversary to effectively carry on the war at some point in the future—a point not necessarily within the time limitations of this game. Consequently, care had to be exercised when making a decision that assets deployed in one location should be deployed somewhere else. In terms of the peripheral offensive campaigns described below, it is probably best to view them as glimpses of what might be possible and as an aid to contemplating future force allocations.

North Norway

The war in Norway began on D-Day, with Red air attacks focused on NATO radar and acoustic sensors at Vardø, North Cape, and Kautokeino. The airfields at Kirkenes, Banak, and Alta were also struck. These attacks were repeated on D+1 and resulted in substantial degradation of NATO intelligence and aircraft basing capability. The first three weeks of the war were characterized by air attacks by both sides, and although hampered by darkness and bad weather, were pressed home against heavy opposition. Indeed, the NWTVD commander had lost about 25 percent of his aircraft by D+6.

By D+7, Blue had assembled five CVBGs south of Iceland, and SACLANT ordered four of them into the northern fjords to support the NATO defense of North Norway, to aid in securing control of the Norwegian Sea, and to carry the war to the Red homeland. Blue B-52s were also tasked for the latter mission. Once the CVBGs were on station in Vestfjord, and the DPC authorized attack on the Red homeland, attacks commenced on Pechenga and, in cooperation with B-52s, on installations in the Kola. B-52 losses were considerable, as Blue found the Kola to be heavily defended and ingress routes restricted by Finnish neutrality. Red troop concentrations on the Norwegian-Red border were also targeted. The Blue CV *Independence* was torpedoed in Vestfjord on D+14. The Red air offensive concentrated not only on the original targets noted above, but also included Tromsø and Andoya. This was the essential character of the war in the north until D+18, when a Red motorized rifle division (MRD) crossed into Norway.

On D+1, Red had moved the 131st MRD to the border, soon reinforced by the 45th and 54th MRDs. These units were joined on D+8 by the 77th MRD. The Blue 10th MAB had been flown to Norway prior to D-Day, and the 2/9th had fallen in on its prepositioned equipment. On D+18, the 45th and 77th MRDs crossed into Norway at Kirkenes.

The NWTVD commander envisioned a land campaign in North Norway as a low-risk operation to keep the Blue CVBGs away from the Central Front, and with brief exceptions for repair of battle damage and belated participation in the amphibious assault on Jutland, there they remained. It is interesting to reflect that both Blue and Red believed that their strategic objectives were best served if the CVBGs were deployed to the north.

Both sides tended to husband their ground forces during the games of the second series. The Red offensive consisted of a slow advance with three MRDs strung out across the Finnmark along a single road. NATO forces fell back, destroying bridges and using small unit actions to delay the advance. NATO did not want to seriously contest the Red advance short of prepared positions of the Tromsø-Skibotn line, and maintained tactical flexibility with the 4,000-man Canadian Air Sea Transportable Brigade (CAST) ashore at Lyngen Fjord and the UK/NL Marines (7,000 strong) embarked and positioned in fjords southeast of Andoya.

The slow advance/retreat continued, with the allies destroying the airfield at Banak on D+27. On D+31, Red moved two MRDs from the Leningrad MD to the Finnish border, posing a threat to outflank Blue by an advance across the "Finnish Wedge." Blue continued its gradual retreat and abandoned Alta on D+37, after destroying the airfield. On D+42, the 77th MRD reached the Skibotn line, and, although the front stabilized, NATO air superiority led to substantial attrition of the 77th, 45th, and 131st MRDs. At this point, the NWTVD commander adopted an essentially defensive posture. Aside from a multiregiment (110 aircraft) raid on Bodø and Evenes that sustained 50 percent losses on D+47, Red had surrendered the initiative.

On D+54, NATO commenced planning for Operation ICE PICK, which was designed to achieve the destruction of Red ground forces in North Norway. The Sixth MAB and the UK/NL marines were to stage an amphibious assault west of Alta against the northern Red flank. This landing was to be coordinated with a frontal attack by Norwegian forces from the Skibotn line, augmented by the CAST brigade.

Operation ICE PICK was completely successful. By the end of D+64, when the attack went in, the 77th MRD was surrounded, and the 131st was under heavy pressure. The end of GWG '87 found the sixth MAB reembarking for future operations and the initiative firmly in the hands of NATO.

Both Blue and Red could view their objectives as having been attained. Red had, with a minimum of risk and force allocation, kept the CVBGs away from the Central Front. Commander North Norway (COMNON), on the other hand, had stopped the Red advance, achieved air superiority, and gained the initiative. The essential question Blue faced was not a new one: how to exploit these advantages to develop leverage against Red.

A primary objective of Blue was to carry the war against the Red homeland by attacks against targets in the Kola that "made a difference." This proved to be both difficult and expensive. The routes of approach were severely restricted by respect for Finnish neutrality, and losses in attacks were heavy. Eight B-52s were destroyed in a single raid on D+8. One of the most controversial events of the entire war occurred on D+37, when a major attack by 32 carrier aircraft struck facilities in the Kola. A Red airfield was put out of action for several days, and, in a striking example of targeting judgment, a nuclear power plant was bombed, resulting in both the degradation of generating capacity and the release of radiation. Twenty-four of the attacking aircraft were lost and only one escaped undamaged. Blue also used TLAM(C), but unreliability coupled with the loss of remotely piloted vehicles (RPV) prevented accurate damage assessment. At game end, a Red violation of Finnish air space prompted the DPC to accede to repeated Blue requests, and a 72-hour window was granted to overfly Finland.

The effects of Blue attacks on the Red homeland did not appear to have had significant military impact. While Blue control of North Norway was imperative to Blue operations in the Norwegian and Barents Seas and a strategic necessity to shield the United Kingdom from Red air attack, the principal impact of offensive air operations against the Kola would appear to have been the tie-down of Red air assets. This may be significant in terms of the impact these aircraft would have had if deployed in the Baltic. It seemed clear that successful operations against the Kola depend on Blue ability to take down Red defenses over time, probably with TLAM(C) playing a major role prior to large carrier air/B-52 raids.

Denmark and the Baltic Approaches

The Jutland Peninsula grew as an area of Blue focus as the Global Series progressed. The initial Blue concern was political: the surrender of Denmark or its occupation by Red would demonstrate the inability of NATO to maintain political integrity. Earlier games had indicated that a Red offensive across the north German plain could not be halted before Denmark was cut off and, further, that NATO units retreating toward the peninsula combined with the indigenous forces available were inadequate to hold the line at the Kiel Canal.

Further analysis demonstrated that there would also be serious military repercussions from a Red conquest of Denmark. Possession of the Danish airfields would permit Red to outflank NATO air defenses on the Central Front, facilitate strikes on the West German and Benelux ports, and aid significantly in contesting air superiority over the North Sea. Also, Norway's centers of both government and population, located as they are to the south, would be subject to attack. The capitulation of Norway would isolate both Sweden and Finland. The military consequences of this capitulation would be the loss of North Norway, and the GIN line would almost certainly revert to the GIUK line.

Clearly, the NATO position in all of northwestern Europe could hinge on the successful defense of Denmark.

Conversely, the maintenance of the NATO position in Denmark could confer potentially important strategic advantage. At a minimum, a Blue/NATO presence in Jutland posed a constant threat to the flank or rear of any Red advance on the Central Front. A "best case" scenario could involve a land/amphibious offensive along the Baltic littoral into the GDR and Poland, as well as the possibility of opening an air or air/sea corridor up the Baltic toward Leningrad and the Red homeland.

For these reasons—political and military, defensive and offensive—the Jutland Peninsula loomed large in NATO planning. Discussions of its importance began on 21 November (D+1) and meshed with an ongoing study of how best to utilize the II MAF. At the commencement of hostilities, the main Red thrust had been against the NORTHAG/CENTAG boundary. The northern flank of the Red advance had been guarded, in the main, by Polish forces, which had crossed into Schleswig-Holstein on 21 November (D+1). On D+5, Blue abandoned Hamburg and withdrew to the line of the Kiel Canal. On this day, 25 November, it was evident that Blue forces in Jutland were not sufficient for its defense and, a day later, the decision was made to land II MAF on the west coast of Denmark at Esbjerg.

Red intentions were not entirely clear to Blue when this decision was made, as the option was still open to Red for a thrust by the ground forces in a southwesterly direction. However, on D+7, the Kiel Canal line was attacked, and on D+8, with 4/9th of II MAF in the Irish Sea, movement of the MPS was begun and the air combat element of the II MAF deployed to Sola, Norway, and Vandel, Denmark. CAS in support of the Kiel Canal line had become the AFNORTH air priority.

On 30 November (D+10), Red intentions became clear. Although the Kiel Canal line was quiet as the heavily attrited Polish forces awaited reinforcements, it appeared that those reinforcements were on the verge of engagement and that an operation by Red airborne and SNI regiments was imminent.

Red forces breached the Kiel Canal line on D+11, and 4/9th of II MAF began landing at Esbjerg. As they came ashore, they were immediately involved in a battle with two Red air mobile brigades that were engaged in a weather-limited helo assault on the Esbjerg airfield. While the marines were fighting to secure the town and airfield, the amphibious force of 46 ships, including the *Coral Sea* battle group, was struck by an eight-regiment (152 planes) SNA attack. This mixed force of Backfire/Badger/Blinder, drawn from the Moscow Air District, augmented by aircraft redeployed from the Kola, launched AS-4 and AS-6 missiles at a range of 150 miles, sinking 27 ships, including the *Coral Sea,* and heavily damaging four others. The Blue NCA had ordered the four

CVBGs in the Vestfjord south to support the operation, but they did not arrive in time to participate. (It should be noted that, while the results of this engagement remained in effect as far as the Blue order of battle was concerned, a replay of the event showed that proper tactics and deployment and effective use of deception and decoys would have held losses to about four ships. This conclusion would tend to be validated by the results of similar future engagements.)

On 3 December (D+13), Red endeavored again to flank the forces falling back from the Kiel line with an amphibious operation designed to put 2,500 SNI ashore on eastern Jutland. Blue/NATO air inflicted 50 percent casualties on this force, sinking 2 DDGs and 7 amphibs and damaging an additional DDG and 7 more amphibs. A follow-on strike on D+14 resulted in the loss of two more of the Red amphibs, but at the cost of 10 out of the 30 attacking Tornados.

From D+15 to the end of GWG '85, activity was essentially confined to Blue efforts to build force and Red attempts to prevent it. Polish forces on the ground were fought out and had been heavily attrited, while Blue was still building combat power. Red air attacks were frequent, particularly efforts to mine the Baltic approaches. Blue was able to make progress along the west side of the peninsula, and while the FRG/Danish border was reached there on D+17, Red was still 50 km north of the border in the east. As the game ended (D+18), Red was pulling out the weakest Polish units and was moving up an armored division, an MRD, airborne units, and naval infantry. The Red intention was to fall back, fighting a delaying action utilizing prepared positions, and to counterattack when a more favorable correlation of forces was possible.

The beginning of GWG '86 found the situation in Jutland as follows: 6/9th of II MAF was engaged, as was the FRG Sixth Panzer Grenadier Division and two mechanized brigades of the Danish army. The UK mobile force, of brigade strength, constituted the reserve. Amphibious shipping was en route Felixstowe, UK, to load the 7th MAB of I MAF, and the 5th MAB was en route, expected to arrive in theater on 13 December. Both were potentially available for deployment to Jutland.

Opposing Red forces consisted of the 6th Polish Airborne at about 35 percent strength, and both the 16th Polish and 20th Red armored divisions at about 65 percent.

The Blue offensive continued with massive air support. The 387 sorties flown on 19 December (D+29) dislodged the 20th Red armored division, which fell back to prepared positions near Logumkloster. On the 20th, all Danish territory was restored to Danish control, and Blue continued to advance with the II MAF, the FRG Sixth Panzer Grenadier and UK Brigade; massive air support continued. Red ordered up the 153rd MRD and the 44th armored divisions, but Blue crossed the Kiel Canal and, by 23 December, held both sides of it.

The movement to and landing of the I MAF plus the 25th Marine Regiment at Esbjerg on 24 December (D+35) precipitated another major Red attack. First, an Oscar SSGN, using targeting intelligence from the beach, fired SS-N-19 missiles from a range of 200nm at the 36 ships involved in the operation. All but one missile was destroyed, but it struck the *Belleau Wood* (LHA 3), causing substantial damage. The Oscar was sunk by a P-3, which had observed the launch.

Two hours later, Red struck again with an 80-bomber raid escorted by 90 fighters and 7 jammers. This force launched 135 AS-4/AS-6 missiles, but effective defense (105 intercepted by SAM/CIWS) and extensive use of decoys limited Blue ship losses to 1 FF and 1 FFG sunk and the *Whidbey Island* (LSD 41) severely damaged. In the air, Red lost 15 bombers, 18 fighters, and 1 jammer; Blue lost 28 fighters.

At the front, Blue was consolidating positions in the vicinity of the Kiel Canal awaiting the closure of I MAF. Red counterattacked at Rendsburg, held by the Danish 1st Jutland division and the 2nd Zeeland brigade and the 1st UK brigade, using the 34th and the 153rd MRDs. Blue, aided by heavy CAS, held on until 26 December (D+36) when the I MAF joined up and Blue regained the initiative.

Blue resumed the offensive and was successful in crossing the Lubeck Canal and entering the GDR, but with the third Red Strategic Echelon engaged, Commander Marine Forces Europe (COMMARFOREUR) prepared defensive positions in depth between the Kiel and Lubeck Canals.

The closure of the Third Strategic Echelon created severe difficulties for NATO on the Central Front, and the Blue NCA was desperate to find an offensive option to try to restore Allied morale. COMMARFOREUR preferred to move eastward along the Baltic toward Rostock, but SACEUR decided on a thrust toward Wittenberge, 120km southeast of Lubeck and about halfway to Berlin, as the most feasible of several unattractive options. In spite of strong opposition from the DPC and various military commanders, the I and II MAF launched the attack on 30 December and reached the outskirts of Wittenberge, but the deployment of the Red Third Strategic Echelon required termination of the offensive and a retreat to the Kiel/Lubeck Canal defensive positions.

On 4 January (D+45), eight WP divisions breached the Lubeck line and advanced toward the Kiel Canal. The FRG Sixth Panzer Grenadiers were surrounded by four WP divisions, but managed to fight their way clear. The British Mobile Force and the Danish 1st Jutland Brigade were destroyed in the heavy fighting between the canals. I and II MAF had assumed defensive positions in the vicinity of the Elbe River/Kiel Canal, and the 82nd Airborne had been ordered to reinforce. One Red division had managed to cross the Kiel Canal, but it was contained, and by 9 January (D+50) the Kiel line was secure.

Coincident with these events (planning started on D+43), SACEUR was devising a scheme to draw Red forces away from the Central Front. The outline of Operation BAMBOO was as follows:

- Bremerhaven to be captured by air-dropped Rangers.
- I and II MAF to link up with Rangers.
- A feint at an amphibious landing in the vicinity.
- Construction of a missile trap for SNA.
- Withdrawal of all forces after 72 hours.

The land portion of this operation was never attempted, as I MAF had to be pulled out of the plan to aid in holding the Kiel Canal line. The naval portion was executed, and on 8 January a multiregiment Red air strike sustained moderate losses, and two Blue ships were sunk.

On 8 January, Red began the use of chemical munitions. These weapons were targeted on Allied forces in Jutland. Persistent and nonpersistent types were delivered by both bombers and SSM. While some casualties were sustained, the adverse winter weather reduced the effect of the Red attack substantially.

The arrival of the Red Fourth and Fifth Strategic Echelons from early to mid-January continued to fuel intense fighting around the Kiel Canal. Red fought desperately to contain Blue forces, which sought to break out of the peninsula and advance toward the southeast as the northern pincer of the SACEUR counteroffensive. While the closure of additional divisions tended to benefit Red, the decision to use chemical weapons was an indication that Red did not see its conventional combat power as adequate to achieve the desired military objectives.

Red resorted to chemical use again on 9 January as bitter fighting continued. The arrival of the 82nd Airborne reinforced the Kiel Canal defenses, and on 10 January, AFNORTH prepared to counterattack toward the Lubeck Canal. This offensive, which began on the 11th, D+52, was vigorously opposed by Red. On D+53, four divisions from the Fourth Strategic Echelon were diverted north to bolster Red defenses, while renewed chemical attacks slowed the Blue advance. Red withdrew across the Elbe on D+54 and continued to reinforce as Blue advanced slowly in bitter fighting. On 14 January (D+55), the Red reinforcements succeeded in halting Blue at the Lubeck Canal. The next day, Red laid a persistent chemical barrier across the LOCs from the Jutland North Sea ports to the Blue forces at the Lubeck Canal. While casualties from the attack were light, the chemical barrier did have a significant impact on Blue ability to support the front. By D+58, the combination of blocked logistics, plus the diversion of other divisions from the Fifth Strategic Echelon, brought the Blue northern pincer to a halt in the vicinity of the Lubeck Canal. A bit to the west, however, Blue was advancing toward Hamburg as GWG '87 concluded.

The progress of this campaign showed clearly that Red was extremely sensitive to Blue initiatives in the Baltic. The massive air attack to disrupt the initial landing, the siphoning off of divisions from the Third, Fourth, and Fifth Strategic Echelons, and the repeated use of chemical weapons made clear that Red was very concerned about the development of significant Blue combat capability along the northern flank. While Blue was not able to accomplish all that it would have desired, it did in fact maintain the integrity of the NATO Alliance, successfully hold Jutland, and create serious problems for Red.

Potential for further development of strategic leverage would appear to depend on the extension of air and sea control eastward up the Baltic. The use of that body of water for offensive purposes had never played in Global, and, while naval actions were ongoing and costly, further study could develop more effective strategies that would facilitate Blue operations. The same can be said for mining, both offensive and defensive. The question of CVBG utilization also arose, particularly with regard to the initial amphibious operation at Esbjerg. Beyond that single operation, the CVBG commander's concern that movement outside the fjords would expose his assets to submarine attack tended to preclude a more flexible utilization of his forces that could have contributed to the success of the AFNORTH offensive scheme.

Southern Europe

Although southern Europe presented the possibility for NATO forces to move north into the flank and LOCs of a Red offensive on the Central Front, such planning had to be conditional because of Austrian neutrality. Developments in the Second Global Series presented players with an opportunity to examine the potential of such a campaign.

The blatant violation of Austrian neutrality by Red presented Blue/NATO with the justification to send Italian troops across the Alps, through Austria, and into the southern FRG. Austrian troops had come under NATO command on D+4, and the Italian movement north was commenced in late November with the Munich-Salzburg area as the initial destination. The force was led by four brigades of Alpini, with the heavier units of the Italian Fourth and Fifth Corps to follow. The advance was discovered by a large Spetsnaz contingent that Red had sent south to destroy bridges and tunnels along the route from the Brenner Pass. This encounter, combined with heavy snowfall in the Alps, retarded the progress of the Alpini and halted the advance of the heavier corps. The Alpini reached Innsbruck on 1 December (D+10).

As the Italians pushed north, units of the Austrian army that had been scattered during the Red offensive began to coalesce with the Italians, and this force reached the vicinity of Munich on D+20. On D+23, motorized units of the Fourth Italian Corps reached Innsbruck, where they halted to replenish for the advance on Munich.

Red had been deceived as to Italian intentions and progress since the initial brush with the Spetsnaz unit, but began to react on 7 December (D+17). Two Hungarian divisions that were to be part of the Red southern pincer on the Central Front were tasked to counter the Italians in the vicinity of Munich and, shortly thereafter, Red pulled two airborne divisions out of the strategic reserve for the same purpose. These two divisions were airlifted to Munich on 16 December (D+26), where their landing was contested by the four Alpini brigades that had gained the outskirts of Munich.

Confused fighting in and around Munich persisted through the end of GWG '85 and into the beginning of GWG '86. In and around the southern fringes of that city, the Alpini fought the Red airborne troops, while to the south of the city, the two Hungarian divisions battled the Italian Fourth and Fifth Corps that were moving to link up with their countrymen to the north. By 20 December (D+30), the Italians occupied an arc from Garmisch to Salzburg, and Red was reinforcing with an additional Hungarian MRD. AFSOUTH was supporting the Italians with heavy air operations, primarily CAS, but with some BAI as well. There was virtually no Red air response and, consequently, few Blue losses.

As GWG '86 ended, the Italian Fifth Corps on the right of the advance had pushed a reconnaissance in force north and east of Munich to threaten the Red LOCs flowing south of the Regensburg-Ingolstadt line. Red was forced to call in two more divisions of the Third Hungarian Army to address this potential problem. As these divisions traversed Austria along the Danube corridor, they were subjected to destructive harassing attacks by reconstituted Austrian light units that overwhelmed personnel of the Ministry of Internal Affairs (MVD) LOC protection organization.

As Global '87 commenced on 1 January (D+41), Red was practicing economy of force operations in the Munich area, endeavoring to defend, reorganize, and reconstitute. On 2 January, Salzburg and Munich were recaptured by the Italians, who then launched a flanking offensive with the Fourth Corps to the west, while the Fifth pinned the opposing Red forces. Red, however, hard-pressed by the SACEUR counterstroke in the central region, launched a nonpersistent chemical attack to halt the Italian offensive. The units most affected were the Italian Fourth and Sixth Armored Brigades, which suffered 70 percent and 75 percent casualties respectively. Both withdrew to the west and were combined into a single unit.

The Italian offensive recommenced on D+51, advancing north and east from Munich into Bavaria. On 12 January (D+53), SACEUR made the decision to launch Phase Three of Operation GOLDEN SWORD, and the Italians were ordered to move on Magdeburg, link up with the southern pincer of GOLDEN SWORD, and thus restore a continuous Allied line. They advanced against light opposition, and by 15 January had put eight brigades across the Danube at Regensburg and were pushing toward Nuremberg, protecting SACEUR's right flank in the process.

On D+57, Red again resorted to chemical weapons use in the vicinity of Munich in an effort to sever the Italian fighting and support elements. Casualties were low, about 2 percent, and the attack a failure because the Italians were moving north, not west as Red believed. In spite of continuing chemical attacks, which slowed but did not stop their advance, the Italians had, by 21 January (D+62), pushed all Red units opposing them out of the FRG and had crossed one division into the GDR. They decisively defeated a group of Hungarian divisions inside Czechoslovakia on 23 January and achieved a link-up with SACEUR forces at Ansbach as GWG '87 concluded.

Balkans

The situation that developed in the Southwestern TVD perhaps most clearly illustrates the uncertainty that Blue offensive operations can create for Red. On D-Day, Red began the movement of five divisions from the Odessa Military District through Romania and into Bulgaria, where they arrived on D+5. On D+4, Red reserve air units were moved to Hungary and, on D+6, Red air in Bulgaria was bolstered by similar additions. Red made frequent attacks on air bases in Italy, with Aviano being particularly hard hit. Red air also struck support facilities at Thessaloniki, airfields in Greece and Turkey, and the 82nd Airborne in Thrace. All this changed on D+13–14, when the VGK ordered the redeployment of the five MRDs from the Odessa MD to the Western TVD and further directed the Southwestern Theater of Military Operations (SWTVD) commander to go on the defensive and transfer all attack aircraft to the WTVD.

Commander-in-Chief South (CINCSOUTH) had planned to seize the initiative as soon as possible. NATO believed that an offensive against Red and selected members of the Warsaw Pact could develop useful military options and exploit potential political fault lines in the Balkans.

The "D-Day shoot-out" in the eastern Mediterranean resulted in the entire Red Eskadra being sunk or driven into neutral ports. An important outcome was the loss by Red of any ability to target Blue CVBGs and BBBGs in the Aegean Sea. This situation contributed to the VGK decision to withdraw its attack aircraft, and the resulting essential immunity from air attack permitted Blue and TLAM shooters to maintain station in the Aegean. While close air support (CAS) was often a priority, the scope of targets and variety of platforms used was extensive. Aircraft involved included not only CVBG assets but also B-52s and B-1s as well. Targets ranged from bridges and railheads to the Red space station at Tyuratam. Mines were air-dropped into the Bulgarian mountain passes to retard the progress of the five MRDs ordered to the WTVD on D+13.

Many of the initial attacks were designed to facilitate the NATO offensive into Bulgaria. Aircraft and TLAMs were used to suppress WP SAM defenses, degrade airfields, destroy command facilities and headquarters, drop bridges over the Danube between Romania and Bulgaria, and to destroy railheads and infrastructure in general.

Targets in the Red homeland included airfields in the Caucasus and Crimea, MRDs, rail and supply facilities, naval installations at Sevastopol, and the aforementioned space station struck by TLAM(C). Blue air was also utilized for mining in the vicinity of the Turkish straits and the ports of Burgas and Varna. Red surface units in the Black Sea were attacked, and a SAG sustained the sinking of one Krivak II and the damaging of an FFL, DDG, and AO. Blue losses in these activities were also considerable; 38 aircraft were lost in the SAG attack noted above. By the last week of Global '87, only one CVBG was on station (*Kennedy*), and the aircraft complement was so depleted that the Sixth Fleet had little CAS capability to respond to the rapidly deteriorating situation of the ground forces.

On D+15, Greek and Turkish forces began limited attacks into Bulgaria, and by D+21, the latter had penetrated to the vicinity of Burgas. The major NATO offensive commenced on D+24, and Bulgarian resistance appeared to falter. Concentrated battlefield air interdiction (BAI) had strained the logistics of the frontline Bulgarian units, and the Turkish III and IV Corps in the east and Greek C and D Corps to the west advanced with heavy artillery support and Blue air superiority. On D+25, the Turkish III Corps surrounded the Bulgarian 3rd MRD and 23rd Infantry Division in the vicinity of Bogdanovo. IV Corps encircled the Bulgarian 15th Infantry near the juncture of the Bulgaria, Greece, and Turkey borders. While some Greek units closed on the Bulgarian 2nd MRD, elements of the Greek 10th Infantry Division (ID) were pursuing the Bulgarian 8th MRD as it withdrew. Burgas fell on D+26, and the Turks advanced on Varna as Red tried to persuade a less than enthusiastic Romania to support the faltering Bulgarians. The Hungarian government was also asked for assistance, but heavy losses sustained while countering the Italian thrust into Austria made Budapest reluctant to commit reserves.

On D+27 the Bulgarian army fell back to a line running from Sofia to Varna. The state of Bulgarian morale was indicated by the surrender of the 15th and 23rd infantry divisions on D+28 and 29. However, by D+34, the Allied offensive stalled before Sofia and Varna. Two Romanian divisions had arrived to stiffen the Bulgarians, and the Red 59th

MRD was en route to the front via Romania. That country, however, refused to permit more than one Red division on its soil, so Red reinforcements were slowed.

A new front was opened on D+29 when Red invaded eastern Turkey. This operation had the military objective of capturing the airfield at Erzurum. While Red hoped that this operation would distract NATO from the Bulgarian offensive, use of the air facilities at Erzurum would permit Red to attack Incirlik from which Blue F-111s were striking the Red homeland. The two-pronged Red offensive moved rapidly at first, but then became slowed by Turkish resistance, bad weather, and difficult terrain. Horasan fell on D+41, but the pace of the attack was so slow that Red resorted to weapons of mass destruction (WMD), utilizing nonpersistent chemicals on the Turkish 51st Division on D+51. Red finally captured Erzurum on D+60, but the retreating Turks had rendered the airfield unusable until D+67–70.

As the eastern offensive plodded toward Erzurum, Red was massing forces in Bulgaria for a counterstroke against the Greeks and Turks. On D+36 the 86th MRD entered Bulgaria, and on D+38 the Kagul MRD began off-loading at Varna. While this landing was opposed by carrier air, the retirement of the *Eisenhower* to Piraeus (D+27) for repair of damage sustained earlier in the war reduced Blue effectiveness. Three Red amphibs were sunk, and the landing of the MRD's equipment and headquarters was delayed. *Eisenhower*'s escorts had joined the *Iowa* BBBG, and that force moved into the Sea of Marmara on D+40. D+40 also saw the commencement of a Red advance down the Black Sea littoral toward Burgas. Both sides resorted to heavy CAS; B-1s were used to attack the 145th MRD. As the Red advance closed on Burgas, the *Iowa* BBBG entered the Black Sea to support the Turks defending that port on D+42. *Iowa* was torpedoed almost immediately by a Foxtrot, went DIW, and was taken under tow for the straits.

The principal Red counterattack was launched by six divisions on D+42. It was supported by heavy CAS and, in an effort to play on NATO political tensions, fell on the Turks, initially sparing the Greeks. The NATO forces were holding a line Sofia-Maritsa-Burgas, and both sides reinforced. The 3rd Romanian Army joined Red forces on D+45, and the 7th MAB augmented the Turks a day later. The following day, D+47, Red forwarded two more MRDs to bolster the front at Sofia and to ensure the free passage of Red supplies and forces through a still reluctant Romania.

The infusion of the 7th MAB stabilized the Allied center, but on D+49, Red achieved a breakthrough west of Burgas, and the MAB was repositioned by helos to plug the gap. Simultaneously, Red launched Operation TOLSTOY, a joint landing of two airborne and one SNI regiments south of Burgas. The *Kennedy* air group opposed it and sank two amphibs and damaged two others. While the naval beachhead was eliminated, the battle to do so diverted ground and air resources from the deteriorating situation west of Burgas.

Red pressure west of Burgas had continued to build, and Blue/NATO had neither the ground nor air assets to hold the line. On D+54, just as the *Eisenhower* was about to leave Piraeus to return to action, Red used HUMINT to target the ship with twelve SS-12 missiles (Operation APOLLO). Five hit, and the *Eisenhower* departed for CONUS, estimating six to eight months to make repairs.

On D+55, AFSOUTH requested permission to employ ten tactical nuclear weapons to prevent destruction of the Greek and Turkish armies and to avoid the loss of the straits. This was denied, as was his request for an additional CVBG and more ground forces. SACEUR told AFSOUTH that he must hold out for another five days to keep Red from shifting forces to the WTVD. B-52s were allocated to AFSOUTH, apparently the only forces available. On D+57, with five more Red divisions en route from Romania, the B-52s, combined with determined resistance on the ground, forestalled a Red penetration west of Burgas.

On D+59, Red broke though the center of the Allied line and wheeled some units to the east to surround Burgas. However, as the SWTVD commander appeared on the verge of victory, the WTVD commander, gravely concerned with the success of NATO counteroffensive that had carried into the GDR, was pressing the VGK for the transfer of five divisions from the SWTVD.

The Allied situation around Burgas became critical on D+60, with six Turkish divisions trapped in the city. Plans were begun for their extraction by sea, and all available B-52s were assigned to halt the Red advance. Severe attrition to the *Kennedy* air group essentially eliminated it as a significant factor in the Allied defense, and on D+61, Red crossed the Turkish frontier west and south of Burgas. On D+62, the evacuation of Burgas by sea began, hampered by Scud Attacks including a lay-down of chemicals on port facilities. These operations were continuing on D+63, Red augmenting the persistent chemical attacks with long-range artillery. The Red advance into Turkey-in-Europe was continuing, although with decreasing momentum, and AFSOUTH saw his primary responsibility as defense of the Turkish Straits.

While the Allied forces were hard-pressed at the end of Global '87, there was clear indication that offensive operations in this area had the potential for both political and military success. With respect to the former, it seemed evident that the morale of the non-Soviet Warsaw Pact (NSWP) countries could be exploited. The early reverses suffered by the Bulgarians seemed to sap their will to fight, as indicated by the surrender of entire divisions. This was particularly significant because the Bulgarians were fighting in defense of their homeland against traditional enemies.

From another perspective, the "fraternal socialist order" seemed to suffer when placed under strain. Hungary demurred in sending troops to aid their Bulgarian neighbors, and Romania was not only chary about providing aid, it actually imposed limitations on Red reinforcements to their beleaguered ally.

From a military perspective, the operation also showed promise. The Red reaction to events in the SWTVD, both in terms of reinforcement and by the opening of a "second front" in eastern Turkey demonstrated concern not only for the situation on the ground but for the ability of Blue to strike a wide variety of targets in the homeland with both aircraft and TLAM(C). This first iteration of a Balkan offensive showed both the problems and the potential of the approach to the homeland.

CHAPTER FOUR

The 1988 Global War Game

Introduction

The essential focus of GWG '88 was war termination; the purpose of the game to assess how relative military, economic, and diplomatic strengths and weaknesses affect the ability of Blue, Red, and their respective allies to conclude the war on a favorable basis. The concept of the game was to spend one week concentrating on each of three different scenarios based on possible culmination points of the strategic battle on the Central Front: Red dominant, Blue dominant, and stalemate.

A "time step" from D+64 (the end of GWG '87) to D+75 provided the means to build in a set of events to transition to the three scenarios used in GWG '88. All three scenarios essentially notionalized the military situation in theaters other than the Central Front in Europe based on the play from Global '87 (GWG '87). In Korea, the DPRK invasion had been thrown back and the FLOT stabilized in the vicinity of the DMZ. Military operations in North Norway had been stalled by force constraints and appalling weather. The balance of power in the Pacific remained unchanged as Blue paused to consider further amphibious options, and Red sought forces from that region to shift west. In Thrace, Red chose not to press the apparent advantage in deference to a maximum effort on the Central Front, and the Red salient toward Erzurum was in danger of being cut off.

As with its predecessors, GWG '88 was a three-sided game with a Blue team and a Red team to represent the principal protagonists and a Green team to play other nations and international organizations such as the United Nations, the Papacy, etc. Unlike the previous games of the series, however, Global '88 was a nonoperational, seminar-style planning game. Time was frozen at D+75 and concentration was on the planning process, with particular emphasis on the NCA level for determination of national goals and the conduct of negotiations, the JCS for coordination and prioritization of military operations, and the CINCs for sequential campaign planning.

Game Objectives

In the military dimension, the objective of the 1988 Global War Game was to identify and analyze the dynamics and leverage that military operations can bring to the war termination process and what constraints or other effects negotiations have on theater initiatives by the armed forces. This objective was pursued and studied in all three scenarios played in Global '88. Of particular interest were the following issues considered during game play:

- The combination and interaction of military, economic, and political instruments that can be used to terminate a global conflict with Red while preserving the Blue global strategic initiative.
- The combinations of regional/theater strategies that best serve the war termination interests of Blue.
- Green (third party) diplomatic initiatives that could be beneficial to enhance the probability of a war termination effort favorable to the West.
- The impact of logistics sustainability and industrial mobilization issues on war termination for both Blue and Red.
- The impact of war termination on moving toward or receding from the nuclear threshold.

Political Objectives Overview

Despite the differences in the three scenarios, Red believed that its basic goals of neutralization of the FRG and the reduction or elimination of Blue influence on the Continent were within reach. Red felt generally comfortable with the military situation and focused on a negotiation process Red believed would ratify what had been achieved in battle. Red became very frustrated by the failure of Blue to recognize what Red saw as "the realities of the situation."

Blue was less dogmatic than Red in terms of objectives and had a tendency to adjust as fortunes fluctuated on the battlefield. This was due in part to the fact that NATO was a genuine alliance, and internal congruence among the members of the Alliance was not always present, particularly regarding the Blue policy that stressed a global, protracted war.

When the war began, Blue objectives centered on the restoration of the territorial and political status quo ante. Specifically, NATO fought to restore the prewar boundaries of its members and neutrals, maintain Alliance cohesion, protect Blue and Western interests around the world, and limit the war to conventional means while eroding some Red strategic nuclear capabilities. While there were occasional thoughts about enlarging these goals in the 1985, 1986, and 1987 games, they remained reasonably consistent throughout. It should be noted that Blue did not thoroughly realize that attainment of these objectives would have far-reaching consequences. For example, the restoration of the status quo ante would mean that the Red military had been in fact defeated, an outcome that would have repercussions in the Warsaw Pact particularly. Further, the defeat of the Red navy would have a significant impact on Red ability to project influence overseas, to import food, and to operate a fishing fleet. Therefore, while return to the status quo ante seemed a relatively modest war aim, the ramifications flowing from its attainment would be profound.

In the Red-dominant scenario, Blue continued to pursue those original aims. The encirclement of the Blue V corps and the anticipated closure of the Red Seventh Echelon prompted Blue to consider settling for less. Blue pondered several status quo ante "minus" outcomes, one example of which was a move in the Congress for Blue to withdraw from Europe and adopt a "fortress America" policy. While Blue studied various possibilities, it never found a palatable alternative to the status quo ante. Indeed, with no apparent threat to the Blue homeland and with the NATO Alliance politically united, no change was deemed essential by the NCA.

On the other hand, Blue believed that the Blue-dominant scenario presented the opportunity for something more than a return to the status quo. Having made great sacrifices, Blue was determined to secure a military victory and to exhaust Red. Buoyed by the encirclement of numerous Red divisions and its access to global resources, Blue wanted to expand objectives to the fragmentation of the Warsaw Pact. The other members of NATO, however, were reluctant to agree.

In the stalemate scenario, Blue remained flexible in determining its final goals. With the potential of the military situation to go either way, Blue alternatives were seen, in theory, to range from something less than the status quo ante to something more. Blue eventually decided to seek military advantage and acknowledged that success on the battlefield or lack thereof would be the ultimate arbiter of war aims. In general, Blue leaned toward the status quo ante as its bottom line but wanted more if military success made this possible at reasonable cost.

Red and Blue approached war termination from quite different perspectives. Having substantially achieved its military objectives, Red was anxious to terminate the war through negotiations. Blue perceived the military situation in Europe to be disadvantageous and, therefore, felt negotiations were unlikely to lead to an acceptable settlement. Consequently, Blue believed it imperative to improve the military situation before joining in a cease-fire or going to the conference table. In all scenarios, Blue always thought in terms of "win" rather than "draw."

Blue Strategy and Operational Planning Overview

Blue strategy and planning was dominated by a preoccupation with the anticipated arrival of the Seventh Strategic Echelon. While the Blue situation worldwide was favorable indeed, the status of the battle on the Central Front remained foremost in each of the scenarios. In essence, Blue felt that losing in Europe would place Blue at a serious disadvantage, no matter how successful elsewhere. Consequently, in each scenario, discussions took place as to the relative military value of forces deployed on the "flanks" as opposed to their concentration on the Central Front. While many transfers of forces were contemplated, few were actually planned.

The situation that confronted SACEUR had a number of points of similarity in each scenario. Dominating all campaign planning, however, was the question of sustainability. Even in the Blue-dominant scenario, logistics concerns forced Blue to regard its advantage as ephemeral. This factor, combined with the closure of the Seventh Strategic Echelon, placed Blue in a situation where the window of opportunity for offensive operations was limited. This combination of factors exerted pressure on SACEUR with regard to the negotiation process: the need to improve the military situation to enhance diplomatic bargaining power essentially required prompt offensive action. However, because the NCA found it impossible to revise political objectives regardless of the military situation, SACEUR tended to be driven toward a recommendation for tactical nuclear use.

The result was the classical mismatch of political ends and military means. Blue could neither retreat nor modify war aims lest NATO disintegrate, did not believe it could negotiate successfully given the military situation, and appeared to lack the military power to achieve its goals either through offensive action or at the conference table. The Blue planning process revolved around this set of problems. As long as the NATO Alliance was firm, there was no pressure on Blue to develop negotiating flexibility. With nuclear use ruled out, it appeared that Blue policy of protracted conventional war was operative, but the short-term requirements for Alliance cohesion and an offensive to build bargaining strength ran counter to that strategy. In the final analysis, few players were given to address the sobering issue: how to fight a war of attrition and keep that war going until Blue industrial mobilization provided the decisive advantage in an estimated D+2 years?

If the nature of the situation on the Central Front could be generalized as "military" and of "impending crisis," that in the Pacific might be termed "political" and "long term." If SACEUR's concern was immediate military success to sustain Alliance cohesion and improve its negotiating position, CINCPAC's was restraint in conducting military initiatives that might have adverse political consequences. Both the political and military situations were most favorable to Blue. The primary strategic question to be resolved was the utilization of PACOM military assets. Aside from reducing his offensive capabilities, CINCPAC raised other arguments in opposition to a "swing" of forces to the west. He argued that, given a strong Blue military presence in northeast Asia, dating from the end of World War II, a significant drawdown of Blue forces could lead various countries to take initiatives detrimental to the long-term interests of Blue. (All three weeks of game play in Global '88 saw Japan planning a rearmament program.) Economically, CINCPAC stressed the vital importance of the Far East industrial and financial strength to the Blue war effort and to postwar recovery. From a military perspective, it was argued that Red should not be permitted to appear the dominant power in the region.

A central issue in CINCPAC planning was whether military initiatives against the Red homeland and the Kuriles had a short-term effect on the war in Europe. In spite of frequent Red statements to the contrary, Red was concerned about events in the Far East, which was the second strategic priority. The question that emerged over the series was that of Blue tying down Red military assets in the Far East. As Blue saw Red forces redeploying from the region, Blue was never sure how much its actions really affected Red.

Global 1988—Scenario One

The D+64 through D+74 scripted events to attain the starting basis for the Red-dominant scenario were as follows:

The military situation on the Central Front had turned decisively against Blue.

- Utilizing extensive operational deception, the Sixth Strategic Echelon had closed with and defeated NATO forces on the Elbe. The Blue V Corps and one FRG division were encircled in the vicinity of Leipzig and a 600-km gap was torn in the NATO line in Bavaria.
- The NATO northern pincer, unable to make progress toward Stendal, had fallen back on the Elbe-Lubeck Canal line.
- The NATO offensive north into the Netherlands had been repulsed by Red, and NATO had failed to eliminate the Red "Bonn pocket" on the west bank of the Rhine.
- Blue was experiencing severe shortfalls in critical items such as "smart" munitions and main battle tanks. Blue held a 1.6-to-1.0 advantage in the air.
- The Seventh Strategic Echelon was moving through western Red.

Blue forces and their allies in western Europe had achieved considerable success in the GOLDEN SWORD counteroffensive, but were dealt a series of disastrous setbacks in the period from D+64 to D+75. The gains of the attack, which had carried NATO forces well into the GDR, had been eliminated. While not routed, Blue had been unable to establish a cohesive defense and Red had penetrated the Bonn-Frankfurt line. Multinational forces of AFCENT stretched from positions on the North Sea in the Netherlands, along the Rhine, and then through Bavaria to and along the Main River, then back to the Swiss and Austrian borders. The failure of the recent counterattack to liberate the bulk of the Netherlands left NORTHAG defending south of the Neder Rhine at Rotterdam and Arnhem. This and other recent setbacks had required the extension of NORTHAG perimeter over hundreds of additional kilometers. The NORTHAG area of responsibility (AOR) met that of CENTAG in the vicinity of Mainz.

Operations out of Jutland had included a four-nation counteroffensive which advanced on Wittenberge but was then thrown back to the Elbe-Lubeck Canal line by elements of the Sixth Strategic Echelon. The combination of remaining Danish, Norwegian, UK, and Blue units provided a sizable force capable of conducting defensive operations.

CENTAG's primary concern was with two forward corps, the V Blue and the III FRG. The crushing Red counterattack that reversed prior NATO gains placed both these corps in extremis. The V Blue was encircled and on the verge of total collapse, while the elements of the III FRG had either been destroyed or were encircled by forces of the Sixth Strategic Echelon. The NATO right flank in CENTAG was in a state of shambles.

The View from Blue

Political. The deteriorating military situation made the NCA's position one of extreme difficulty. On the one hand, Blue needed some kind of military success to support any negotiating position, but military advisors took the position that tactical nuclear weapons would be required to attain the required result on the battlefield. Congress, on the other hand, which had turned distinctly hawkish when the news from the front was good, now supported a virtual surrender and a retreat to a vague "fortress America" concept. Further, the NCA had to deal with NATO members who wanted the war to end without the use of nuclear weapons and were resentful of the large Blue commitment of forces to other theaters.

The NCA formulated the following set of Blue options and they provided the basis for discussion at all levels of command:

1. Return to the status quo ante without use of nuclear weapons.
2. Return to the status quo ante with nuclear weapons use.
3. Preserve as much of the territory of the FRG as possible.
4. Settle for a continental defense line west of (outside) the FRG.
5. Develop a new Blue political/military order with a focus outside Europe.

The NCA considered that options 4 and 5 were simply not politically acceptable and tended to dismiss any tactical nuclear option for two reasons, in spite of SACEUR's vigorously pressed recommendation for such use. First, he believed that the time frame in which tactical nuclear weapons would have utility had passed, and second, the NCA was concerned that the Red response to Blue limited use would be broad-based and result in Blue losing the war. The choice and implementation of the remaining option(s) was, essentially, a military question.

Military. Taken on a worldwide basis, the Blue situation was favorable. Red was essentially isolated, and a massive global coalition had been constructed to support Blue/NATO. However, Blue faced the imminent possibility of collapse of the European theater. The problem was to sustain a viable military presence on the Continent until negotiations could terminate the war successfully or sufficient global military and industrial mobilization occurred to overwhelm Red. While Blue retained a 1.6 to 1 air superiority, Red had regained all of the territory lost to the Blue GOLDEN SWORD counteroffensive, the V Corps was surrounded, and Red was moving 21 divisions of the Seventh Strategic Echelon toward the FLOT. While the Blue retreat was organized, Blue forces had not been able to establish a viable defensive line to hold Red.

SACEUR was tasked by the NCA to develop a conventional option to regain territory to buy time for and provide a basis for substantive negotiations. The following alternatives were discussed:

- Retake the Netherlands and the Ruhr (nuclear use open).
- Establish a defensive line in the FRG and then either continue a war of attrition or negotiate a cease-fire.
- Use nuclear weapons to improve the military situation or to compel Red to withdraw to prewar boundaries.

The fact of the matter was that the SACEUR analysis of the military situation did not support the ability of Blue/NATO forces to retake any territory in Europe, nor was there much basis for believing that Blue could win a war of attrition given the lead time required for industrial mobilization. The nuclear option, as noted above, appeared to have limited utility and risked Red escalation. Given these circumstances, SACEUR proposed to the NCA the "3+" plan based on the NCA's third option to "preserve as much of the FRG as possible." The salient features of this proposal were:

- Form a defensive line along the Rhine and thence to Munich, which, it was estimated, could hold for nine to fourteen days.

- Establish another defensive line running from Lubeck to Emden. It was estimated that this line could be held for 30 days.
- Use deep interdiction strikes against the Red LOCs, targeting in particular the Seventh Strategic Echelon.

In order to implement this plan, the following shifts in assets to support the Central Front would be required:

- Transfer of the three CVBGs from the Norwegian fjords.
- All TACAIR, a total of 800+ aircraft including the CV A/C.
- The BBBG from the Caribbean.
- B-52s from the SIOP, conventionally armed.
- TLAM(C).
- Blue USMC forces deployed in Norway to bolster the Lubeck-Emden line.

While this was not entirely satisfactory, SACEUR felt it was the best that could be done. The surrounded V Corps would have to be sacrificed, and, by falling back in the center and south, the line could be consolidated with prospects of holding out for two weeks. The longer term was uncertain, with the speed of Blue/Japan industrial mobilization a major determining factor.

CINCPAC viewed the situation in Asia with considerable confidence. Theater objectives had been achieved, and the CINC sought ways to aid the global war effort in general and make a contribution to the beleaguered Central Front in particular. The theater commander was, to some extent, faced with a "Hobson's Choice." Aggressive use of assets was required lest they be "swung" to Europe. However, offensive operations faced the problem of "attrition without replacement," as all noncommitted forces were prioritized for the Central Front.

CINCPAC's objectives were:

- Wear down Red.
- Seize additional islands in the Kurile chain.
- Destroy the remainder of the Red Far Eastern Fleet.
- Support the ROK against the DPRK.
- Encourage the cooperation of the PRC against Red.
- Encourage deeper involvement of Japan.

CINCPAC believed that Vladivostok was too heavily defended to attack and proposed the seizure of three more islands in the Kuriles to cut the SLOCs to Petropavlovsk, facilitate ASW operations in the Sea of Okhotsk, and divert Red forces aiding the DPRK. The JCS approved this plan.

CINCPAC's major concerns were political. Japan was contemplating a more assertive role in the region, both as a military power and as a source of capital. This as well as the possibility of a reunited Korea would have substantial impact on the relatively stable relationships that had existed since the end of the Korean War.

The View from Red

Political. The Red perspective on the war was somewhat less complex than that of Blue. Essentially, the VGK believed that the war had been won. All that remained was to convince Blue/NATO of this truth, but if they failed to grasp this reality, the Seventh Strategic Echelon would secure military victory.

Red, however, did have some concerns. First, while Red fortunes appeared favorable on the Central Front, there were sufficient vulnerabilities and uncertainties to put pressure on Red to end the war and to do it expeditiously. A key emerging problem was agriculture. Never a strong point of the Red regime, wartime dislocations were certainly going to impact the winter wheat harvest and probably spring planting as well. Further, with so much of the national transportation assets devoted to the military logistical effort, food distribution, a chronic problem in peacetime, had become exacerbated. In more general terms, the cost of the war to the Red economy had been enormous, and the sooner the war ended, the quicker this drain could be abated.

Among the major international uncertainties was the PRC. That nation had provided assistance to Blue in a number of ways, particularly since the invasion of the ROK by the DPRK. China's large military potential and the historic enmity between the two nations weighed on the VGK.

Finally, Red did not want a long war. Along with the factors noted above, Red was aware that the eventual mobilization of the Free World economies would doom Red militarily. Consequently, Red needed an end to the war—preferably by negotiation, but by whatever means—quickly. The problem for Red was to find a lever to bring this about, and there was substantial frustration in the VGK over the Red inability to obtain a cease-fire. Red groped for solutions; the possibility of holding the V Corps hostage instead of destroying it was discussed. However, the fact remained that while Red might win militarily in Europe, Red could not compel a Blue capitulation, and a protracted war with a Blue that dominated the oceans could blockade Red and keep its fishing fleets in port—a prospect Red did not look forward to.

Military. Red felt extremely confident in terms of the military situation. Most military objectives had been achieved, the Seventh Strategic Echelon was en route, and even Blue tactical nuclear use was viewed as inadequate to reverse the favorable outlook on the Central Front. Consequently, much of the General Staff thinking focused on initiatives that could facilitate negotiating success.

A major planned initiative was to try to demonstrate to Blue that their homeland was not invulnerable and thus develop pressure from public opinion and Congress for serious negotiations. Red therefore decided to launch conventional "demonstration" attacks on the Blue mainland, timed to occur just prior to a Presidential address to the nation. One strike was to be delivered by an Akula-class submarine against military and aerospace facilities on the West Coast. Meanwhile, Spetsnaz teams based in Cuba were tasked to destroy railroad facilities and marine terminals in North Carolina.

Global 1988—Scenario Two

The D+64 through D+74 scripted events to attain the starting basis for the Blue dominant scenario were as follows:

The military situation on the Central Front had turned markedly in favor of Blue.

- The Sixth Strategic Echelon had failed to break the NATO line on the Elbe, and the Blue/NATO forces were advancing on Stendal, which had been taken by NATO airborne assault.
- The NATO northern pincer had broken though Red defenses and was advancing on Stendal from the northwest.
- The imminent linkup of these Blue/NATO forces in Stendal would cut the LOCs to 60 Red divisions (attrited to about 32 division equivalents) between the Elbe and the Rhine.
- The NATO offensive north into the Netherlands had failed to gain ground.
- NATO had, essentially, eliminated the "Bonn pocket" on the west bank of the Rhine.
- Blue maintained a 1.6-to-1.0 ratio of air superiority over the FLOT; Red was assembling the Seventh Strategic Echelon in western Red.

The Blue military outlook on the Central Front had swung from the precarious brink of defeat and force exhaustion of D+42 to a more positive posture of cohesion and stability because of recent military success achieved by the mutually supporting counteroffensives conducted by AFNORTH and AFCENT.

The situation in AFCENT found the NATO Alliance holding positions from the North Sea in the Netherlands through the southern FRG to the Swiss and Austrian frontiers, with a sizable portion of the forces maintaining a salient in the GDR. The Northern

Army Group had strengthened its defensive line from a northern anchor at Kampen, thence to the Rhine at Arnhem, and then south along the west bank of the Rhine to the confluence with the Main at Mainz. The air campaign of the combined NATO air forces in the Central Region had achieved some measure of dominance over those of the WTVD commander.

In the Jutland area of NORTHAG operations, Danish, Norwegian, UK, and Blue forces represented six divisions and approximately 18 brigade equivalents of combat power. While these forces could sustain their positions for the next few weeks, reinforcements would be required for the execution of subsequent offensive operations. In the air, as in CENTAG, NATO maintained a degree of air superiority over Jutland and the North Sea. However, air defense of the area was a problem. The lack of an effective SAM network forced heavy reliance on all-weather interceptors, which were in short supply.

The View from Blue

Political. The second scenario of the 1988 Global War Game found Blue with a tactical advantage that the military believed marginal and transitory, and which the NCA saw as an opportunity to be exploited. This led to a tension that permeated the strategic planning process for the "Blue-dominant" scenario as an aggressive President demanded offensive options from a concerned military that sought to conserve territorial gains.

The President focused particularly on what the world would look like after the war. He told SACEUR: "You have a temporary victory on the Central Front and a strong advantage throughout the rest of the world." He then asked, "How can we use this situation to our advantage?" The Presidential view of war aims had much to do with his desire for offensive operations. He wanted to end the war with all Red forces back in their homeland, self-determination for the nations of eastern Europe, and the demilitarization of the GDR. He did not view the military situation extant conducive to the attainment of those ends.

The NCA gave the JCS three broad options to consider:

- Seek further military advantage by accepting high short-term risk; seek a fundamental change in the world balance of power.
- Consolidate military dominance by accepting moderate near-term risk; maximize diplomatic leverage to gain a Europe more Western than at the start of the war.
- Consolidate military gains to those that can be defended with minimum risk over the long term (strategic defense); utilize protracted diplomacy to achieve status quo ante.

When SACEUR proposed the consolidation option combined with active defense and expedited negotiations to terminate hostilities or the alternative of withdrawal to

France or beyond, he was taking into consideration a sustainability problem the President did not accept. The President rejected the SACEUR defensive recommendation and directed him to develop an offensive option and to define his requirements.

The NCA was not unaware that risk was attendant to this position. However, the President believed that the logistical situation, coupled with a parochial perspective on the part of the Blue theater commanders, contributed to a pessimism that prevented them from exploiting the present advantage. Hungary had dropped out of the war and Rumania, Czechoslovakia, and Poland appeared to be wavering. If Blue could collapse the Red sixty-division pocket, the NCA believed dissolution of the Warsaw Pact might result. Further, the President was convinced that the logistical shortfall could be overcome by pooling free world resources toward that aim. He was so confident in this regard that he assured an extremely skeptical SACEUR that he could count on his logistical needs being met.

Military. The SACEUR perspective was dominated by two concerns:

- The anticipated imminent arrival of the Seventh Strategic Echelon, the 27 divisions of which would shift the initiative to Red.
- The estimate that Blue forces had 21–30 days of sustainability if maintaining an active defense—less than that if offensive operations were to be conducted.

Other SACEUR concerns involved the sixty-division Red "pocket." Analysis showed that the so-called "pocket" was so large that it was in fact a series of multiple "fronts" occupying most of the FRG. Further, air superiority existed only over NATO-occupied territory. Air parity could be said to exist over the NSWP countries, and Blue air losses were running at 40 percent over the Red homeland. Two-thirds of Red combat aircraft were outside the WTVD, and the current air force superiority ratio of Blue in CENTAG was seen as tenuous. What this meant, as far as SACEUR was concerned, was that Blue air could not stop the Seventh Strategic Echelon, collapse the Red "pocket," gain air superiority over the NSWP, and destroy important targets in the Red homeland.

SACEUR's outlook, therefore, was that while all NATO territory had not been regained and access to Berlin not assured, GOLDEN SWORD had been a resounding NATO success and had placed the Alliance in the most favorable negotiating position it was likely to have.

SACEUR concluded that offensive operations anywhere (North Norway, Central Front, or Balkans) would endanger current positions in the other areas. Therefore the recommendation to the DPC was as follows:

- Consolidate and actively defend in all regions.

- Seek out and destroy the logistical support for the sixty "surrounded" Red divisions and delay the arrival of the Seventh Echelon.
- Utilize deception operations.
- Expedite negotiations.
- If negotiations break down, use nuclear weapons against the Seventh Echelon when it arrives, or withdraw to French territory or beyond.

There appeared to be a degree of confusion regarding planning in the CINCPAC AOR. The Navy interpreted the NCA's instructions to mean the continued execution of the global strategy they had been pursuing since the war started. Therefore, the theater commander made plans to support ROK initiatives with amphibious landings in the DPRK, with a longer range objective of threatening Vladivostok, urging Japan to take greater responsibility for air defense, and to carry out other aggressive actions when and where appropriate. However, the President made it clear that what he really meant was to use global assets to win on the Central Front, and he was not interested in a lot of "meaningless" activity in other theaters.

The View from Red

Political. The Red political viewpoint changed substantially during the play of the Blue-dominant scenario. At the outset, the General Secretary was anxious to negotiate. He evidenced a distrust for the Red military, which he believed should have concluded the war long before D+75; yet not only was it still engaged but was fighting at a tactical disadvantage as well. He ordered the General Staff to put their plans on hold for ten days while he pursued a diplomatic solution. He felt relatively comfortable doing so, based on a VGK appraisal that Blue could hold in place but do little else.

The General Secretary wished to reach a cease-fire agreement as soon as possible and put forth a "bottom line" proposal that he thought would be acceptable to Blue. He was taken aback and frustrated by the outright rejection of his offer and by the Blue refusal to even negotiate. When a subsequent diplomatic initiative designed to fragment NATO was unavailing, the General Secretary resolved on a prompt military solution.

There was unanimous agreement among the VGK that hostilities must be terminated before the "long war" phase was reached. Red believed that Blue industrial capacity combined with Red isolation would doom Red to defeat. Red frustration over failed negotiations with Blue, a sense that Blue had decided to seek a military solution, and the perceived requirement to end the war quickly led the General Secretary to declare the sixty divisions in the "pocket" a "Red vital interest" and, therefore, that Red was prepared to use tactical nuclear weapons to preserve that army's integrity.

Military. The Red General Staff was optimistic regarding the situation on the Central Front. The current situation was seen as but a temporary tactical disadvantage, soon to be redressed by the arrival of the Seventh Strategic Echelon supported by an additional 350 combat aircraft drawn from other military districts. The Military Intelligence Directorate (GRU) estimates of NATO force accretions saw the possibility of a maximum of ten new divisions in an undefined time frame. The General Staff saw no requirement for nuclear use.

Red concerns focused on the safe passage of the Seventh Echelon forces to the front and the preservation of the divisions in the "pocket." Heavy use of chemical weapons was planned to facilitate both objectives. Initially, Blue air operational capability was to be decreased by heavy and repeated use of CW, both persistent and nonpersistent. Scuds were to be used as the delivery system, and Red was planning for attacks over a fifty-day period, if necessary. Artillery would be used to pour chemicals on the northern and southern pincers of the encircling Blue forces for at least several days. Further, Red planned to mass forces to open the rail LOC south of Berlin. An initial force correlation of 4 to 1 was intended for this operation, with chemical weapons utilized there as well.

Concentration on the Central Front was total. If necessary, all peripheral theaters would be stripped of forces and aircraft to provide an Eighth Strategic Echelon. The General Staff had identified 30–40 divisions that could be moved west from the Chinese border. Under this proposal, one Red division would remain at the PRC frontier to act as a "trip wire," with a Red promise of nuclear retaliation if it were attacked. The General Secretary believed that Red war aims had been achieved and his task was to end hostilities as rapidly as possible.

Global 1988—Scenario Three

The D+64 through D+74 scripted events to attain the starting basis for the stalemate scenario were designed so that neither Blue nor Red had a clear military advantage.

- The Red Sixth Strategic Echelon and Blue/NATO forces along the Elbe had fought each other to a standstill. While unit cohesion remained intact on both sides, neither possessed offensive capability.
- The northern NATO pincer, objective Stendal, had stalled, and a weak but cohesive defensive position had been established in the vicinity of Wittenberge.
- The NATO offensive north into the Netherlands had failed, and NORTHAG was forced to consolidate in defensive positions along the Neder-Rhine line.
- All Red forces had been cleared from the "Bonn pocket" on the west bank of the Rhine.

- Blue/NATO air was in a high state of readiness to aid in the defense against any renewed Red offensive and to provide limited offensive air operations.
- The Seventh Strategic Echelon was assembling in western Red.

The land situation in Europe was relatively favorable to Blue because of the recent success achieved by the mutually supporting counteroffensives conducted by AFNORTH and AFCENT. NATO forces in the Central Region were holding a stable line, and the front from Rostock to Vienna was essentially quiet. While the WP had experienced heavy attrition, the balance of conventional power on the ground lay with Red, offset, however, by NATO air superiority.

The FLOT in AFCENT ran from the North Sea in the Netherlands along the Rhine and through Bavaria to Leipzig in the GDR, then back to the Swiss and Austrian frontiers. The failure of recent counterattacks in the Netherlands had left NORTHAG defending south of the Neder-Rhine at Rotterdam to Arnhem, then south along the Rhine to a junction with CENTAG at the confluence of the Main.

The north flank was held by the small but well-entrenched elements of the I Netherlands Corps. To the right of the Dutch, the Belgian Corps, while relatively light, was capable of defending well-prepared positions and could be relied on to deter any crossing of the Neder-Rhine. Next in line, the Blue XXX Corps held a small bridgehead on the north bank of the Neder-Rhine. It sustained heavy casualties in the unsuccessful attempt to liberate North Holland and, while capable of defending for the next week to ten days, would require reinforcement. Various other forces along the Rhine contributed to defense in depth. Overall, the CENTAG posture was a relatively good one, capable of defending current positions over the coming weeks. However, any offensive operations would require reinforcements.

The multinational force based on Jutland and Zealand had made substantial gains over the last two weeks of the war. The XVIII Blue Corps, composed of two MEFs, one armored, one mechanized, and one airborne division, and two heavy brigades, had taken Rostock. However, the current lines of this corps were stretched thin, and any appreciable pressure could not be held for more than a week without reinforcements.

The View from Blue

Political. The NCA began the stalemate scenario trying to ascertain what military options were available to improve the Blue negotiating position. The first issue that had to be resolved was that of sustainability of the NATO forces. The NCA believed that until they were able to know the ramifications of the logistical situation, they would be unable to delineate offensive options and did not want to engage in immediate, substantive negotiations if military initiatives were available that could improve the Blue posture.

The President did, however, state the Blue objectives:

- Maintain the cohesion of the NATO Alliance.
- Restore prewar boundaries.
- Fracture the Warsaw Pact and neutralize Eastern Europe.
- Advance Blue/Western vital interests worldwide and amputate Red global reach.
- Avoid the use of nuclear weapons except to:
    - prevent Red victory in Europe
    - counter massive Red CW use.
- Initiate full-scale Alliance economic mobilization as a part of "long-war" strategy.

The President was entirely committed to a long-war concept and worked to facilitate it, diplomatically and logistically, while trying to develop a military strategy that would permit it to succeed. Congressional resolutions indicated solid support for the administration and the military and public opinion polls showed a majority endorsing the President's war aims. In the Far East, Japan and the PRC were forming a North Asia Security Council, and China had agreed to provide bases to Blue for limited attacks on Red. Global allies were pressed for military assistance in terms of men, supplies, and the buyback of military equipment previously provided by Blue. While it appeared that NATO was divided on negotiating objectives, this was due in part to the reluctance of the Blue chief executive to be specific until military options had been determined. Information provided by the Director of Central Intelligence lent credence to the validity of the long-war policy. The Red homeland was essentially destitute of trucks, the harvest was in danger, and famine was a distinct possibility.

The question of military strategy was finally resolved in favor of an offensive. The President had initially been opposed to this course of action, fearing it would be wasteful in terms of supplies. He acceded only because he became convinced that a defensive strategy would result in military defeat.

Military. SACEUR viewed the situation in Europe with far more concern than appeared evident in the NCA and Congress. Sustainability was the central issue. A JCS assessment showed that NATO forces had experienced significant losses in capability, particularly because of shortages of ammunition and major end items, such as tanks. Air sortie generation was dependent on fuel distribution capacity, and, while ports were open, infrastructure damage restricted the flow of POL. Significant resupply from

CONUS would exceed D+100. Taking these factors into consideration, the JCS estimated that NATO could sustain an offensive for from one to three weeks, could hold in place for three to six weeks, and fight a delaying action for six to eight weeks.

It was in part because of these sustainability problems that the use of tactical nuclear weapons was reviewed. SACEUR recognized that retaliatory strikes would be costly but believed that there would be a "window of opportunity" created for negotiations. He proposed an offensive that envisioned the use of twenty-five 70kt nuclear weapons, but planned to proceed with offensive operations even if nuclear release was not granted. SACEUR believed that even a temporary advance was better than standing on the defensive. He requested the transfer of other assets to Europe, which raised the issue of theater priorities. CINCPAC was extremely concerned that moving the CVBGs could lead to a questioning of Blue political and military resolve and lead to a perception that Red was the dominant military power in the region. Similarly, SACLANT would not accede to the movement of the three CVBGs from the Norwegian fjords because of the priority of SLOC protection.

At the insistence of NATO, SACEUR prepared a plan for a strategic defensive dubbed Operation OSTRICH. This plan was based on instructions to disregard initial mission guidance and to select the best defensive position that would be both to the east of France and would include a portion of the GDR. SACEUR developed the plan but was adamant in opposition to it. In the event, SACEUR's offensive plan was approved by the NCA and the DPC, although both were extremely concerned about escalatory ramifications. SACEUR was granted "conditional nuclear release," but launch authority was withheld. Convinced that doing something was better than doing nothing, SACEUR was prepared to try to close the northern and southern pincers at Stendal, with or without nuclear weapons.

CINCPAC's fundamental objection to the "swing" of the CVBG force has been noted above. Further, CINCPAC believed that the crisis on the Central Front would be resolved, one way or the other, before they could get there. The theater commander was also mindful that a perceived reduction in Blue interest in the Far East could lead to unilateral initiatives on the part of other states in the region that might seriously complicate postwar relations. CINCPAC was very sensitive to the political, economic, and military relationships that would be critical in sustaining and enhancing Blue worldwide influence. It was the CINC's position that an unquestioned Blue security commitment during the war would be essential to regional stability and access when hostilities ended.

Therefore, CINCPAC proposed the following potential options for his forces:

- Consolidate and declare victory.

- Use two CVBGs and one BBBG to support the ROK.
- Capture two more of the Kurile Islands.
- Launch an attack on the Red fishing and merchant fleets to complicate Red postwar problems.

The View from Red

Political. The VGK viewed the situation at the outset of the "stalemate" scenario with confidence. It believed that Red was in a position of military superiority and a primary objective—the neutralization of the FRG—had been accomplished. As Red forces occupied almost all of West German territory, the VGK sought to ratify military success through negotiations with Blue while keeping the military pressure on. To this end, all military effort was to be concentrated on the Central Front at the expense of other theaters.

Red opened negotiations with Blue and was initially quite optimistic. The VGK accepted an initiative by the UN Secretary General, pressed for bilateral meetings with France and the FRG, and tried to involve Blue in substantive negotiations. When the bilateral efforts failed and Blue refused to move from the initial position, Red, clearly frustrated and feeling isolated, took the following actions:

- Withdrew all existing proposals.
- Refused to negotiate under UN auspices.
- Refused a Blue offer for a "walk in the woods."
- Established a provisional socialist government in the occupied FRG.
- Withdrew French immunity from nuclear and chemical attack.

Red was so confident of military success that it was not seriously concerned with Blue tactical nuclear use. The VGK agreed that as long as such use by Blue was not decisive, Red would not retaliate.

Military. The General Staff believed that Red had a decided military advantage over Blue. Aware of the potential for Blue to attempt a double envelopment, Red was not concerned because of the belief that Blue lacked the staying power, even if successful, to sustain an encirclement long enough to discomfort Red forces to the west. Further, the closure of the Seventh Echelon and, if necessary, the mobilization of an eighth, would unquestionably seal the military victory.

Contrary to Blue, Red had a short war, Central Front focus. Although defeated at sea and on the defensive in other sectors, Red felt comfortable in moving whatever assets were necessary to Germany. Matters in other theaters could be taken care of once the war on the Central Front was concluded.

Again, even Blue theater nuclear use did not greatly concern Red. The General Staff was convinced that by the time Blue/NATO could make a nuclear decision, it would be too late because Blue would lack the conventional capability to follow up and exploit. Consequently, the General Staff faced its tasking from the VGK with considerable confidence.

The Negotiating Process

The primary focus of GWG '88 was "to identify and analyze the dynamics and leverage that military operations in all theaters can bring to a war termination negotiation process and what constraints or other effects negotiations have on theater military operations." The stated political objectives of the belligerents are the starting point for an analysis of negotiations. These can be summarized as follows:

Blue/NATO

- To restore the territorial status quo ante of allies and neutrals and maintain the cohesion of NATO.
- To protect Blue interests worldwide, but especially in the Caribbean, Latin America, the Pacific Basin, the Indian Ocean, and the Persian Gulf.
- To keep the conflict at the lowest possible level of intensity by avoiding the use of nuclear weapons and destroying Red nuclear capabilities through conventional means.
- To defeat Red conventional forces while minimizing Alliance casualties.

Red/Warsaw Pact

- To solve the "German problem" once and for all on Red terms—a demilitarized Germany.
- To destroy or seriously weaken NATO by demonstrating the inability of the Alliance to protect its most important continental member.
- To diminish or eliminate Blue influence in Europe.
- To attain these objectives while avoiding escalation to nuclear war.

Negotiations to D+64

Demands for war termination began immediately following the outbreak of hostilities. The government of India sponsored a plea from the "nonaligned" movement for an immediate cease-fire. Then, and as the Warsaw Pact invasion of Austria unfolded, the government of Yugoslavia presented a more comprehensive proposal that called for the withdrawal of forces to premobilization positions (those as of 1 November 1990) immediately following a cease-fire. Subsequent calls for negotiations evoked the following Red proposal on behalf of the Warsaw Pact.

"In contrast to NATO's apparent aim of prolonging the war, reestablishing a militarized West German regime, and overthrowing democratically elected governments in eastern Europe, we seek to end the fighting as soon as possible and eliminate the conditions that gave rise to the current conflict. We seek neither the destruction of free societies nor the occupation of territory and we are determined to make a breakthrough for peace. Accordingly, we put forward the following proposal:

- That both sides agree to a cease-fire in place and tactical withdrawals of 5km by both sides to assure that military incidents do not occur.
- That both sides agree to begin negotiations in Geneva at the foreign minister level that have the following agreed central objective:
- Establishment of a West Germany and an East Germany that would be demilitarized, belonging to no military alliances and having no military forces on their territory and no indigenous military forces beyond those required for maintaining internal order and the security of their borders.

"If the NATO side will agree to this proposal, we are prepared to begin immediately to implement a mutual withdrawal from western Europe and other theaters of all Pact and NATO forces introduced since 1 November 1990 and to complete such withdrawals within 60 days. Agreement to this proposal would also set the stage for the discussion of further objectives:

- The abolition of all military alliances.
- The reduction of conventional forces from the Atlantic to the Urals to levels well below those existing on 1 November 1990.
- The elimination of all tactical and medium-range NATO and Red nuclear weapons from Europe and the surrounding seas.

"It should be clear from this proposal that we do not seek to impose our will on anyone. Under its terms, Germans and other peoples would resume their rightful place as sovereign masters of their own territories. It should also be clear that if NATO seeks to impose by military actions the withdrawal of Pact forces that we offer to carry out peacefully, it can only be for the purpose of reimposing militarism and revanchism in the center of our continent. This we will not tolerate." (This proposal is quoted at length because the language and terms are typical of the Red negotiating position throughout this series.)

Blue and its NATO partners totally rejected the substance of the Red proposal, but agreed to negotiate. On 15 December 1990, the President of Blue announced that he was sending his Secretary of State to Geneva to negotiate "a return to pre-hostilities boundaries as provided for in the Yugoslav Proposal." By 18 December the negotiations had made no progress. In a hotline message to the Red General Secretary, the President stated that "cease-fire in place without essential guarantees of immediate, phased withdrawal to the pre-hostilities lines" was unacceptable and that "we will never stop fighting until the pre-war boundaries have been re-established."

The week before Christmas, 1990, the Pope and the United Nations General Secretary proposed a 48-hour cease-fire over Christmas. This initiative was rejected by both sides—Red because of concern that a pause would break their offensive momentum, and Blue out of fear that any halt would result in a de facto cease-fire in place.

The week following Christmas, a modalities working group consisting of representatives from Blue, Red, and NATO, chaired by the Secretary General of the United Nations, was formed to work out the details of a phased withdrawal as a precondition for a cease-fire. The terms of reference used by the working group were:

- A phased withdrawal of Warsaw Pact forces combined with a cease-fire.
    - Withdrawal to begin within 24 hours of agreement and completed within 10–30 days.
    - The goal of withdrawal by phases to be restoration of prehostilities borders.
    - No flights or hostile acts to take place in or over the buffer zone to be created as part of the time-phased withdrawal.
- A commission to be formed composed of representatives of those forces in contact to:
    - Investigate incidents reported to the commission.
    - Establish "police" or specially designated units contributed by the combatants to patrol the buffer zone phased withdrawal areas.

The working group for these modalities was to assume that a cease-fire agreement would be agreed to and determine the procedure that would facilitate a withdrawal should the principals resolve outstanding points of disagreement, such as the posture of reinforcements. Blue proposed possible withdrawal lines, but by D+48 military events rendered the proposal obsolete.

As the Warsaw Pact advance stalled in the Benelux, and the NATO 1st Allied Army counterattack succeeded, war aims and consequently negotiating positions became less well defined for both Blue and Red. Escalation to chemical warfare and changing peripheral strategies, with their theater-oriented political considerations, tended to cloud the intentions of the opposing camps, not only in Europe but globally.

The success of the NATO 1st Allied Army thrust was a cause of substantial concern to the Red leadership. After some vacillation and much discussion within the VGK, Red surmised that the NATO attack was a last-resort effort that would have to be contained. Upon reaching this conclusion, several Red planning adjustments were made:

- A decidedly more aggressive posture in peripheral theaters.
- A delay in Central Front offensive operations until a more favorable correlation of forces was created with the arrival of the Sixth Strategic Echelon.

By D+64, Red leaders had regained confidence in the strength of the European position and, further, felt that implementation of pending initiatives in other theaters would enhance the Red negotiating stance.

The Blue/NATO military position in Europe had indeed improved, and this led to a rather euphoric mindset at D+64. The successful counteroffensive had helped to bolster Alliance morale, but the self-assessed improbability of sustaining those gains much beyond D+70 did not translate into an impetus for timely and aggressive negotiations. What "window of opportunity" for successful negotiations NATO might have had while Red was trying to adjust to the reality of the success of GOLDEN SWORD was quickly lost. However tardy, the Blue President requested a projection of the NATO post–D+70 position in preparation for exploiting the recent military gains by reviving what was, in essence, the earlier Yugoslav proposal.

Consequently, D+64 found both sides far from any mutual accommodation over how to end the war. Although plagued with uncertainty over each opponent's nuclear threshold, particularly after both had used chemical weapons, the combatants felt that the other was "on the ropes" and that near term events on the field battle would enhance leverage at the bargaining table. NATO was less confident than the Warsaw Pact, but neither side was convinced that all political objectives could be realized by diplomacy.

Negotiations in Global 1988

Introduction

Red, with its military objectives secured or apparently within reach, sought a termination of the war that would ratify Warsaw Pact military success and limit losses. From a military perspective, Red, at D+75, was in about as favorable a position (Red-dominant scenario) as it had been at D+46, yet had sustained substantial losses due to the inability to translate military conquest into political victory. Red in fact had become quite frustrated trying to persuade Blue to accept what Red perceived to be inevitable.

Blue generally believed that military success was prerequisite to satisfactory negotiations. Blue viewed neutralization of the FRG as equivalent to the end of the NATO Alliance and was convinced that Red would settle for nothing less. As long as the NATO Alliance remained politically united and the Blue homeland was not threatened, it appeared that Blue would continue to spurn negotiations in favor of a protracted conventional war strategy. Blue also believed that a cease-fire in place would be the equivalent of a Red victory, as Blue felt that public opinion would not countenance resumption of hostilities should subsequent negotiations fail.

Both Blue and Red, then, believed that military success was the key to political victory. Red, having achieved most of the military objectives, was eager to negotiate. Blue saw the perceived military advantage of Red, both in terms of position and the closure of the Seventh Echelon, precluding any success at the bargaining table. As negotiations showed little prospect of fruition, the focus shifted to other options. Both sides saw the nuclear option as counterproductive, while conventional war, "soldiering on," gave Blue the prospect, however remote, of regaining parity or of attaining victory.

The crux of the matter, however, was that the minimum conditions for war termination for both sides, or even any compromise positions that were reasonably available, were mutually exclusive. Given this circumstance, negotiations were essentially certain to fail.

Red-Dominant Scenario

With Red dominant on the Central Front, Blue was unable to develop a bargaining strategy and concluded that circumstances did not provide a basis for negotiations. The Blue NCA considered five options ranging from a territorial status quo ante to a new Blue political/military order with focus away from Europe. However, it was perceived that negotiating from a position of less than military superiority by Blue was impossible, and any cease-fire under such conditions was viewed as surrender. Further, any cease-fire would give a short-term resupply advantage to Red. Blue believed that, given the conditions postulated by the scenario, some substantial military achievement would be necessary to allow successful negotiations. The major negotiating strategies for Blue, and indeed for Red, were played out on the battlefield and in private bilateral discussions, not at the general conference table. Blue dominance in theaters other than Central Europe did not appear to provide sufficient leverage for Blue to use in that theater.

Red felt that in this scenario it had achieved its war aims and sought to conclude negotiations that would give political ratification to its military achievements. Although Red put forward a very demanding set of proposals, Red was willing to compromise, a premise that Blue never tested. Influenced by this set of proposals and a self-perception of a hopelessly weak negotiating position, Blue walked out.

The salient points of the initial Red proposal were:

- Dissolution of NATO.
- Restoration of prewar boundaries for FRG and GDR.
- FRG army abolished.
- Demilitarized zone in Benelux.
- Repatriation of forces.
- Return of occupied Kuriles to Red.
- Reduction in Blue nuclear forces.
- Separate negotiations with France over nuclear weapons.

The "bottom line" for Red was actually:

- A demilitarized FRG.
- Blue out of Europe (or, possibly, just Blue nuclear forces out of Europe).
- Return of the Kuriles.

The minimum criteria for a negotiated settlement developed by Blue were:

- Freedom for the FRG and Netherlands.
- Continuation of the NATO Alliance.
- Blue forces to remain on the Continent.

Negotiations did resume, with Blue under the impression that Red had accepted these minimum conditions as a basis for negotiations. This was not the case, and the Secretary of State endeavored to sidestep the critical issue with a cease-fire proposal subject to a number of conditions, one of which would have required Warsaw Pact forces to be withdrawn behind prewar borders within two weeks. This was clearly unacceptable to Red, as it left open entirely both the future status of the FRG and of Blue military forces on the Continent.

Red sought other negotiating avenues in an effort to circumvent the impasse. Specifically, Red tried to both convince and demoralize the French with news of the Seventh Echelon and an overture to favor France by conferring nonbelligerent status. Fortunately for NATO, France spurned the offer.

Red also failed to understand that Blue's inability to monitor world events during a cease-fire due to the attrition of space assets was of considerable concern, and some sort of arrangement to facilitate a space cease-fire could have been a start for negotiations.

In summary, then, Red wanted a quick war termination to secure military and political victory. Although the Red negotiating strategy appeared to have substantial flexibility, the minimum conditions were not acceptable to Blue. Blue, although running out of supplies on the Central Front, rejected negotiations due to the solidarity of the NATO Alliance, its long-term industrial strength, and its dominance over the other theaters, and the possibility of assistance from a variety of heretofore noncombatants. Blue therefore made a deliberate choice to spurn negotiations in favor of a long-war strategy.

Blue-Dominant Scenario

The negotiating process in the Blue-dominant scenario was strongly influenced by a perception, shared by both sides, that the Blue advantage was short term. Red believed that the military objectives had been attained and that it was time to stop the war. The General Secretary was, therefore, serious about negotiations, but saw no reason to modify the terms offered with the Seventh Strategic Echelon moving to the front. Given this perspective, the General Secretary presented Blue with a "bottom line" proposal that contained the following points:

- A demilitarized and neutralized FRG and GDR under existing governments.
- An immediate, in-place cease-fire.
- Withdrawal of all NATO and Warsaw Pact forces from the FRG and GDR within 90 days.
- FRG and GDR forces demobilized within 90 days.
- Withdrawal of NATO and Warsaw Pact forces to prewar territories within 90 days.
- FRG and GDR citizens free to decide for themselves how they wish to live, as long as political union is not an option.

The VGK proposal was in anticipation of a Blue status quo ante position, which would in fact imply Red defeat and erode Red legitimacy. The longer term implications of the Hungarian situation, and by possible extension, the Eastern European bloc, would be difficult enough with legitimacy intact. Therefore Red proposed what amounted to a vacuum in Central Europe.

Blue felt, as in the Red-dominant scenario, that the military situation was not favorable enough to negotiate successfully; that it could not negotiate what it had not won militarily. Blue went to the table reluctantly and with no position, apparently for the sake of public opinion and to lay the groundwork for strategy. In the event, Blue rejected all points of the Red proposals except those calling for a cease-fire coupled with the withdrawal of NATO and Warsaw Pact forces to their prewar territories within 90 days. The General Secretary received this Blue response with a certain amount of disbelief, concluding that Blue either had no understanding of the Red position or had no desire to negotiate and was pursuing a military solution. The next Blue response tended to confirm that view. Blue proposed, among other things, the payment of reparations to the nations that had suffered economic damage as a result of Red aggression and self-determination for all countries, east and west alike.

As the "negotiations" proceeded, both sides endeavored to secure advantage in other ways. Blue sought through military success in other theaters to exploit worldwide dominance, but Red kept the issue focused on the Central Front. Red held to its termination objectives and stood by its proposal while making diplomatic overtures designed to fracture NATO. France was a primary target, but neither they nor any other Alliance members were willing to negotiate with Red. Eventually a "back channel" was opened that allowed Red to expand the proposal to include the demilitarization of western Czechoslovakia and the return of Austrian neutrality. This "back channel" served to clarify positions and, had the scenario continued, could have proved beneficial.

In general, negotiations in the Blue-dominant scenario were characterized by significant perceptual mismatches. Blue was looking for leverage. NATO was considering options to terminate the war before faced with a choice of surrender, nuclear escalation, or protracted war. Red, depending on the Seventh Strategic Echelon as the arbiter of victory, preferred a diplomatic settlement to sustained military action. In the final analysis, Blue was not seriously interested in negotiations because of the perception that the military situation had to be improved before Alliance political objectives could be successfully negotiated.

Stalemate Scenario

As in the other two scenarios, the stalemate construct was dominated by the Seventh Strategic Echelon and the concomitant perception of Blue disadvantage. Red, as in previous scenarios, believed that a negotiated settlement could prove advantageous. Red felt it had achieved its military objectives and wanted to convert this achievement into lasting political advantage. A confident General Secretary instructed the VGK to think "bold ideas" and to pursue economic initiatives with special attention to the Far East. Accordingly, the following proposal was presented to Blue:

- Immediate withdrawal of all foreign forces from the FRG, GDR, and the Netherlands preparatory to:
  - Permanent withdrawal of all NATO forces from FRG and the Netherlands.
  - FRG and the Netherlands withdrawal from NATO.
  - Restructured FRG and Netherlands armed forces for internal security only.

- Red forces in GDR to retain defensive capability only and to guarantee external security of the FRG jointly with Blue forces stationed elsewhere on NATO territory.
- No Blue or Red nuclear forces anywhere in Europe.
- Red forces to be withdrawn from Norway provided the following undertakings are agreed to:
    - Reaffirmation that no foreign forces will be permanently based in Norway or Denmark.
    - No stockpiling of foreign military equipment to be permitted in Norway or Denmark.

This proposal was tabled at the first negotiating session, chaired by the Secretary General of the United Nations.

The Blue perspective was that Red must be convinced that the war could not be won, but was dubious that NATO military power was sufficient to accomplish this. However, Blue intelligence was reporting that there was political unrest in both Hungary and Poland and, further, that the possibility of famine existed in the Red homeland. These factors, combined with Blue success everywhere except on the Central Front, led Blue to stall. Blue entered negotiations halfheartedly and sought to improve its standing in world public opinion, to bolster Allied national will, and to maximize the potential for assistance from other countries.

Another problem that Blue had in entering negotiations was that there were considerable differences between the goals of the President and the objectives of other Alliance members. The President's initial position was no cease-fire without withdrawal to prewar boundaries in Europe, neutralization of Eastern Europe, and the fracturing of the Warsaw Pact. NATO did not agree that the Warsaw Pact should be fractured, and there were further divisions within NATO as to the approach to a cease-fire. It seemed apparent that the Blue actions were directed toward buying time to plan global offensive operations rather than to achieve a negotiated settlement.

The Red proposal elicited the response that it contained little to encourage Blue/NATO to end the war and, due to the inability of Blue/NATO to formulate a position, the status quo ante was put forth yet again. The Blue Congress passed a resolution calling for an eastern European "buffer zone" consisting of a neutralized Poland, Czechoslovakia, and Romania as well as an open corridor to Berlin as part of the FRG.

After a delay that frustrated Red, NATO finally put together a counteroffer consisting of the following:

- Acceptance of a cease-fire conditional on Red withdrawal from all NATO territory.

- All nations, east and west, to be allowed without coercion to determine alliances and regional arrangements.
- Discussion of postwar environment must be based on negotiating political arrangements in Central and Eastern Europe that satisfy the aspirations and security interests of the states concerned.
- Norway and Denmark have no intent to have permanent stationing of foreign forces.
- The stockpiling of military equipment is a decision for each sovereign government.

While NATO was developing this proposal, the President of Blue was seeking the advice of the principal negotiator. Two options were proposed:

- Reject the Red proposal.
- Begin negotiations on Central Front based on cease-fire, withdrawal of forces, and some restrictions on stationed and indigenous troops/weapons within the region, including Eastern Europe.

The second option seemed more pragmatic, and the Secretary of State suggested a counterproposal based on that option. At this juncture, there was no agreement between Blue and NATO on specific counterproposals. Some distinct national views had emerged: Norway and the Benelux wanted an immediate cease-fire; the FRG, UK, and France wanted some measure of retribution—the status quo ante was not adequate for them; the Italians and the Turks supported the Alliance; and the Greeks were wavering. Consequently, without a Blue/NATO position, negotiations stalled.

Red, unaware of the internal problems in formulating an allied position, again sought to end the impasse by a diplomatic offensive. Bilateral talks were offered to several NATO countries and overtures extended to the PRC and Japan. All of these initiatives came to naught, and, feeling isolated internationally, Red withdrew all proposals, broke off negotiations, and decided to seek a military solution with a goal of occupying the FRG and establishing a provisional government in Frankfurt.

CHAPTER FIVE

Industrial Mobilization, Logistics, and Sustainability

Introduction

Prior to the outbreak of hostilities in Global '85 both NATO and the Warsaw Pact conducted extensive mobilization of personnel. The vast majority of the war-fighting to D+64 had been accomplished using resources immediately available to the theater commanders and by deploying reserve assets as rapidly as possible. The very nature of this global conflict had caused massive losses in a relatively short period of time. Consequently, national decision makers and theater commanders confronted political and military decisions with options seriously constrained by equipment shortages and supply problems.

The related issues of mobilization, logistics, and sustainability were critical to the ability of Blue/NATO to fight a protracted conventional war. The NCA addressed these issues with a continuing, multifaceted approach throughout the series.

Authorities and Controls

The President declared a national emergency when the war broke out, and the Congress promptly declared war on Red and the other members of the Warsaw Pact. Economic controls and consumer rationing were not deemed necessary early on, and authority for wage, price, and rent controls was not requested from the Congress.

Congress also passed timely legislation amending the Defense Production Act of 1950 to permit closer industry-to-industry cooperation in the war effort by ameliorating antitrust provisions and allowing government intervention in the economy if other methods of meeting defense needs failed.

Several Defense Production Act authorities were utilized to:

- Ensure the production and delivery of defense requirements ahead of commercial items.

- Expand production capacity and supply.
- Integrate industry leaders and experts with the government's mobilization management force.
- Convene industry representative committees to solve defense production problems.
- Enable emergency (streamlined) contracting and financing procedures.

Industrial Base

After the initial production surge, capacity expansion efforts were intensified. Measures adopted included:

- Conversion of plants and the development of supporting plants.
- Financial assistance to expand prime contractor and subcontractor capacity, particularly munitions.
- Overtures to allied and friendly nations for the provision of supplies.
- Recommendations for funding authority to activate machine tool trigger orders across the board.

However, production capacity improvements were limited by the unavailability of components and manpower limitations.

Economy

At D+75, Blue industry was operating at or near full-surge capacity. However, that capacity was only about 10–25 percent higher than prewar levels, and because it was achieved at the cost of drawing down lower priority pipelines, it was not sustainable. It was estimated that 12–30 months would be required to convert plants from peacetime to wartime production and to expand capacity by construction of new facilities.

Two potential production problems that plagued Blue involved shipbuilding and ammunition. The former was constrained by few yards, a lack of critical resources and materials, and skilled talent. The latter was plagued by lack of manufacturing plants, which necessitated both prioritization and work-around. Indeed, this condition regarding ammunition was expected to worsen as short-term substitutes were depleted before new plants came on line. Alternatives, such as the offshore building and repair of ships, were considered as well as foreign procurement of ammunition, but some players believed that the ammunition problem could not be remedied in the short term.

Farm production levels had not diminished in spite of the labor demand; labor was close to the full employment level with some near-term shortages anticipated. Increases in productive capacity, combined with increased military manpower demands, would eventually mandate occupational deferments for those with critical skills.

Manpower was sufficient to match the production capacity and, with increased working hours, would sustain the maximum level of output to D+135. The increase in requirements to man new production facilities coming on line in D+2 years outstripped the ability to train and provide competent personnel. Early and extensive training programs were viewed as essential to alleviate some of the impact and to offset the needs for potentially scarce skills.

At D+75, the economy in general was strong and undamaged. Although the economic expansion of the service industry had been halted as assets were shifted from the civilian sector to government use, the average citizen had yet to feel an economic impact from the war. Consideration was given to the implementation of wage and price controls, and the intent was to delay these steps as long as possible. Inflation was moderate, but some consumer discontent had developed as wartime demands preempted civilian production and distribution.

The Blue domestic transportation system could meet essential defense and civil movement requirements in both the short and the long term. The Defense Production Act, Title I, DOT, established a priority control movement system to handle essential defense and civilian traffic before routine market goods.

Over 1,200 Blue-flag and NATO ships were supporting the sealift requirements of the war in Europe. All Blue ports were operational, and Canada made both eastern and western ports available for ammunition out-load. Other allied nations and reliable Third World carriers were providing adequate capacity to meet essential Blue economic shipping needs. Air transportation was relying heavily on the use of chartered, foreign flag aircraft. Transportation capacity was adequate for military requirements in both the short and the long term.

The outlook for providing the petroleum necessary to meet military and civilian needs did not provide a cause for concern. Foreign sources of supply had not deteriorated, and alternate refinery capacity existed to meet expected growth of requirements. Electrical generation capability was limited in some parts of the country and remained vulnerable to sabotage. The long lead-time required to construct these plants and their associated transmission lines mitigated against a near-term solution. Conservation measures such as close management of industrial work periods and controls on public use as required were coupled with increased levels of Canadian imports to ameliorate the problem. Supplies of most raw materials were generally satisfactory and expected to remain so as long as Blue retained access to certain key foreign suppliers.

The prospect of a long, conventional war mandated a shift in planning priorities toward financial requirements and the development of technological and production solutions for problems associated with sustainment, reconstitution, and force-level expansion. Because revenue-raising measures were in place, the outlook for long-term financing of the war, 50 percent pay as you go, appeared favorable. However, the cost of the war was going to be staggering. For example, it was estimated that reconstitution to prewar levels would require 25 percent of GNP over a two to four-year period, and expanding to planning force levels would consume 41 percent over the same period. Therefore, in order to avoid the financial depletion that struck Great Britain after World War II, careful planning was essential if Blue were not to share a similar fate. Not only the pay-as-you-go plan alluded to above, but other alternatives including a luxury tax, a national sales tax, an increase of $1.50 per gallon in the gasoline tax, and an income tax surcharge were identified and reviewed. Japan was seen as an essential partner, both from a credit management standpoint and for financial and industrial assistance. Other non-NATO nations might be willing to reduce the overall burden, but there was no question that the major cost would end up being a Blue responsibility.

CHAPTER SIX

Weapons of Mass Destruction

Introduction

The use of weapons of mass destruction (WMD) was far more frequent in the first Global series than in the second. Indeed, it was not until GWG '87 when a Red chemical attack occurred on D+49, and nuclear weapons were not used. Red had in fact contemplated earlier use of CW when the military situation in Bulgaria began to deteriorate, but did not do so. Blue/NATO considered nuclear use on several occasions to stem the Red advance in Central Europe, but could not make a credible case that such use would provide military or political advantage. Red was very much aware that nuclear use was under consideration by Blue and, while using all means available to deter such use, did study targeting options for a retaliatory strike should Blue escalate.

Chemical Weapons Use (to D+64)

Red had initiated the use of chemical weapons on the Central Front and in eastern Turkey. Both persistent and nonpersistent types were employed to facilitate offensive and defensive operations. NATO forces were not well prepared to operate in a chemical environment and perceived that their capacity to retaliate was limited. By D+60, the reality of chemical warfare was accepted by both sides, although unfavorable weather conditions led to generally inconclusive results.

Status of Nuclear Forces (to D+64)

The central strategic systems of each side, including command and control, remained essentially intact. Although Red had lost about one-half of their SSBNs, their land-based nuclear arsenal remained undamaged. The tactical and theater systems of both sides had been substantially depleted by conventional means, but significant capabilities remained.

Nuclear Considerations (to D+64)

Blue and Red were well aware that on several occasions the use of tactical nuclear weapons had appeared to make good military sense, but political concerns combined with the uncertainty over nuclear escalation led to a decision against such use. Typical of the latter aspect of the problem was uncertainty of the other side's nuclear doctrine. For example, would "limited" or "tactical" use by Blue be the signal—or excuse—for a massive riposte by Red? As the games progressed and the perceived stakes mounted, the resort to nuclear use seemed to come closer to a realistic option in the minds of some players.

Blue/NATO held firmly to its position that it would not initiate nuclear use unless Warsaw Pact forces achieved a major breakthrough, even though there was no clear determination as to how such use would solve the problem, especially in view of the assumed Red response. Blue considered nuclear use against the DPRK after their invasion of South Korea but rejected such use because of the expected adverse political consequences, particularly from Japan.

Red began to consider nuclear use as a means of terminating the war. A principal Red objective was an early end to hostilities because of a concern that the economy, and especially agriculture, would be unable to sustain a protracted (one-year-plus) conventional war. Red perceived that it had, for all practical purposes, won the war in Central Europe based on its territorial conquests and that Blue/NATO was refusing to recognize this reality. Some in the VGK believed that the use of nuclear weapons would so shock public opinion that war termination would be forced upon the Western governments.

Red also considered the use of nuclear weapons to stem the Greek-Turkish invasion of Bulgaria. Red reasoned that such use would be non-escalatory because:

- Use would be on Warsaw Pact territory and thus defensive.
- No Blue forces would be involved
- The theater was geographically isolated.

Red concluded, however, that the allied offensive was not sustainable and, therefore, with the danger quite limited, the risk of first use was not commensurate with any obvious benefit. However, Red did believe that if the Central Front offensive bogged down, the Balkans might be ideal for a nuclear "demonstration shot."

In the Pacific, Red had debated the feasibility of a nuclear strike on Blue CVBGs to eliminate some of their problems. Because Blue/NATO homelands were not involved, Red saw such an attack as a horizontal rather than vertical escalation that would greatly reduce the Blue conventional offensive assault on the Red Pacific rim, possibly drive Japan into neutrality, and send a strong message to a potentially aggressive PRC. From the Red perspective, Blue would not have an in-theater, symmetric retaliatory target and would be faced with the prospect of a nuclear response in Europe or in the Red homeland itself. Red believed that in either case, world public opinion would focus blame on Blue for escalating the war, which might result in NATO disintegration and a war termination decidedly favoring Red political goals.

Nuclear issues were always in the forefront of Red thinking and planning. The specific concerns varied—contingency planning for Red nuclear employment, concern over possible Blue/NATO use, etc., but the nuclear question was always close to the surface in VGK deliberations.

Early in the war, Red was definitely worried about a possible "penalty for success" that a rapid advance by Warsaw Pact forces would lead to Blue/NATO nuclear use. However, as the war progressed and what Red perceived as several nuclear "gates" (e.g., crossing the Rhine) were passed without escalation, the Kremlin's fears tended to diminish. However, Red remained wary that if Blue shared their belief that the military objective had been essentially attained, the temptation to escalate would increase. An interesting side issue involved France and the possible use of the "force de frappe." Early in the war, Red tried to avoid invading France for reasons both political and military, with French nuclear weapons a subject of discussion. Although most were more conservative, one Red leader quipped that perhaps the best thing that could happen from the Red perspective would be unilateral French employment of nuclear weapons against Warsaw Pact forces. The logic was that, in accordance with their goal of early termination, Red wanted a "war stopper" and nuclear use might very well provide it. Further, if France chose to engage in a nuclear exchange with Red, the result was a foregone conclusion. The troubling unknown was the degree of linkage between a France-Red exchange and Blue/NATO use.

Throughout the war, Red seriously considered the employment of tactical nuclear weapons as a viable military option. However, while Moscow struggled with the possibility that tactical nuclear use might lead inexorably to a central systems exchange, not all VGK members viewed this possibility as a major deterrent.

One issue that often arose in Red deliberations was the possibility of "decoupling" in the use of tactical nuclear weapons by using them against the Blue CVBGs or outside the Western TVD. This was a concept that had been utilized in games of the first series, and Red speculation was that Blue did not have a symmetrical response to such use. Further, and as noted above, Red believed that any Blue nuclear use would be viewed as escalatory by world opinion and would redound to Blue disadvantage. In the event, however, Red always assessed the risks as needless given the generally acceptable results of the conventional offensive on the Central Front. Indeed, through D+64, the final analysis always showed that there was no point in jeopardizing the already attained successes in Europe.

There were two other nuclear related issues that arose during the games. The first involved the Blue air carrier raid on the nuclear power plant located in the vicinity of the Kola. This attack was executed without consultation with either the DPC or the Blue

NCA. Expert opinion differed regarding the precise effects of a successful strike, but, if the Chernobyl accident could be taken as a valid guide, damage and casualties would presumably be widespread and serious. Further, with the recent disastrous chemical leak at Bophal, India in mind, the issue was raised that attacks on chemical plants also had the potential for massive destruction. Two points emerged from these discussions:

- There was a need for a Blue/NATO targeting policy and
- Defense of similar installations in Blue and NATO countries from attack or sabotage should not be overlooked.

A second issue concerned the destruction or capture of Blue/NATO tactical and theater nuclear weapons based in western Europe. The early Red independent air operation against these weapons would seem certain to have resulted in the release of radioactive material, and this situation was not addressed in terms of its possible effects on military operations and civilian populations. Of additional concern was the possible over-run by advancing Red forces of these same weapons. Here again, little thought appeared to have been given to planning for this contingency.

Weapons of Mass Destruction: GWG '88

Week One—Red-Dominant Scenario

As might be expected, discussions of the use of tactical nuclear weapons were prominent in a scenario where Blue/NATO forces were threatened with military defeat. Off-line simulations were utilized to provide Blue players with an analysis of several "what ifs." Although Blue perceived the situation as desperate, Blue players were unable to frame a plan of nuclear use that provided a clear military advantage. While it was conceivable that the Red offensive could be blunted with nuclear use, Blue lacked the conventional capability to counterattack and exploit any advantage that nuclear weapons might provide. Further, off-line gaming suggested that, at this stage of the war, any nuclear use could rapidly escalate to a central systems exchange.

Red clearly wished to avoid nuclear weapons given the enhanced prospects for success. The two possible exceptions were the ongoing friction with the PRC, a major cause for concern, and a contingency plan by the FETVD commander to attack the Blue CVBGs, considered most unlikely to be implemented. Curiously, the French situation continued to cause Red some concern. When Paris declared a 15-kilometer "kill zone" along the border, Red took this threat seriously. While the Kremlin did not believe that Blue would resort to nuclear weapons use, it did feel that French use in defense of or in retaliation to conventional attacks on France was a distinct possibility.

Week Two—Blue-Dominant Scenario

The primary Red concern in this scenario was the large number of troops in the Central Front "pocket." This force had been designated a "national asset" by the General Secretary, who had threatened nuclear use if its destruction appeared imminent. Red military planning was, however, that should Blue develop the combat power to threaten collapse of the pocket, Red would use a heavy chemical attack to aid in establishing a relief corridor to the trapped forces. Massive amounts of persistent, thickened chemical weapons would be delivered by tube artillery and multiple rocket launchers to protect the corridor flanks, and nonpersistent CW would be used on Blue forces threatening the corridor. It was judged that Blue casualties would be minimal due to experience gained from previous chemical attacks and good defensive posture. It was thought, however, that the protective measures would have a detrimental impact on NATO fighting ability, leaving the forces vulnerable to follow-on conventional attack. Further, decontamination would be required.

The planned Blue response was to use persistent chemicals on the Red front-line divisions in order to prevent Red from attaining total control. Given an excellent defensive capability, Red casualties probably would have been minimal and impact on Red fighting ability nominal.

Red planning envisioned the strong possibility of a Blue nuclear reaction to the proposed large-scale use of chemicals. Therefore, the Red off-line planning involved a preemptive nuclear attack to reduce the risk and effectiveness of such an event. Red would use 200 Scud-delivered, high-altitude (to minimize fallout) 10kt to 200kt weapons against Blue C3 nodes and nuclear delivery systems. The Blue response in this off-line excursion was to detonate one 350kt weapon at high altitude over Mosowka, Lithuania, a WP naval port without a large civilian population. Red perceived this Blue response as a signal and, having suffered no military damage, did not respond.

Week Three—Stalemate Scenario

The Red position at the beginning of week three was that the "stalemate" would not last long and would quickly be resolved in the favor of Red. While the General Secretary tried at first to seek a diplomatic solution, he abandoned negotiations altogether when faced by Blue/NATO intransigence. While the PRC appeared restive, and while Red appeared to be totally isolated, the VGK position toward nuclear weapons was unchanged. Red was not afraid to use nuclear weapons in retaliation or if Blue was able to severely attrite the Seventh Strategic Echelon. But Red was so confident of the strength of its position that even Blue tactical nuclear use was viewed with, essentially, lack of concern. In summary, Red believed that the use of nuclear weapons by Blue would be insufficient to disrupt the offensive, that Blue realized it was "too late" for their use, and that Blue knew that it did not have the combat capacity to follow up and exploit any temporary advantage nuclear use might confer. While Red did select targets such as troop concentrations for retaliatory strikes, Red even questioned whether the damage Blue might inflict was even worthy of a nuclear response.

The Blue situation was one of a classic mismatch of ends and means. While the President urged the military to "be bold," the lack of combat power and logistical support meant that offensive operations would create an enormous drain on sustainability. Therefore, Blue planning had to turn to consideration of tactical nuclear use. The Blue NCA and NATO reluctantly concurred that if SACEUR's conventional offensive failed, then nuclear use would be authorized provided both agreed. SACEUR then planned a campaign that involved the use of twenty-five 70kt weapons on specific military targets. It was his belief that if he were going to conduct an offensive—and he felt that was better than remaining on the defensive—tactical nuclear use would be essential. The game ended without the final decision.

Summary

Military considerations aside, there were several political considerations that mitigated against Blue first use:

- NATO Allies were opposed to options in some of the scenarios because the weapons would be detonated on their soil.
- Red retaliation might cause the loss of positions gained in other theaters as well as increase the possibility of Blue losing advantage at sea.
- Japanese neutrality might result.
- Separately negotiated treaties could result in dissolution of the NATO Alliance.

Each side seriously questioned the utility of nuclear weapons, as was clearly demonstrated by their failure to use them in situations that appeared to warrant that use. Therefore, both sides tended to believe that the other would not escalate across the nuclear threshold. An example of this mindset occurred in the Blue-dominant scenario when the Blue President ordered the destruction, by conventional means, of encircled Red troops that the Red General Secretary had declared a "national asset" to be defended by nuclear use if their annihilation were threatened. Conversely, unaware of how frequently and intensively Blue had debated first use, Red did not believe Blue would resort to nuclear use unless there was profound provocation. The consideration of nuclear use was event-driven, and both sides seemed to lack an appreciation for what their opponent might consider critical.

The War in Space

The war in space was ongoing throughout the game series and had a substantial impact on Blue intelligence, reconnaissance, and command and control capabilities. This was an important constraint on Blue military operations. For example, by D+48, only a limited Blue space reconnaissance capability remained. UHF SATCOM was sporadically jammed, making it an unreliable medium 60 percent of the time. SHF SATCOM channels lacking anti-jam features were effectively lost.

Red commenced an active antisatellite campaign on D-Day. Nearly all Blue LEO reconnaissance satellite systems were neutralized early in the war. Blue counterattacked in space, but ran short of antisatellite (ASAT) weapons before Red ran out of replacement satellites. Blue then attacked Red space launch and antisatellite targets on the ground using TLAM(C) and B-1 bombers.

Blue used alternative, nonspace means as a substitute for its losses. Air-breathing reconnaissance platforms (SR-71, U-2, RC-135, EP-3, RPV, etc.) were particularly important.

After about D+20, both sides "stood down" from their antisatellite campaigns. Red had accomplished the objective of neutralizing the Blue LEO reconnaissance threat but had sustained damage to their ASAT lasers at Sary Shagan and co-orbital ASAT launch facilities at Tyuratam. In the face of the Red reconstruction of satellite assets, Blue decided to conserve its remaining antisatellite weapons for use at a critical time against high priority targets. Faced with the prospect of a protracted war, both sides found it necessary to take a hard look at the availability of space systems over the long term.

Blue space warfare planners and operators had the following goals:

- Deny Red use of their space systems through such means as operational deception, attacking launch/control facilities, jamming, and other electronic countermeasures.
- Regain superiority in space over the long term through improved ground site security, accelerated production of satellite and antisatellite weapons, development of cheaper satellites, use of the shuttle, and increased space asset survivability.

After D+46, space action was at a reduced level as each side concentrated mainly on reconstituting space reconnaissance assets and ASAT capabilities lost or utilized in the opening days of hostilities. Blue particularly played a catch-up game on reconnaissance satellites, starting with 11 on D+43 and ending with 17 on D+64. Red was able to recover their losses more effectively. Starting with ready replacement units, by D+64 Red had 40 orbiting missions and 23 ready replacement units with associated booster assets.

ASAT capabilities for both Blue and Red were reduced due to successful attacks on their launch bases. Inventories were low on both sides: Blue was down to four ASAT satellites; Red had an estimated five. Both had begun exploring new ASAT technology and recommended increased ASAT production rates.

In the satellite communications area, Blue was severely hampered (FLASH priorities on occasion being delayed up to six hours) by communication jamming in the SHF/UHF bands. This situation was particularly acute in the European Theater. Red attacks on ground communications stations had less effect on Blue very-low-frequency submarine communications. Some relief from jamming was attained from Blue raids on Red jamming facilities; eight Red jamming sites were destroyed or severely damaged.

By D+64, Red had made two ASAT attempts against the Space Shuttle, neither of which succeeded. Blue had made a decision to expend its remaining ASATs against the Red Cosmos 929 RECON satellite and the Red Space Station, but had not yet launched.

Red had been quite successful in the war in space; Blue less so. Blue was hampered in its recovery of space assets, partially due to the sophisticated technology integrated into both the orbiting hardware and ground control systems. Simpler satellite designs that could be put in orbit more quickly and were still adequate, at least as gap fillers, to provide the strategic and tactical intelligence and communication required for the near-term war effort were discussed. The judicious use of nonspace reconnaissance assets and more conventional communication networks appeared to be the near-term solution.

The three-scenario GWG '88 found the situation little changed. Blue strategic warning capabilities were intact and not in jeopardy as were its navigation and weather satellites. Satellite communications, however, were subject to intensive jamming, and non-satellite systems were severely overloaded, extending message time from the minutes expected for the satellite-supported system to up to ten hours. Commander-in-Chief, Space, devised a plan to counteract Red jamming and restored communications to 75 percent of the prewar level.

A new consideration that emerged in GWG '88 was that of preserving an imaging capability to monitor a cease-fire or compliance with terms of a peace treaty. While Blue did in fact preserve assets for this purpose, the point was raised that it might be desirable for both sides to have such capability—lest confidence be lost and war resumed as a result. During the "Blue-dominant" scenario, Blue was confident enough to consider negotiating a cease-fire in space.

In its approach to the space war, Blue largely neglected the space assets of other nations. In none of the three scenarios of GWG '88 did either side feel completely comfortable with the quantity and quality of intelligence it was receiving, and Blue especially suffered due to the loss of space intelligence collection assets. Occasionally,

Blue civilian and military intelligence analysts differed regarding Red capabilities. And, indeed, Red was closer to exhausting its assets than Blue realized. Although frustrating to the players, these battles were probably close to what would have been an actual situation.

Conclusions

Summary

One of the definitions of the Global War Game was "a joint forum to test and refine national strategies and doctrine in a crisis environment." As research games, the first two GWG series, 1979-1988, resulted in a number of changes in the way a potential war between Blue/NATO and Red/Warsaw Pact was perceived. The following tables summarize how effectively the "test and refine" aspect of game purpose influenced thinking on some major issues.

TABLE 1
Shifts In Naval Thinking
First Global Series 1979–1983
General War

BEFORE	AFTER
Defend to avoid losing	Attack to win
Concerns about survivability in D-Day shoot-out at sea	Confidence in ability to defeat Red
Safety of SLOCs a major concern	Aggressive use of SSNs relieves SLOC pressure
Use SSNs in barrier to protect SLOCs	SSNs attack to control Norwegian Sea
Red SSBNs secure in bastions	Red SSBNs heavily attrited
Pessimism regarding survivability of CVs	Moderate confidence in ability to use CVs offensively
Keep naval surface ships out of eastern Mediterranean	Use surface forces to control eastern Mediterranean
Persian Gulf/Southwest Asia a major concern	Considerably less so
Plan for early use of theater nuclear weapons by Blue	No advantage to Blue from theater nuclear use
Non-Central Front battles trivial and of no concern to Red	Non-Central Front battles interactive and heavy

TABLE 2
Shifts In Military Thinking
Second Global Series 1984–1988
Long War

BEFORE	AFTER
Use nuclear weapons early or lose	Reason for optimism in conventional campaign
NATO fight Red as far forward as possible	NATO stresses maneuver vs positional defense
Blue concerned about Red 4th generation air	Blue deep penetration air strikes for FOFA
Naval concern for SLOC protection	Naval emphasis on power projection
Little prospect for USMC employment	Extensive MAF/MEF operations
AFNORTH, AFCENT, AFSOUTH fighting separate wars	Coordinated, integrated strategy in Europe
AFSOUTH concentrates on defense of Turkish Straits	AFSOUTH exploits offensive opportunities
Blue forces in Pacific react to Red	Blue takes offensive to sink/bottle up Red

The 1988 Global War Game was the last global to focus on war between the two Superpowers.

Some Concluding Thoughts on Major Issues

Aside from the "shifts" in military and naval thinking alluded to above, the game had substantial influence on some major issues that deserve examination in greater depth.

One of the principal benefits of the game was that it provided both the opportunity and a forum for people with similar concerns to work and interact with each other. Although the number of participants was lower in the final game of the series (primarily because it was a seminar planning-type evolution instead of an operational game), approximately ninety different government departments and agencies, educational and research facilities, and various military commands participated. As noted above, there was foreign participation as well, both on the military and civilian level. Certainly, no other simulation, seminar, or other event existed that brought such a depth and breadth of expertise to bear on the issue of potential superpower conflict. Clearly, the issues raised and potential solutions to problems envisioned benefited from bringing these people together. But the benefits extended beyond the game. Virtually all participants left the game with the business cards of individuals they had met and worked with in Newport, with whom they could consult and advise in their "real world" jobs. It seems beyond question that the defense planning establishment benefited from associations begun at Global.

One of the primary reasons for the existence of Global had been then CNO Admiral Thomas B. Hayward's concerns, expressed in 1978, that the navy did not have a clear perception of its role should war occur between the United States and the Soviet Union. Consequently, one of the most important products of the Global War Game Series was a most significant contribution to what came to be known as "The Maritime Strategy." That strategy might be summarized as follows:

- The war will be non-nuclear.
- A protracted war with sequential rollback operations would be planned.
- Offensive sea control operations were to be stressed.
- War termination leverage would be sought.
- Sea control was stressed to take advantage of U.S. economic mobilization.

It is evident from the contents of this paper that the GWG series contributed to all of these points in the course of its games.

There was considerable criticism of the Maritime Strategy from a number of quarters. Regardless of the accuracy of that criticism, however, the value of the game as a guide to naval operations is not to be overlooked, both strategically and operationally. At the strategic level, it became clear that, despite apparent risks, a forward, offensive employment of naval forces not only protected the SLOCs, but paid dividends in providing Blue with options that were not attainable through passive defense. At the operational level, among other examples, the folly of deserting the Eastern Mediterranean was a lesson learned very early on. That being the case, study had to be given to how carrier operations could be conducted, what tactics needed to be invented, what technologies utilized or developed to facilitate such operations. Therefore, the impact of the game on naval thinking went well beyond the Maritime Strategy per se.

Another over-arching issue that received much attention was what constituted victory for each of the superpowers? Red was aware of its limitations and wanted a short war followed by early negotiations. The VGK, however, was constantly frustrated by its inability to bring about substantive talks with Blue. Further, lacking control of the sea and the air, Red found it extremely difficult to force Blue to negotiate or to surrender. Red had, generally, succeeded in attaining most of its military objectives, but with Blue unwilling to ratify that success at the conference table, Red faced the protracted war that it desperately wanted to avoid.

Blue, fighting a defensive war within a defensive alliance, usually expressed its principal war aim as the restoration of the territorial status quo ante bellum. This seemed, in the early games, to be a relatively modest goal. As the series progressed, however, Blue began to realize that achievement of that objective would probably have enormous repercussions for Red and the Warsaw Pact. Huge losses to the Red Army, struggling economies, and agricultural disasters would challenge the political cohesion of the Warsaw Pact countries, both internally and externally, and, quite possibly, the primacy of the CPSU itself. Blue felt it needed a better military situation on the Central Front as a prerequisite to negotiations, but realized that sustainability and alliance cohesion problems could be fatal.

While nuclear weapons were not used in the game, their influence permeated the proceedings. Real world questions, such as the likelihood and feasibility of limited nuclear war at sea and whether or not chemical use by Red signaled nuclear use were discussed. The game itself, however, tended to raise questions regarding nuclear use that tended to be original.

In general, Red saw no reason to contemplate first use of nuclear weapons. It was believed that Blue retaliation for such use could negate the assumed conventional superiority of the Red Army, and that further escalation would threaten the safety of the homeland. However, the question of possible nuclear use was, for at least one General Secretary of the CPSU, intimately connected to the issues of military success and war termination. While previous games tended to show Red modifying military objectives if NATO resistance took the offensive off its time-line, his belief was that, if the NATO conventional defense was successful and the Central Front stabilized without the attainment for the Red minimum military objective, the failure of the vaunted Red Army would:

- Threaten total collapse of the Eastern/Central European security structure, the degradation of which had precipitated hostilities in the first place and
- Leave Red in an intolerable negotiating position vs. Blue.

As far as this General Secretary was concerned, Blue long war strategy was not the issue, the total Red security structure, internally and externally, would be threatened with catastrophic collapse if Blue just stabilized the Central Front, let alone restored the territorial status quo ante bellum. Thus the VGK considered the use of nuclear weapons and asked the General Staff for a "survival strategy" utilizing them in circumstances that Blue did not anticipate.

At the time these games were conducted, it was assumed by the majority that a war in Europe between the United States and the Soviet Union would see the use of tactical/theater nuclear weapons in a fortnight, and that Blue defense on the Central Front required early use of them. A goal of this series was to test the concept of protracted, conventional war, but players did have the option to go "off line" to discuss the ramifications of nuclear use. Excursions of this nature did take place, and Blue found the results unpalatable. Blue usually envisioned the use of ten to twenty weapons in the 20 kt range to eliminate Red salients or to stem Red breakthroughs. The Red response was based on the principal of "no first use but first decisive use" and involved retaliation in the form of several hundred weapons across the entire front. Thus, although Blue did, on occasion, see possible advantage in modest nuclear use, the probable Red response was a most effective deterrent.

Thus, the games tended to indicate, in certain circumstances, the unexpected possibility that events could lead Red rather that Blue to contemplate the first use of nuclear weapons.

Just inside the door of the Conolly Hall spaces formerly occupied by the Office of Naval Intelligence Detachment at the Naval War College stood a towering, cutout figure of a Soviet military officer. This was the original "ten-foot tall" Russian, whose purpose was to remind those who worked there of the dangers of "worst casing" the Red threat.

In spite of this, events of the late 1980s and early 1990s would appear to show that the Global "Red Team" seriously overestimated the capabilities of the Warsaw Pact, particularly with regard to the seemingly endless parade of Red Strategic Echelons thrown against NATO forces on the Central Front.

Be that as it may, the overall series result was significant. While the first Global series indicated that nuclear escalation worked to neither side's advantage, the second tended to demonstrate that such escalation by NATO was not in fact necessary. Indeed, as later events in Eastern Europe and the Soviet Union made clear, the lessons learned in the Global War Games might have prevented nuclear catastrophe had war between the two alliances actually occurred.

CHRONOLOGY: 1984 GLOBAL WAR GAME

AUGUST 1990		
1	D-15	80% of Red submarines and surface combatants sortie
2	D-14	
3	D-13	
4	D-12	Red begins to mobilize air and ground forces Red begins Spetsnaz operations in SWTVD/Med area
5	D-11	
6	D-10	Blue marines arrive in Norway
7	D-9	
8	D-8	
9	D-7	Blue begins military mobilization
10	D-6	
11	D-5	
12	D-4	
13	D-3	
14	D-2	Red submarines mine anchorages at Augusta and Souda Bays Suez Canal blocked by sinking of Red minelayer
15	D-1	
16	D-Day	Warsaw Pact offensive begins-concentration on NORTHAG Red invades North Norway with 2 MRDs Extensive and intense naval battles commence, worldwide
17	D+1	Red Spetsnaz attacks in Japan, Guam, and Hawaii
18	D+2	Red attacks on Adak, Shemya, and Amchitka Red aircraft and SS-22s strike Chitose and Misawa
19	D+3	
20	D+4	NATO counterattacks to northeast from Fulda
21	D+5	Red bombs Diego Garcia
22	D+6	NATO counterattack withdrawn after minimal success
23	D+7	
24	D+8	
25	D+9	
26	D+10	Two CVBGs originally stationed off Cuba redeployed to UK Red offensive reaches outskirts of Hamburg and Hanover
27	D+11	Two Polish armies invade Scheeswig-Holstein, cut off Denmark Red invades Hokkaido
28	D+12	Warsaw Pact offensive in NORTHAG resumes
29	D+13	Red forces cross Elbe River, Bremerhaven captured Warsaw Pact begins southern offensive toward Munich
30	D+14	
31	D+15	Munich and Augsburg fall, Red presses on toward Stuttgart North Korea invades South Korea
SEPTEMBER 1990		
1	D+16	
2	D+17	
3	D+18	

4	D+19	NATO stabilizes NORTHAG line at Weser River Red advance on Stuttgart halted Red Second Strategic Echelon Closes
5	D+20	Red opens strong attack on Frankfurt Red reinforces Jutland, renews offensive into Denmark
6	D+21	
7	D+22	NATO amphibious landing on western side of Jutland Weser line holds in NORTHAG Red drive on Frankfurt contained
8	D+23	Warsaw Pact suspends offensive to await reinforcements TLAM C strikes by Blue against Murmansk area
9	D+24	
10	D+25	Blue pulls SSNs out of Kara Sea and reduces those in Barents
11	D+26	NATO counterattack begins; French divisions attack toward Halle NORTHAG attacks south of Hamburg toward Magdeburg
12	D+27	NATO airborne units capture Halle
13	D+28	
14	D+29	French link-up with airborne in Halle NATO northern pincer held by Red at Luneburg Jutland beachhead stable CENTAG attacking toward Brunswick Red Third Strategic Echelon arriving
15	D+30	NATO offensives continue against heavy Red opposition French cross IGB headed for Magdeburg and Leipzig NORTHAG pincer swings south toward Celle Red deploys 14 SSN/SSGN for anti-SLOC campaign Blue SSNs foil Red amphibious attempt to flank Skibotn line
16	D+31	
17	D+32	Massive Red attack damages LINCOLN and MIDWAY off Japan Red begins withdrawal of Hokkaido invasion force
18	D+33	NATO northern and southern pincers meet at Celle
19	D+34	
20	D+35	Red pressure causes withdrawal of all three NATO offensives Red sorties 11 diesel SS against CVBGs operating in North Sea
21	D+36	Full closure of Third Strategic Echelon restores initiative to Red
22	D+37	Red offensives in progress toward Bremen, Frankfurt, Stuttgart
23	D+38	Red OSCAR SSGN launches only successful ASCM attack of war
24	D+39	RANGER heavily damaged by massive Red air attack off Japan
25	D+40	North Korean invasion stalled, Seoul retained by South Korea
26	D+41	
27	D+42	
28	D+43	
29	D+44	
30	D+45	
OCTOBER 1990		
1	D+46	
2	D+47	NATO offensive commence in Thrace
3	D+48	End of GWG '84

CHRONOLOGY: 1985, 1986, AND 1987 GLOBAL WAR GAMES

NOVEMBER 1990		
10	D-10	Blue notes indication of widespread Red/WP mobilization Red issues demarche to Norway; offers French neutrality
11	D-9	
12	D-8	WP forces move to "threat of war" readiness level Congress votes "State of Emergency"; mobilization ordered NATO declares "simple alert" NATO "Rapid Reinforcement Plan" (RRP) implemented
13	D-7	
14	D-6	
15	D-5	
16	D-4	
17	D-3	Red/WP forces at state of "full combat readiness"
18	D-2	
19	D-1	NATO declares "reinforced alert"
20	D-Day	Red/WP commences multi-front offensive into FRG NATO declares "general alert" Extensive and intensive naval battles commence worldwide *Eisenhower* torpedoed in Med, operational after 24 hrs.
21	D+1	France mobilizes, lead elements sent to FRG *Clemonceau* sunk, FOCH damaged by Red sub in Med
22	D+2	Red SAG attacks Panama Canal; closed for one week
23	D+3	Red/WP commences attack through Austria toward Bavaria *Kennedy* torpedoed in Med, OOA for six hours *Nimitz* torpedoed, in Pacific, under tow
24	D+4	Austrian forces come under NATO command Red surface ships in Indian Ocean eliminated
25	D+5	*Nimitz* hit by ASCM attack, under tow to Hawaii
26	D+6	Hamburg falls to Red Polish offensive on Denmark held at Kiel Canal AFNORTH authorized by DPC to attack Red homeland
27	D+7	Red achieves breakthrough in vicinity of Kassel
28	D+8	Blue III Corps counterattacks to seal breakthrough Blue four-carrier CVBG enters Norwegian Sea
29	D+9	CVBGs launch strike on Kola
30	D+10	French 1st and 2nd armies defending WP drive on Munich Italian battalion size units advance toward Innsbruck
DECEMBER 1990		
1	D+11	Blue MAF successfully ashore at Esbjerg, Denmark *Coral Sea* sunk by Red air to surface missile attack Red/WP forces cross Kiel Canal
2	D+12	
3	D+13	
4	D+14	*Independence* torpedoed in Vestfjord, taken under tow
5	D+15	*Independence* torpedoed again, under tow, Trondheim Greek and Turkish units stage limited attacks in Bulgaria

6	D+16	*Kitty Hawk* to Osaka, damaged by SSGN/SNA strike *Lincoln* to Yokosuka , damaged in same attack
7	D+17	Italians enter Innsbruck
8	D+18	End of GWG '85 Red invades North Norway
9	D+19	Beginning of GWG '86
10	D+20	Italian Alpini reach outskirts of Munich
11	D+21	Red attacks between Stuttgart and French border with 29 divisions *Ark Royal* torpedoed, under tow for Bergen
12	D+22	Red crosses Rhine at Mannheim Italian mechanized units in slow advance toward Munich
13	D+23	
14	D+24	Red Second Strategic Echelon Closes Greeks and Turks commence major offensive in Bulgaria
15	D+25	
16	D+26	Red offensive breaks NATO defenses, crosses Weser Italians fighting Red/Hungarian forces in Munich Burgas falls to the Turks Red attacks Japan with SS-12 missiles and aircraft *Kitty Hawk* hit in dry dock, OOA for one year
17	D+27	Blue/NATO begin insertion of surface ships in Black Sea PRC sends additional five divisions to border of Red
18	D+28	
19	D+29	Red invades eastern Turkey
20	D+30	*Forrestal* torpedoed and sunk off Norfolk
21	D+31	
22	D+32	
23	D+33	Red Third Strategic Echelon Closes
24	D+34	Blue III and UK Corps destroyed Greek/Turkish offensive stalls at Sofia and Varna
25	D+35	Red offensive penetrates into Benelux and south France French armies come under NATO command
26	D+36	
27	D+37	Blue air strike into Kola damages nuclear power plant
28	D+38	
29	D+39	1st MAB takes Shikotan by heliborne assault
30	D+40	SACEUR opens five-phase offensive Dikes opened east of Amsterdam to slow Red advance I and II MAF commence attack toward Wittenberge
31	D+41	
JANUARY 1991		
1	D+42	End of GWG '86 Red launches counter attack against Turks in Bulgaria *Iowa* enters Black Sea *Iowa* torpedoed, taken under tow Red offensive reaches Skibotn line in North Norway

2	D+43	Beginning of GWG '87
		Munich and Salzburg fall to Italians
3	D+44	Red begins limited anti-SLOC campaign
		Eisenhower severely damaged in Pireaus by SS-12s
4	D+45	
5	D+46	VGK authorizes use of chemical weapons by WTVD CDR
6	D+47	
7	D+48	
8	D+49	Red uses chemical weapons vs NATO units in Jutland
		Red Fourth Strategic Echelon begins to arrive, piecemeal
9	D+50	Red uses chemical weapons vs CENTAG on Rhine
10	D+51	VGK, concerned about escalation, prohibits chem. use
11	D+52	Blue retaliates with chem. attack on two Czech airfields
12	D+53	SACEUR launches GOLDEN SWORD counteroffensive
13	D+54	Spetsnaz sinks ship in Panama lock, closes it three wks.
14	D+55	
15	D+56	NATO forces break out of Jutland
		Italians cross Danube
16	D+57	GOLDEN SWORD advancing 50 km/day
		Red resumes chemical weapons use
		Jutland breakout halted by heavy Red resistance
		Italians come under AFCENT command
17	D+58	Fifth Strategic Echelon closes
18	D+59	
19	D+60	Erzurum (Turkey) falls to Red
20	D+61	NATO forces cross IGB into GDR
		Red forces cross into Turkey south of Burgas
21	D+62	Leipzig falls to NATO; Elbe River reached
		Italians, AFCENT units link up at Ansbach
		Operation ICE PICK conducted in North Norway
		Multi-regiment air attack on CVBG in Vestfjord
		DPRK invades South Korea
		Operation PISTOL PETE, Blue invasion of Uturup
		Red attacks Alaska with missiles from two SSGNs
22	D+63	
23	D+64	End of GWG '87

Partial List of Participating Organizations

Department of Commerce
Department of Defense
Department of Energy
Department of Justice
Department of Labor
Department of State
Department of Transportation
Department of the Treasury

Bureau of Mines
Bureau of Selective Service
Central Intelligence Agency
CNO Executive Panel
Defense Intelligence Agency
Federal Emergency Management Agency
General Accounting Office
Joint Chiefs of Staff
National Aeronautics and Space Administration
National Security Agency
National Security Council
World Bank

Applied Physics Laboratory
David Taylor Model Basin
Lawrence Livermore National Laboratory
Los Alamos National Laboratory
Naval Civil Engineering Laboratory
Naval Research Laboratory
Naval Underwater Systems Command
Sandia National Laboratory

Air University
Army School of Command and Staff
Army War College
National Defense University
Naval War College
Navy Postgraduate School

Also participating were about twenty Corporations and numerous military organizations representing joint and unified comands and all of the armed services and the Coast Guard.

Glossary

Abbreviations

A	**A/C**		aircraft
	ACE	NATO	Allied Command Europe
	ADM		atomic demolition mines
	Aegis	Blue	USN Integrated Antiair Warfare Weapons System
	AFCE	NATO	Allied Forces Command Europe
	AFCENT	NATO	Allied Forces Central Europe
	AFNORTH	NATO	Allied Forces Northern Europe
	AFSOUTH	NATO	Allied Forces Southern Europe
	AG	NATO	army group
	AI		air intercept
	Alpini		Italian Light Infantry trained and equipped to fight in the mountains
	AMPHIBS		slang expression for amphibious warfare ships
	AOR		area of responsibility
	ASAT		antisatellite weapon
	ASCM		air-to-surface cruise missile [or] antiship cruise missile
	ASUW		antisurface warfare
	ASW		antisubmarine warfare
	AWACS	Blue	Airborne Warning and Control System
B	**BAI**		battlefield air interdiction
	BBBG	Blue	battleship battle group
	Benelux		Belgium Netherlands Luxembourg

Blue		United States of America
Boomer		slang expression for ballistic missile submarine
BW		biological weapon(s)/warfare
C3		command, control, and communications
C3I		command, control, communications, and intelligence
CAP		combat air patrol
CAS		close air support
CAST	NATO	Canadian Air-Sea Transportable Brigade
CENTAG	NATO	Central Army Group
CHOP		change of operational control
CINCLANT	Blue	Commander-in-Chief Atlantic
CINCPAC	Blue	Commander-in-Chief Pacific
CINCSOUTH	NATO	Commander-in-Chief South
CIWS		Close-in Weapons System
CJTF	Blue	Commander Joint Task Force
CNO	Blue	Chief of Naval Operations
COMMARFOREUR	NATO	Commander Marine Forces Europe
COMNON	NATO	Commander North Norway
COMSECONDFLT	Blue	Commander Second Fleet
COMSTRIKEFLTLANT	NATO	Commander Striking Fleet Atlantic
CONUS		Continental United States
COSMOS 929	Red	reconnaissance satellite
CPSU		Communist Party of the Soviet Union
CVBF	Blue	aircraft carrier battle force
CVBG	Blue	aircraft carrier battle group
CW		chemical weapon(s)/warfare

D	**D-Day**		day on which war begins
	DIW		dead in the water
	DMZ		demilitarized zone
	DOT	Blue	Department of Transportation
	DPC	NATO	Defense Planning Committee
	DPRK		Democratic People's Republic of Korea (North Korea)
E	**EASTLANT**		Eastern Atlantic Area
	ENWGS		Enhanced Naval Warfare Gaming System
	Eskadra	Red	squadron (Russian)
	ETA		estimated time of arrival
	ETR		estimated time of repair
	EW		early warning [or] electronic warfare
F	**FEBA**		forward edge of battle area
	FETVD	Red	Far Eastern Theater of Military Operations
	Finnish Wedge		that part of Finland north and west of the juncture of the borders of Finland, Norway, and the USSR
	FLOT		forward line of troops
	FRG		Federal Republic of Germany (West Germany)
G	**GCI**		ground control intercept
	GDR		German Democratic Republic (East Germany)
	GIN GAP		ocean spaces between Greenland, Iceland, and Norway
	GIUK GAP		ocean spaces between Greenland, Iceland, and United Kingdom
	GRU	Red	military intelligence directorate controlled by the General Staff
H	**HFDF**		high frequency direction finding

HUMINT		intelligence obtained from human sources
I and W		indication and warning
ID		infantry division
IGB		inter-German border
INF		Independent Nuclear Force (France)
JCS	Blue	Joint Chiefs of Staff
KIA		killed in action
LEO		low earth orbit
LOC(s)		line(s) of communication
LRA	Red	long-range aviation
MAB	Blue	Marine Amphibious Brigade
MAC	Blue	Military Airlift Command
MAF	Blue	Marine Amphibious Force
MARDEZLANT	Blue	Maritime Defense Zone Atlantic
MCM		mine countermeasures
MD	Red	military district
MERSHIP(s)		slang expression for merchant ship(s)
MEF	Blue	Marine Expeditionary Force
MIDEASTFOR	Blue	USN Middle East Force
MODLOC	Blue	modified location—a geographic point about which ships maneuver
MPS	Blue	maritime prepositioning ships
MRD	Red	Motorized Rifle Division
MVD	Red	Ministry of Internal Affairs
NATO		North Atlantic Treaty Organization
NCA	Blue	National Command Authority

NGFS		naval gunfire support
NORTHAG	NATO	Northern Army Group
NSC	Blue	National Security Council
NSWP	Red	Non-Soviet Warsaw Pact
NWACM		Navy War Air Combat Model
NWC		Naval War College
NWTVD	Red	Northwestern Theater of Military Operations

O

OCA		offensive counter air
OPLAN		plan of operations
OTHR		over-the-horizon radar

P

PACAF	Blue	Pacific Air Forces (USAF)
PACOM	Blue	Pacific Command (headed by CINCPAC)
PLA		People's Liberation Army (PRC)
POL		petroleum, oils, and lubricants
PRC		People's Republic of China

Q

Q ROUTES		protected shipping lanes swept for both mines and submarines

R

Rangers	Blue	Army unit trained for long-range reconnaissance and special operations
RC-135	Blue	electronic reconnaissance aircraft
Red		Soviet Union
REFORGER	NATO	Return of Forces to Germany
REINFORCED ALERT	NATO	alliance mobilization step
ROK		Republic of Korea (South Korea)

S

SACEUR	NATO	Supreme Allied Commander Europe
SACLANT	NATO	Supreme Allied Commander Atlantic
SAF	Red	Soviet Air Forces

SAG		surface action group
SAM		surface-to-air missile
SHF SATCOM		super-high-frequency satellite communications
SIGINT		signals intelligence
SIOP	Blue	single integrated operational plan for nuclear war
SLOC(s)		sea line(s) of communication
SNA	Red	Soviet Naval Aviation
SNI	Red	Soviet Naval Infantry
SOF	Blue	special operations forces
SOSUS	Blue	sound surveillance system
SOVINDRON	Red	Soviet Indian Ocean Squadron
SOVMEDRON	Red	Soviet Mediterranean Sea Squadron
SPETSNAZ	Red	special operations forces USSR designation: troops of special designation
SQR-19	Blue	passive long-range towed sonar array
SRF	Red	Soviet Rocket Forces
SUBACLANT	NATO	Submarine Allied Commander Atlantic
SWAPS		southwestern approaches (to the English Channel)
SWTVD	Red	Southwestern Theater of Military Operations

T

TACAIR		tactical aircraft operations
TACNUC		tactical nuclear weapon
TACOPS		theater and corps operations and planning simulation
TASM	Blue	Tomahawk antiship missile
Thin line array	Blue	towed passive sonar system
TVD	Red	theater of military operations

U

UHF SATCOM		ultra-high-frequency satellite communications

	UK		United Kingdom
	USA	Blue	U.S. Army
	USAF	Blue	U.S. Air Force
	USCG	Blue	U.S. Coast Guard
	USMC	Blue	U.S. Marine Corps
	USN	Blue	U.S. Navy
V	**VACAPES**		Virginia Capes—just seaward of Norfolk
	VGK	Red	Supreme High Command
W	**WESTLANT**		Western Atlantic
	WMD		weapons of mass destruction
	WP		Warsaw Pact
	WTVD	Red	Western Theater of Military Operations

Platforms and Weapons

A	**A-6**	Blue	two-seat carrier-based bomber for CAS, interdiction, and deep strike
	AGI		auxiliary vessel general intelligence purposes
	Akula	Red	fleet submarine (SSN)
	AOE		fast combat support ship
	AS-4	Red	air-to-surface missile with a range of about 185nm (Kitchen)
	AS-6	Red	air-to-surface missile with a range of about 185nm (Kingfish)
B	**B-1**	Blue	long-range multirole strategic bomber
	B-52	Blue	long-range multirole strategic bomber
	Backfire	Red	twin-jet medium bomber and maritime reconnaissance and attack A/C (Tu-26)
	Badger	Red	twin-jet medium bomber and maritime reconnaissance and attack A/C (Tu-16)

BB		battleship
Bear	Red	four-turboprop long-range bomber and maritime reconnaissance A/C (Tu-95)
Blinder	Red	twin-jet supersonic bomber and maritime reconnaissance A/C (Tu-22)
BLKCON 5	Red	aircraft carrier (CV) 67,000 tons *(Leonid Brezhnev)*
C		
CA		cruiser (all-gun armament)
CapTor	Blue	deep-water antisubmarine mine (encapsulated Mk-46 torpedo)
CG		guided missile cruiser
Charlie	Red	cruise missile submarine (SSGN)
CV		aircraft carrier
CVN		nuclear-powered aircraft carrier
D		
DD		destroyer
DDG		guided missile destroyer
E		
E-3	Blue	airborne warning and control platform (AWACS)
Echo	Red	cruise missile submarine (SSGN)
F		
F-14	Blue	twin-seat carrier-based multirole fighter
F-111	Blue	twin-seat multirole attack aircraft
Fencer	Red	two-seat attack aircraft (Su-24)
FF		frigate
FFG		guided missile frigate
FFL		light frigate
Flanker	Red	single-seat all-weather fighter with attack capability (Su-27)
Flogger	Red	single-seat fighter (MiG-27)
Forger	Red	ship-based V/STOL aircraft (Yak-38)
Foxhound	Red	two-seat all-weather interceptor (MiG-31)

	Foxtrot	Red	submarine (SS)
	FPB		fast patrol boat
	Fulcrum	Red	all-weather fighter with attack capability (MiG-29)
H	**Harpoon**	Blue	medium-range antiship cruise missile
	HAWK	Blue	land-based medium-range surface-to-air missile
I	**IL-38**	Red	intermediate-range shore-based ASW/maritime patrol aircraft (MAY)
J	**Juliett**	Red	cruise missile submarine (SSG)
K	**Kara**	Red	cruiser (CG) USSR designation: large antisubmarine ship
	Kashin and Mod Kashin	Red	guided missile destroyer (DDG) USSR designation: large antisubmarine ship
	Kiev	Red	VSTOL aircraft carrier (CV) USSR designation: tactical air-capable cruiser
	Kilo	Red	submarine (SS)
	Kirov	Red	battle cruiser USSR designation: nuclear-powered missile cruiser
	Koni	Red	frigate (FF) USSR designation: escort ship
	Kresta I	Red	cruiser (CG) USSR designation: missile cruiser
	Kresta II	Red	cruiser (CG) USSR designation: large antisubmarine ship
	Krivak I & II	Red	guided missile frigate (FFG) USSR designation: escort ship
	Kynda	Red	cruiser (CG) USSR designation: missile cruiser
L	**LHA**		amphibious assault ship (general purpose)
	LHD		amphibious assault ship (multipurpose)
	LSD		landing ship dock

M	**Mainstay**	Red	early warning and control aircraft (IL-76)
	MiG-21	Red	single-seat fighter (Fishbed)
	MK-57	Blue	submarine or ship-laid moored mine
	MPA	Blue	maritime patrol aircraft
N	**Nanuchka**	Red	missile corvette USSR designation: small missile ship
	November	Red	submarine (SSN)
O	**Oscar**	Red	cruise missile submarine (SSGN)
P	**P-3**	Blue	maritime patrol aircraft
R	**Ro/Ro**		merchant ship with vehicle roll-on, roll-off design
	RPV		remotely piloted vehicle
S	**SA-6**	Red	surface-to-air missile (Gainful)
	Scud	Red	Army battlefield missile (SS-1)
	Sierra	Red	submarine (SSN)
	SL-7	Blue	fast merchant ship
	Slava	Red	cruiser (CG) USSR designation: rocket cruiser
	SM-1	Blue	standard missile 1—shipboard surface-to-air missile
	SM1-ER-BTN	Blue	standard missile 1—extended-range nuclear warhead
	SM-2	Blue	standard missile 2—shipboard surface-to-air missile
	Sovremenny	Red	destroyer (DD) USSR designation: destroyer
	Spetznaz	Red	special operations forces USSR designation: troops of special designation
	SR-71	Blue	strategic reconnaissance aircraft
	SS		submarine (nonnuclear)

SS-12	Red	tactical surface-to-surface missile (Scaleboard)
SS-22	Red	tactical surface-to-surface missile
SSBN		nuclear-powered ballistic missile submarine
SSGN		nuclear-powered cruise missile submarine
SSM		surface-to-surface missile
SSN		nuclear-powered attack submarine
SS-N-12	Red	surface or subsurface launched antiship missile (Sandbox)
SS-N-19	Red	supersonic antiship cruise missile
SUBACLANT	NATO	Submarine Allied Commander Atlantic
Sverdlov	Red	cruiser (CA) USSR designation: cruiser
T **T-AGOS**	Blue	auxiliary ocean surveillance ship (civilian manned)
TANGO	Red	submarine (SS)
TLAM(C)	Blue	Tomahawk land attack missile (conventional)
TLAM(N)	Blue	Tomahawk land attack missile (nuclear)
Tornado	NATO	twin-engine all-weather multipurpose combat aircraft
U **U-2**	Blue	high-altitude reconnaissance aircraft
Udaloy	Red	destroyer (DD) USSR designation: large antisubmarine ship
Y **Yankee**	Red	ballistic missile submarine (SSBN)

About the Author

Captain Robert H. Gile was sworn into the Navy as a midshipman in the fall of 1952. He attended Dartmouth College on an NROTC scholarship, and graduated with a commission in 1956. Captain Gile served six years on active duty and twenty-four in the Naval Reserve. During his last reserve tour, he began working with Bud Hay, then Director of Advanced Concepts at the Center for Naval Warfare Studies. Captain Gile's affiliation with the Global War Game began in 1983, and he has been involved with every Global since that time. He and Mr. Hay coauthored the first volume of Global War Game history, which was published as Newport Paper Number Four in 1993.

Mr. Gile is Vice President, Investments, in the Concord, New Hampshire, office of a national brokerage company. He has served as an elected representative in the New Hampshire State Legislature and as Chairman of the Board of Education in Franklin, New Hampshire. He is Coach of Debate at St. Paul's School in Concord, New Hampshire, and President of the Debating Association of New England Independent Schools.

Titles in the Series

"Are We Beasts?" Churchill and the Moral Question of World War II "Area Bombing," by Christopher C. Harmon (December 1991).

Toward a Pax Universalis: A Historical Critique of the National Military Strategy for the 1990s, by Lieutenant Colonel Gary W. Anderson, U.S. Marine Corps (April 1992).

The "New" Law of the Sea and the Law of Armed Conflict at Sea, by Horace B. Robertson, Jr. (October 1992).

Global War Game: The First Five Years, by Bud Hay and Bob Gile (June 1993).

Beyond Mahan: A Proposal for a U.S. Naval Strategy in the Twenty-First Century, by Colonel Gary W. Anderson, U.S. Marine Corps (August 1993).

The Burden of Trafalgar: Decisive Battle and Naval Strategic Expectations on the Eve of the First World War, by Jan S. Breemer (October 1993).

Mission in the East: The Building of an Army in a Democracy in the New German States, by Colonel Mark E. Victorson, U.S. Army (June 1994).

Physics and Metaphysics of Deterrence: The British Approach, by Myron A. Greenberg (December 1994).

A Doctrine Reader: The Navies of the United States, Great Britain, France, Italy, and Spain, by James J. Tritten and Vice Admiral Luigi Donolo, Italian Navy (Retired) (December 1995).

Chaos Theory: The Essentials for Military Applications, by Major Glenn E. James, U.S. Air Force (October 1996).

The International Legal Ramifications of United States Counter-Proliferation Strategy: Problems and Prospects, by Frank Gibson Goldman (April 1997).

What Color Helmet? Reforming Security Council Peacekeeping Mandates, by Myron H. Nordquist (August 1997).

Sailing New Seas, by Admiral J. Paul Reason, U.S. Navy, Commander-in-Chief, U.S. Atlantic Fleet, with David G. Freymann (March 1998).

Theater Ballistic Missile Defense from the Sea: Issues for the Maritime Component Commander, by Commander Charles C. Swicker, U.S. Navy (August 1998).

International Law and Naval War: The Effect of Marine Safety and Pollution Conventions during International Armed Conflict, by Dr. Sonja Ann Jozef Boelaert-Suominen (December 2000).

The Third Battle: Innovation in the U.S. Navy's Silent Cold War Struggle with Soviet Submarines, by Owen R. Cote, Jr. (2003).

The Limits of Transformation: Officer Attitudes toward the Revolution in Military Affairs, by Thomas G. Mahnken and James R. FitzSimonds (2003).

Military Transformation and the Defense Industry after Next: The Defense Industrial Implications of Network-Centric Warfare, by Peter J. Dombrowski, Eugene Gholz, and Andrew L. Ross (2003).

The Evolution of the U.S. Navy's Maritime Strategy, 1977–1986, by John B. Hattendorf (2004).

Printed in Great Britain
by Amazon